SELF-BLAME AND MORAL RESPONSIBILITY

Self-blame is an integral part of our lives. We often blame ourselves for our failings and experience familiar unpleasant emotions such as guilt, shame, regret, or remorse. Self-blame is also what we often aim for when we blame others: we want the people we blame to recognize their wrongdoing and blame themselves for it. Moreover, self-blame is typically considered a necessary condition for forgiveness. However, until now, self-blame has not been an integral part of the theoretical debate on moral responsibility. This volume presents twelve new essays by leading moral philosophers, who set out bold theories of the nature and ethics of self-blame, and the interconnection between self-blame and moral responsibility. The essays cast new light on traditional problems in the debate on moral responsibility and open exciting avenues for research in moral philosophy, moral psychology, and the philosophy of punishment.

ANDREAS BREKKE CARLSSON is Associate Professor at the Inland Norway University of Applied Sciences. He is the author of several articles on blameworthiness, guilt, and shame.

SELF-BLAME AND MORAL RESPONSIBILITY

EDITED BY

ANDREAS BREKKE CARLSSON

Inland Norway University of Applied Sciences

CAMBRIDGE
UNIVERSITY PRESS

Shaftesbury Road, Cambridge CB2 8EA, United Kingdom

One Liberty Plaza, 20th Floor, New York, NY 10006, USA

477 Williamstown Road, Port Melbourne, VIC 3207, Australia

314–321, 3rd Floor, Plot 3, Splendor Forum, Jasola District Centre, New Delhi – 110025, India

103 Penang Road, #05–06/07, Visioncrest Commercial, Singapore 238467

Cambridge University Press is part of Cambridge University Press & Assessment, a department of the University of Cambridge.

We share the University's mission to contribute to society through the pursuit of education, learning and research at the highest international levels of excellence.

www.cambridge.org
Information on this title: www.cambridge.org/9781009179249

DOI: 10.1017/9781009179263

First published 2022
First paperback edition 2024

A catalogue record for this publication is available from the British Library

Library of Congress Cataloging-in-Publication data
NAMES: Carlsson, Andreas, author.
TITLE: Self-blame and moral responsibility / edited by Andreas Brekke Carlsson, Inland Norway University of Applied Sciences.
DESCRIPTION: Cambridge, United Kingdom ; New York, USA : Cambridge University Press, 2022. | Includes bibliographical references and index.
IDENTIFIERS: LCCN 2021059297 | ISBN 9781009179256 (hardback) | ISBN 9781009179263 (ebook)
SUBJECTS: LCSH: Faultfinding. | Blame. | Criticism, Personal. | Responsibility. | BISAC: PHILOSOPHY / Ethics & Moral Philosophy
CLASSIFICATION: LCC BJ1535.F3 S45 2022 | DDC 158.2–dc23/eng/20220121
LC record available at https://lccn.loc.gov/2021059297

ISBN   978-1-009-17925-6   Hardback
ISBN   978-1-009-17924-9   Paperback

Contents

Contributors

GUNNAR BJÖRNSSON is Professor of Practical Philosophy at Stockholm University.

ANDREAS BREKKE CARLSSON is Associate Professor of Philosophy at Inland Norway University of Applied Sciences.

RANDOLPH CLARKE is Professor of Philosophy at Florida State University.

JUSTIN D'ARMS is Professor of Philosophy at Ohio State University.

DANIEL JACOBSON is Bruce D. Benson Professor of Philosophy at the University of Colorado, Boulder.

MICHAEL MCKENNA is Professor of Philosophy at the University of Arizona.

DANA KAY NELKIN is Professor of Philosophy at the University of California San Diego and Affiliate Professor at the University of San Diego School of Law.

DERK PEREBOOM is Susan Linn Sage Professor of Philosophy and Ethics at Cornell University.

DOUGLAS W. PORTMORE is Professor of Philosophy at Arizona State University.

PIERS RAWLING is Professor of Philosophy at Florida State University.

DAVID SHOEMAKER is Professor of Philosophy at the Sage School of Philosophy, Cornell University.

KRISTA K. THOMASON is Associate Professor of Philosophy at Swarthmore College.

HANNAH TIERNEY is Assistant Professor of Philosophy at the University of California, Davis.

Acknowledgments

I would like to thank the authors for their contributions. Most of the chapters in this volume were presented at the workshop "Self-Blame and Moral Responsibility" at the University of Oslo, in September 2019. I am very grateful to the Centre for the Study of Mind in Nature and ConceptLab, both at the University of Oslo, which generously provided funding for this event. Thanks to all the participants of the workshop for helpful feedback on the papers. I am grateful to Hilary Gaskin, and Thomas Haynes at Cambridge University Press and to Suganiya Karumbayeeram at Lumina Datamatics Limited. Special thanks to Dana Nelkin and Michael McKenna for their support with this volume.

Introduction

Andreas Brekke Carlsson

Self-blame is an integral part of our lives. We often blame *ourselves* for our failings, and we experience a familiar set of unpleasant emotions such as guilt, shame, regret, or remorse. Self-blame is also often what we aim for when we blame *others* – we want the people we blame to recognize their wrongdoings and blame themselves for it. Moreover, self-blame is typically considered to be a necessary condition for forgiveness. If the wrongdoer has not blamed herself for her action, say by experiencing guilt or remorse, forgiveness may seem inappropriate. Yet so far, self-blame has not been an integral part of the theoretical debate about the nature of blame and its relation to moral responsibility. This volume seeks to remedy this omission.

Until recently, philosophers working on blame and moral responsibility have focused almost exclusively on other-directed blame. In the Strawsonian tradition, the emphasis has been on anger, resentment and indignation, and the communication of these emotions (Wallace, 1994; Watson, 1996; McKenna, 2012; Macnamara, 2015a; Shoemaker, 2017). Alternative views have seen blame as a way of modifying one's relation with others (Scanlon, 2008), as a belief-desire pair (Sher, 2006), or as an expression of protest (Hieronymi, 2001; Smith, 2012; Talbert, 2012). It is unclear how self-blame fits into these accounts of the nature of blame. On the face of it, self-blame is not obviously a form of communication, a modification of relationships, or the expression of protest.

It is also unclear how a focus on self-blame will affect accounts of moral responsibility. An agent is blameworthy to the extent that it would be appropriate to blame her. The question of what makes it appropriate to blame other people is arguably the central issue in the literature on moral responsibility. But the question of what would make self-blame appropriate has received far less attention. Self-blame thus raises new questions. It also makes old questions take on a new significance. One of those is the question of whether wrongdoers can deserve pain or harm for their wrongdoings. On many accounts, self-blame is intrinsically unpleasant or painful, for example if self-blame is identified with guilt. This raises the question of whether and how this particular form of pain can be justified. For example, is the pain a mere side effect of a fitting recognition of one's own wrongdoing, or is this pain something that wrongdoers deserve in the sense that it is noninstrumentally good and just that they experience it?

The contributions to this volume show that thinking carefully about self-blame might change or challenge our perspectives on traditional problems in the debate on blame and moral responsibility and open new avenues for research in moral philosophy, moral psychology, and the philosophy of punishment.

The issues that will be discussed in the chapters that follow can be divided into three groups of questions that intersect in interesting ways.

(1) The *nature* of self-blame: There are many competing accounts of other-directed blame. How does self-blame fit into a comprehensive account of blame? It seems that we blame ourselves both for our moral and nonmoral failures. What is the difference between moral and nonmoral kinds of self-blame? It is common to understand moral self-blame as the emotion of guilt. If so, what is the nature of guilt? Is it possible to blame oneself without experiencing guilt? The nature of self-blame is importantly connected to its justification. Our reasons for blame are often backward-looking: We tend to think it is appropriate to blame an agent simply in virtue of what they have done. However, sometimes our justifications are forward-looking. We blame in order to influence, educate, or generate other beneficial consequences. Can there be forward-looking reasons for self-blame and is it possible to develop an account on which self-blame is only justified by forward-looking considerations?

(2) The *ethics* of self-blame: There is a thriving debate concerning the norms of other-directed blame. But what are the norms governing self-blame? Is self-blame something that we should express to those who we have wronged, or should it rather be suffered in silence? There are interesting asymmetries between the normative expectations concerning blaming oneself and others. For example, there are many cases where it may seem appropriate to blame ourselves, but where it is less clear whether it is appropriate for others to blame us. Are there different standards for blaming oneself than for blaming others? Finally, we often experience emotional reactions that are at

odds with our own evaluations and judgments. Are these reactions something for which we should blame ourselves?

(3) The relation between self-blame and theories of *moral responsibility*: Given that self-blame and other-directed blame differ in many respects, which of them should be fundamental in our conception of blameworthiness? Many theories on moral responsibility focus on the communicative aspects of blame. How does self-blame fit into this picture? Other theories emphasize that blame is sometimes harmful. As a result, it is often assumed that agents must fulfil certain conditions for other-directed blame to be justified. Does the fact that guilt is intrinsically painful support a strict control condition on moral blameworthiness and is the painfulness of guilt something we deserve?

These three topics correspond with the three parts of the volume.

Part I concerns the nature of self-blame. What is it to blame oneself? According to a traditional view, self-blame is identified with the emotion of guilt. In their chapter, Justin D'Arms and Daniel Jacobson develop an account of what guilt is and how it relates to moral responsibility. The Strawsonian approach to responsibility tries to explain what it is to be morally responsible for one's actions in terms of being an appropriate object of the reactive attitudes, such as resentment, indignation, and guilt. How informative such explanations can be depends in part on whether an adequate characterization of these attitudes can be given without appeal to the concept of responsibility itself. Guilt, D'Arms and Jacobson argue, is the most promising candidate for a Strawsonian account of the first-personal case of holding oneself morally responsible. The question is whether guilt can be characterized without appeal to responsibility or any similar concept. D'Arms and Jacobson argue that it can. This chapter offers a theory of guilt as a motivational state involving a goal and specific action tendencies that constitute direct and urgent means of meeting that goal. Despite its cognitive complexity, guilt is like simpler emotions such as anger and fear in how its goals and action tendencies are discontinuous with practical reasoning. The motivational theory of guilt, developed in this chapter, provides an important tool for theorizing about first-personal responsibility practices in Strawsonian terms.

If we focus on moral wrongdoing, it seems natural to think of self-blame as guilt. But once we consider self-blame for nonmoral failures, the picture may look very different. The starting point of David Shoemaker's contribution is *athletic* self-blame. When Tom Brady throws an interception, he yells at himself and pounds his fists on his helmet. When Serena Williams misses a shot, she breaks her racket. These athletes, Shoemaker argues, are clearly blaming themselves. Surprisingly, though, current theories of blame have a hard time accounting for such cases. Most theories of blame take other-blame as their paradigm, typically thought to be a response to poor quality of will or moral wrongdoing and consisting in some kind of relationship modification, communication, or protest. None of these features seem to apply in the cases of athletic self-blame. Recently, some theorists have taken self-blame to be a more fundamental paradigm than other-blame. But they are focused on self-blame as guilt, which again, according to Shoemaker, can't capture the athletic cases, because Tom Brady and Serena Williams are not feeling anything like guilt when they blame themselves. In reply to these problems, Shoemaker offers a new theory of self-blame, one that takes athletic cases as its starting point. He draws on recent interesting psychological work on the phenomenon of *self-talk* to make the case that the emotional core of self-blame is in fact very different than that of other-directed blame.

Douglas Portmore, by contrast, develops a unified account of self-blame and other-directed blame. Portmore's goal is to provide a *comprehensive* account of blame, on which deserved guilt, regret, and remorse play an integral part. It is widely noted that blame is multifarious. It can be passionate or dispassionate. It can be expressed or kept private. We blame both the living and the dead. And we blame ourselves as well as others. What is more, we blame ourselves, not only for our moral failings but also for our nonmoral failings: for our aesthetic bad taste, gustatory self-indulgence, or poor athletic performance. And we blame ourselves both for things over which we exerted agential control (e.g., our voluntary acts) and for things over which we lacked such control (e.g., our desires, beliefs, and intentions). Portmore argues that, despite this manifest diversity in our blaming practices, it is possible to provide a comprehensive account of blame. Blame, according to Portmore, essentially involves representing the wrongdoer as not having experienced all the guilt, regret, or remorse the wrongdoer deserves. Based on this idea, he proposes a set of necessary and sufficient conditions of blame and argues that this proposal has a number of advantages over competing theories.

Portmore's account of blame and self-blame presupposes a notion of deserved guilt, regret, and remorse. In his chapter, Derk Pereboom develops a notion of self-blame that *does not* invoke the notion of deserved pain or harm. In previous work, Pereboom has argued that causal determinism and the absence of control that indeterminism implies will undermine this kind of desert. In this chapter, he focuses on developing a *nonretributive* conception of other-directed blame and self-blame. On this account, to blame is to take on a nonretributive stance of moral protest. The reasons for moral protest are forward-looking: moral formation or reconciliation in a relationship that has been impaired due to wrongdoing, protection from wrongdoing, and restoration of the integrity of those who were wronged. To blame oneself, according to Pereboom, is to take on a stance of moral protest toward oneself in virtue of an action one regards as morally wrong. The reasons one has for doing so are forward-looking and include moral formation and reconciliation in a relationship that has been impaired as a result of one's wrongdoing. Which emotional reactions would aptly accompany this form of self-blame? According to Pereboom, guilt presupposes desert. But *regret*, that is, a painful response to one's own wrongdoing, does not involve the supposition that the pain it involves is basically deserved and can thus be apt even if no one deserves to experience pain or harm.

Part II concerns the ethics of self-blame. Are there different standards for blaming oneself than for blaming others? Dana Nelkin begins her contribution by observing that there is a striking asymmetry in our normative expectations of degrees of self-blame and degrees of other-directed blame. There are many situations in which it seems intuitively plausible that a person should blame herself to a certain degree, while at the same time, it is also appropriate for others to blame her to a lesser degree. This calls out for explanation. Nelkin canvasses the prospects for rejecting the idea that there is any systematic explanation to be found. She also critically discusses a variety of possible explanations that purport to justify a genuine asymmetry between the norms of self-blame and other-directed blame. The latter group includes explanations according to which it is a virtue to over-blame in one's own case and in which it is a virtue to be disposed to under-blame in the case of others. Instead, Nelkin argues that a central and systematic explanation relies in part on a general moral principle according to which asymmetric risk imposition between self and others is justified. Nelkin concludes by exploring the implications of this view for whether we should privilege intuitions about self-blame, other-directed blame, or neither in philosophical theorizing.

Self-blame may but need not be expressed. *Should* self-blame be expressed, and if so under what conditions? Hannah Tierney's chapter develops an important norm for the expression of self-blame that she calls "Don't Suffer in Silence." When we blame ourselves, we ought not do so privately. Rather, we should, *ceteris paribus*, express our self-blame to those we have wronged. Tierney centers her discussion around a paradigmatic form of expressing self-blame: expressing guilt. She notes several important reasons for expressing one's guilt. Such expression does important interpersonal work. In confessing our guilt to those we have wronged, we begin the process of repairing our relationships with them. Expressions of guilt can ease victims' suffering, restore something important that they have lost (or that was taken from them) and reaffirm their standing in the moral community. But such expressions can also serve as an ameliorative function for the wrongdoer. A failure to express one's guilt can make the wrongdoer suffer more guilt than she deserves. Tierney ends her chapter by exploring how the "Don't Suffer in Silence" norm can contribute to our understanding of the ethics of self-blame as well as the nature of blame-worthiness itself.

Interesting normative questions concerning self-blame arise in cases when we evaluate our own emotional responses. Krista Thomason's chapter explores an important moral experience: that of judging ourselves for our emotional responses. Often the emotions that we criticize are *recalcitrant*: they are emotions that we do not endorse or that conflict with our considered judgments. Thomason notes that most of the philosophical literature on recalcitrant emotions focuses on whether and how they are possible or whether and how they are irrational. Thomason focuses instead on the ways we blame ourselves for recalcitrant emotions. She argues that it is harder than it looks to explain self-blame for recalcitrant emotions. Recalcitrance alone does not give us a reason to feel any particular way about our emotions, and it does not provide sufficient grounds for self-blame.

Part III investigates the relationship between self-blame and moral responsibility. In his chapter, Michael McKenna examines the role of both self-blame and guilt within the context of his conversational theory of moral responsibility. According to McKenna's own theory as well as communicative theories of responsibility more generally, the central examples of blame involve others overtly and directly blaming the one who is blameworthy and so communicating with the culpable party. Some philosophers have recently placed guilt and self-blame at the heart of moral responsibility's nature. They also have made the deservingness of guilt the most fundamental normative consideration in justifying the harms of blaming. Doing so appears to threaten conversational and other communicative theories of moral responsibility. In response, McKenna argues that guilt and self-blame cannot play the fundamental grounding role in a theory of moral responsibility. As a result, conversational and other communicative theories are not in jeopardy. Rather, what is required is a proper appreciation of the aim and norms of our blaming practices wherein guilt and also self-blame are meant to fit as responses to the blame of others as well as oneself. Along the way, McKenna also argues that self-blame and guilt are distinct things. While it is natural to think that to experience guilt just is to blame oneself, this, according to McKenna, is not so. Although the two are tightly connected, the relationship is nevertheless contingent; one can blame oneself without experiencing guilt, and one can experience guilt without blaming oneself.

In my own chapter, I focus on an often overlooked aspect of blameworthiness. The literature on moral responsibility is ripe with accounts of what it takes for an agent to become blameworthy. By contrast, very little has been written about what it takes for an agent's blameworthiness to cease or diminish. It seems that there are certain things a wrongdoer can feel or do that might make her less blameworthy than she would otherwise have been. She might experience guilt, atone, apologize, and make reparations. I argue that prominent accounts of blameworthiness are unable to explain how such actions and emotions can influence one's blameworthiness. I then present an alternative account. If we understand blameworthiness in terms of deserved guilt rather than fitting resentment, we can give a plausible account of how blameworthiness can change over time. The fact that a wrongdoer has already experienced guilt, atoned, or apologized will make her less deserving of guilt and therefore less blameworthy.

Gunnar Björnsson's chapter also concerns the connection between guilt, desert, and blameworthiness. Central cases of moral blame suggest that blame presupposes that its target deserves to feel guilty and that if one is blameworthy to some degree, one deserves to feel guilt to a corresponding degree. This, some think, is what explains why being blameworthy for something presupposes having had a strong kind of control over it: only given such control is the suffering involved in feeling guilt deserved. Björnsson argues that all this is wrong. By considering a wider range of cases, Björnsson proposes that blame does not presuppose that the target deserves to feel guilt and does not necessarily aim at the target's suffering in recognition of what they have done. In addition to that, he offers an explanation of why, in many cases of moral blameworthiness, the agent nevertheless deserves to feel guilt. The explanation builds on a general account of moral and nonmoral blame and blameworthiness and a version of the popular idea that moral blame targets agents' objectionable quality of will.

We often feel guilty for our wrongdoings. But do we have any reason to feel guilty, and can the pain of guilt be deserved? In the final chapter of this volume, Randolph Clarke and Piers Rawling argue that the facts that make an agent blameworthy also provide the agent with a reason to feel guilty. For example, the facts in question might be that the agent acted freely, with knowledge that the action was wrong, and was moved by ill will. The same set of facts that makes an agent blameworthy also suffices for the agent to deserve to experience the painful emotion of guilt. Clarke and Rawling argue that desert is essential to moral responsibility, that it can be permissible to induce a feeling of guilt in people who are blameworthy, and that it is noninstrumentally good that people who are blameworthy are subject to a fitting feeling of guilt.

PART I

The Nature of Self-Blame

CHAPTER I

The Motivational Theory of Guilt (and Its Implications for Responsibility)

Justin D'Arms and Daniel Jacobson

The Strawsonian approach to responsibility tries to explain what it is to be morally responsible for one's actions in terms of being an appropriate object of the reactive attitudes (see Strawson, 1962).[1] In order to succeed, the approach must first explain what the relevant attitudes are and what is meant by appropriateness. Although there are both negative and positive reactive attitudes, corresponding to blame and praise, most of the discussion following Strawson focuses on the negative side. It can therefore only hope to capture blameworthiness, not responsibility in general, since to be morally responsible in a good (or neutral) way is surely not to be the appropriate object of a negative attitude. We, too, will focus on blameworthiness, which Strawsonians hope will provide the foundation for a general theory. This chapter develops and answers an important challenge to any such account of responsibility, whatever the reactive attitudes to which it appeals. Our discussion centers on guilt, for reasons to be explained, and hence specifically concerns self-blame. A similar problem arises for other-directed blame, which will require an analogous solution.

The challenge facing the Strawsonian project also faces the sentimentalist project we have been developing for some time, and we will suggest that the same solution applies to both cases. *Sentimentalism*, as we understand it, refers to those views that explain (at least some) values in terms of the emotions; and our own view, *rational sentimentalism*, does so specifically in terms of the fittingness of emotions – or, equivalently, of what merits them – where merit and fit are understood to be notions of correctness. We have argued that considerable confusion arises from the failure to differentiate between fittingness and other forms of appropriateness.[2]

---

[1] There are other ways to read Strawson's classic paper, but this is what we shall mean in referring to the Strawsonian tradition. McKenna (2012), Rosen (2015), Shoemaker (2017), and Wallace (1994), among others, are all Strawsonians in this sense.

[2] See D'Arms and Jacobson (2000) for more on differentiating such notions of appropriateness.

An influential challenge presented by Philippa Foot observes that sentimentalist explanations are informative only if the emotions they appeal to do not already include the evaluative concept they attempt to explain. In her view, sentimentalism fails that challenge because "the explanation of the thought comes into the description of the feeling, not the other way round" (1978, p. 76). Foot adopts a cognitivist theory of the emotions, in which they are type-identified by some constitutive thought necessary for having the emotion. In order to be proud of something, for example, one must believe it to be splendid and one's own. As she puts it: "I do not mean, of course, that one would be illogical in feeling pride towards something one did not believe to be in some way splendid and in some way one's own, but that the concept of pride does not allow us to talk like that" (1978, p. 76).

According to Foot's challenge, sentimentalism gets the order of explanation wrong. Emotions are to be explained in terms of values, not values in terms of the emotions. If to be prideworthy is to merit pride, and pride is even partly constituted by the thought that something is splendid and mine, then it seems to follow that for something to be prideworthy is just for it to be splendid and mine.[3] But if the prideworthy can be understood via a pride-independent notion of *splendid and mine*, then sentimentalism would be otiose: pride drops out of the explanation of the prideworthy. A distinct but related problem is suggested by Foot's cognitivist claim that the order of explanation goes from the evaluative concept to the emotion, "not the other way round." Some sentimentalists propose to adopt both directions of explanation in an overtly circular fashion: the value gets explained in terms of the response, which in turn gets explained in terms of the value (see Wiggins, 1987). We are skeptical of the claim that such an explanation is not viciously circular; at any rate, we do not think that it can explain much.

The same issues arise for the Strawsonian account of responsibility. If blameworthiness should be understood via some reactive attitude whose content can be given in terms of concepts that are attitude independent, then the attitude seems to drop out of the explanation. If to be blameworthy is to have violated a requirement of respect, for instance, then – even if there is some reactive attitude that involves the thought that someone has disrespected you – the attitude seems inessential to this account of

---

[3] At any rate, this is so if fittingness is tantamount to the truth of the emotion's constitutive thought. Indeed, cognitivism's ability to explain fittingness in this straightforward way is one of its features.

blameworthiness (cf. Graham, 2014). Such an explanation renders the attitude otiose.[4] Yet, if blameworthiness must be explained in terms of a reactive attitude that is even partly constituted by a thought containing concepts such as *blameworthiness* or *responsibility*, then the explanation would be rendered circular.

We suggest that Foot's challenge sets the ground rules for a successful Strawsonian account. The reactive attitude to which it appeals must meet two conditions: (1) *Priority*. The attitude's content must not be capable of being given in wholly response-independent terms, or the attitude will drop out as otiose. And it must not be given in terms of responsibility or any concept that presupposes responsibility, on pain of circularity. (2) *Rational assessability*. The attitude must be amenable to assessment of its appropriateness in the relevant respect, such that it is appropriate to respond that way specifically to blameworthy (or otherwise responsible) action. The trouble is that the most straightforward way to meet the second condition seems to presuppose a cognitivist theory of emotion that cannot meet the first condition.

Philosophers tend to conceive of reactive attitudes as propositional attitudes, and to characterize them in terms of certain thoughts, beliefs, or judgments necessary for their possession. This approach risks violating the priority condition. In our view, a core class of what we term natural emotions are the most promising candidates for a Strawsonian account, because they have a psychological character that is independent of the concepts the account tries to explain. Many of Strawson's examples of reactive attitudes are emotions, including indignation, resentment, and guilt – but these emotions differ in one crucial respect. If indignation and resentment are second- and third-personal attitudes whose content involves the notion of wrongness, as is often claimed, then Foot's challenge looms, and it threatens the priority of these attitudes. If wrongness can be understood in wholly response-independent terms – say as what violates the categorical imperative – then the appropriateness of indignation and resentment drops out; it does not contribute to the account of blameworthiness. But if wrongness must be understood even partly

---

4 One might be tempted to resist this conclusion by appeal to a distinction between the concept and the property of blameworthiness. It might be said that our concept of blameworthiness is response dependent, involving an essential appeal to some reactive attitude, even if the property of blameworthiness is a response-independent one such as *having engaged in disrespectful behavior*. But this would not vindicate a Strawsonian approach. Whatever one says about the metaphysics of properties and about the conditions of blameworthiness, it is crucial to a genuinely response-dependent approach to responsibility that the reactive attitudes figure in the explanation of why the conditions are as they are, and why this particular property has the significance it has.

in terms of moral responsibility (or blameworthiness), then that would render the account circular.[5]

We have argued elsewhere that resentment and indignation are best understood as *cognitive sharpenings* of anger – a subclass of anger instances that are defined in part by including some thought involving a moral complaint (D'Arms & Jacobson, 2003). Roughly, they involve being angry with someone over her wrongdoing. This suggests that neither of these other-directed reactive attitudes is well positioned to meet the priority condition. David Shoemaker's (2017) recent development of a Strawsonian theory proposes instead that to be blameworthy is to be a fitting target of anger in general. Anger has the advantage of being a paradigm of the core class of emotions that plausibly satisfy the priority condition. But there are difficulties with this suggestion as well. Anger is coarse-grained in some respects, and it is controversial whether its conditions of fittingness match those for (negative) moral responsibility.

The first concern is that there may be a variety of anger, which Shoemaker calls *goal-frustration anger*, that can be fitting without anyone being blameworthy.[6] Another concern is that some actions seem to be suitable targets of self-blaming responses but do not merit the anger of others – cases where one does what one should do, all things considered, but in doing so betrays someone to whom one has special obligations. If so, then the form of blameworthiness that captures responsibility might be better modeled on self-blame than on the blame of others. Finally, Andreas Carlsson (2017) has argued that guilt is uniquely positioned to explain and justify why agents are blameworthy only for what they directly or indirectly control. All of these issues are complex, and they deserve attention in their own right that we cannot offer here. For present purposes, we simply note them as reasons to think that although anger and its cognates have been discussed more and received more of Strawson's attention, there are substantial advantages to a Strawsonian approach that is focused on guilt and, hence, on self-blame.

---

[5] This poses an interesting problem for Gideon Rosen's *alethic* view. If the thoughts he claims to be integral to resentment can be understood in response-independent terms, and blameworthiness is simply the truth of those thoughts, then resentment would be otiose. Blameworthiness would cease to be response dependent in anything like the way Strawson suggests. It is unclear to us whether Rosen (2015) accepts the first part of the antecedent – the evidence seems equivocal. If he does, he may yet think that he has an answer to the challenge of otioseness, insofar as resentment explains why the conditions of responsibility are as they are. That is a point he makes explicitly. But we think that this explanation would be substantially undermined if the content of resentment can be fully captured in terms of thoughts that are response independent. We cannot pursue that issue further here.

[6] Shoemaker (2018) worries about this possibility and tries to distinguish this sort of anger from what he terms *blaming anger* without circularity.

Guilt, too, must answer Foot's challenge, since its content is also often held to be constituted by thoughts about wrongdoing. We have a theory of guilt to offer, however, which proves helpful because it is suited to play the right sort of role in this dictum:

> (*) For A to be blameworthy for *x* is for it to be appropriate for A to feel guilt for *x*.

We do not here aspire to defend an account of responsibility or blameworthiness on the basis of appropriate guilt, but to develop the building blocks of such an account. Our main contribution is to offer a theory of guilt that can satisfy the priority condition because it is grounded in a sentimentalist-friendly theory of the natural emotions. We can only sketch this motivational theory of emotion here, though we develop it in detail elsewhere. We will then offer some reasons for thinking that appropriateness should be understood as a matter of fittingness rather than some other normative notion. The accounts of guilt and appropriateness we put forward flesh out (*) in a way that avoids problems besetting other Strawsonian accounts. They provide the most promising way to develop a theory of blameworthiness grounded in self-blame.

1   The Motivational Theory of Natural Emotions

We reject the cognitivist theory of emotion, understood as those views that make some constitutive thought a necessary condition for having the emotion and use that thought to type-identify the emotions.[7] As Martha Nussbaum claims: "It seems necessary to put the thought into the definition of the emotion itself. Otherwise, we seem to have no good way of making the requisite discriminations among emotion types" (2001, p. 30). In our view, the putatively response-independent thoughts that cognitivists use to type-identify emotions are either subject to manifold counterexamples or else must become tacitly response dependent. "This is splendid and mine," for example, can be held of many things that are not prideworthy; to take just one example, consider your winning a lottery ticket. Although it is both splendid and yours, it does not seem to merit your pride. Since Foot identifies this thought as a necessary condition for being proud of

---

[7] This is not to claim that emotions are mere feelings with no cognitive aspect, or to deny that there are conceptions of what it is to have a thought (e.g., "this is dangerous") or to possess a concept (*danger*) such that they can be attributed to an agent simply by virtue of his having an emotion (fear). Such interpretivist views are compatible with the priority thesis, however, unlike traditional forms of cognitivism that challenge sentimentalist and Strawsonian theories.

something, not a sufficient one, it is open to her to elaborate further on the thought – though she never suggests that she sees any need to do so. But in order for her view to belie the sentimentalist order of explanation, as she claims, the additional content must not be pride-dependent. She cannot explain away the lottery ticket example by saying that in order to be pride-worthy, something must be *splendid and mine in the pride-y way*.

Other reasons to reject the cognitivist theory have to do with the nature of emotional motivation and with problems concerning how to adjudicate disputes between cognitivists over the content of these constitutive thoughts. These questions ought to be primarily empirical, but cognitivism seems to make them matters of semantics or conceptual analysis. Moreover, cognitivism has an inadequate explanation of important phenomena such as *emotional recalcitrance* (where an agent has an emotion that is unfitting by his own lights) and *acting without thinking* (where an agent in the throes of an emotion acts on its goal in ways contrary to her ends and sometimes pursues predictably bad means for achieving even the goal of the emotion itself). A motivational theory can do better. Its compatibility with sentimentalism and the Strawsonian approach to responsibility is not the reason to accept the theory so much as a felicitous implication of its acceptance.

Our motivational theory does not attempt to capture all the states commonly called emotions, let alone every affect-laden attitude, but focuses on what we term the *natural emotions*. The natural emotions are pan-cultural psychological kinds that figure in the explanation of various familiar phenomena that would otherwise be mysterious. We are not claiming that everything commonly called an emotion counts as a psychological kind or that only these states should be called emotions. Rather, we use this term to differentiate this core class from cognitive sharpenings (like resentment, as opposed to anger) and from a broad class of affect-laden attitudes (such as love and grief) that the theory does not purport to capture. The natural emotions – which we hereafter will refer to simply as emotions – are goal-directed states characterized by specific *action tendencies*: urgent motivations toward certain actions that are especially direct ways to satisfy the emotion's generic goal, in paradigmatic circumstances.

The goal of fear is threat avoidance, for example, but the state of fear prejudices the means taken to avoid a threat. It favors the most direct and urgent goal-directed actions, such as fleeing. Those threats that are best avoided by calm negotiation or through complex mental calculation still cause fear. Though it may be possible to take these better means despite being afraid, fear impedes its own goal in such cases, because its action tendency must be overcome in order for the threat to be avoided. Moreover, people in a state of fear are often inhibited in their ability to pursue ends more important to them than avoiding the feared threat – and similarly for other natural emotions. These are respects in which the emotions are discontinuous with practical reasoning, and this is the kernel of truth in the clichéd (and exaggerated) opposition between emotion and reason. Although the motivational aspect of emotions is central to their function, emotions are syndromes that are also typically characterized by other things, including feeling, selective attention, typical elicitors and palliators, bodily changes, and thoughts.

The motivational theory can explain emotional recalcitrance, because it takes the emotions to be discrete motivational systems that are partially encapsulated and, hence, not reliably responsive to certain beliefs and ends that may be contrary to them. The self-aware phobic who is afraid of flying judges it to be less dangerous than many activities she engages in without fear; yet she is disposed to be afraid of flying, nonetheless. Notice how implausible it is to think that she makes conflicting judgments about the safety of flying, given her calm attitude toward the prospect of other people – even those she loves – flying. If she has contradictory beliefs, those are specific to her own flying. The introduction of conflicting beliefs in some such cases seems like a desperate attempt to salvage a theory.[8] Much better to say that her fear motivates her to direct and urgent means of avoiding what it appraises, contrary to her judgment, as dangerous. The motivational theory can offer a similar explanation of acting without thinking. Agents in the grip of an emotional bout are motivated to pursue the generic goal of their emotion in the most direct and urgent ways, regardless of whether these are the best ways to pursue the goal and whether this is the most important goal to pursue.

While various aspects of the motivational theory require further explication, some of them are not crucial for present purposes. What is important here is that it offers a way of understanding the emotions on which they are well suited to satisfy the priority condition. The question is whether there is such a natural emotion that is a likely candidate to play the lead role in a Strawsonian account of blameworthiness. We will argue that guilt is such a state. It is a psychological kind, open to

[8] Although it is possible for cognitivists to hold that agents in the grip of a recalcitrant emotion have contradictory beliefs or conflicting thoughts, those forms of the theory strong enough to undermine the priority thesis have no explanation for why such conflicts persist after their recognition, as ordinary cases of conflicting belief do not – that is, for why they are so recalcitrant to considered judgment.

empirical investigation. It is not even partly constituted by a thought
of blameworthiness or by some emotion-independent thought that can
explain blameworthiness without appealing to a reactive attitude.

Any theory that attempts to capture blameworthiness in terms of
guilt will need a normative component, since it is obviously implausible
to understand the blameworthy as whatever actually makes people feel
guilty. The fact that someone feels "survivor guilt" over being the only
one to survive some catastrophe – assuming for the sake of argument
that survivor guilt is a genuine phenomenon and is genuinely a form of
guilt, as seems plausible – must not entail that she is blameworthy for
surviving. Similarly, for something to be blameworthy is not for it to
elicit guilt but for it to make guilt in some sense appropriate. Rational
sentimentalism takes the relevant sense of appropriateness to be fittingness. We will assume this position for now and defend it (briefly) later.
The question is how to capture what it is for an emotion to be fitting,
consistent with the priority criterion. How can one give standards of fittingness for the emotions without appealing to the truth of some constitutive thought? We defend a proposal for how to get fittingness without
cognitivism elsewhere, which we can only sketch here (see D'Arms &
Jacobson, forthcoming).

Begin with an *empirical* characterization of the general emotional syndrome: the cluster of feelings, patterns of attention, typical elicitors and
palliators, characteristic thoughts, and especially the motivational role
occurring in paradigmatic episodes of the emotion kind. In light of this
data, give an *interpretation* into language of how someone in the grip of
such an emotion appraises its object as specifically good or bad. Appraisals
in this sense are not constitutive thoughts or components of emotion, but
ways of understanding how the emotion as a whole evaluates its object.
Any gloss into language will be imperfect and can at most help to point in
the direction of the distinctive way that the emotion appraises its object.
Since these emotional appraisals are derived from the emotion holistically,
including its motivational element, they must be understood as response
dependent – even if their terms have response-independent senses in ordinary language. In deciding whether the gloss applies in any given case,
one must understand it in a way that is informed by the emotion whose
appraisal it attempts to articulate. A minimal condition of adequacy on
such a gloss is that it rings true to those who have experienced the emotion. Consider the case of fear and danger.

An empirical characterization of fear favors the suggestion that it should
be interpreted as appraising its object as dangerous, for example; this makes

sense of how fear engages with its object – as something to be avoided directly and urgently. Notice too that the manner in which a feared object is to be avoided differs from the way that disgust motivates avoidance. It can be enjoyable to observe something fearsome from safety, whereas one typically wants to avoid perceiving the disgusting. The claim that fear concerns danger is not a surprising suggestion, of course, though interpretive matters are subtler in other cases. What is distinctive about our approach is *how* it understands the claim that fear is about danger: not as a response-independent thought one must have in order to count as afraid, but rather as an effort to articulate the distinctive emotional appraisal involved in the combination of feelings, goals, and action tendencies of fear.

Yet one might be puzzled about how our claim that fear appraises its object as dangerous differs from the cognitivist claim that fear includes a thought about danger. The difference depends on what is meant by saying that fear is (at least partly) constituted by such a belief or thought. We reject a specific and substantive thesis, articulated by Foot and embraced by other cognitivists, which threatens sentimentalist and Strawsonian accounts by violating the priority condition. This is the thesis that emotion types are individuated by some constitutive thought or defining proposition – something explicable independent of other aspects of the emotion, in particular its motivational component, which provides a necessary condition on being in the state. If that were true, then sentimentalism would be otiose; however, these supposedly constitutive propositions are either subject to manifold counterexamples, such as *splendid and mine* with pride, or have to be understood as tacitly response-dependent (see Deigh, 1994; Scarantino, 2010).[9]

On the other hand, if the claim that fear involves a thought of danger does not import these traditional cognitivist commitments, it might be compatible with our view. In particular, if thoughts of danger are attributed to the agent simply on the basis of the fact that she is afraid, then the concept of *dangerous* being imputed can be granted to be tacitly response-dependent. In which case, such a thought or construal may not differ substantively from our notion of emotional appraisal. We find our terminology more perspicuous for making the crucial point, which is that this proposal is compatible with the priority condition and, hence, does not threaten a sentimentalist or Strawsonian account.

[9] Although this is our central and novel objection to the cognitivist theory of emotion, it is not the only important criticism of this theory. It has problems explaining recalcitrant emotions and emotional motivation, as previously noted, but also with attributing emotions to infants and animals, and with unconscious emotions.

What it is for an emotion to be fitting then is for it to appraise its object correctly. Whether that is so in any given case is an evaluative question about which people can differ – for instance, when they disagree about whether riding a bicycle without a helmet merits fear. But such differences on evaluative questions constitute real disagreement only insofar as there is some shared way in which their fear appraises things. It seems clear that this is true of many natural emotions, and it is possible to find a way of expressing that appraisal in language that all parties to such a dispute can accept.

2 The Motivational Theory of Guilt as a Natural Emotion

Moral philosophers tend to suppose that there is a sharp distinction between states such as anger and fear, which they typically grant to be psychological kinds and continuous with states of beasts, and those sophisticated social emotions with which philosophical moral psychology tends to engage, such as guilt, regret, shame, envy, and jealousy. Paul Griffiths (1997) argues that the former class constitutes a kind that, following Paul Ekman, he calls *affect programs*; but that the latter, which he calls the *higher cognitive emotions*, differs so drastically that the two classes do not belong to any common kind.

Subsequent critics have noted that Griffiths's influential argument for this popular distinction is hasty. His treatment of the affect programs understates the variety and complexity of states such as fear and disgust, which, at least in humans, are neither as systematically encapsulated from higher cognition nor as stereotypical in their behavioral output as he initially suggested.[10] And his focus on the differences between affect programs and higher cognitive emotions, such as the presence of clear biological markers and the automaticity of some of their symptoms, leads him to overlook motivational similarities that cut across this distinction. Even if some instances of fear, anger, and disgust form a biological kind as affect programs, there might also be a broader psychological kind that includes other instances of those emotions as well as guilt, jealousy, and the like.[11] Indeed, Griffiths seems open to this possibility in more recent

---

[10] Roberts (2003) makes this point among others against Griffiths's disunity argument.

[11] Prinz (2004) and Deonna and Teroni (2012b) press this point as well. Both also note that the category Griffiths calls "irruptive motivations" appears to include both affect programs and the examples of higher cognitive emotions mentioned earlier. We agree entirely on these points and develop them further, in what follows, by illustrating the explanatory power of the motivational theory in the case of guilt.

work (see Scarantino & Griffiths, 2011). Although some contemporary psychologists are skeptical that *any* emotions are natural kinds, we find their standards for such claims overly demanding and doubt some details of their arguments.[12]

Guilt is a good example of an emotion that recruits sophisticated cognitive faculties and lacks some of the physiological symptoms of bodily preparation for action characteristic of fear and anger, but which exhibits the peculiar motivational features distinctive of natural emotions. Guilt typically arises in response to voluntary action of the agent that gives others grounds for anger. Two familiar examples are personal betrayals (which give a specific person such grounds) and breaches of moral rules (which give them to all). Bouts of guilt display the *control precedence* characteristic of emotional motivation: they prioritize the emotional goal in attention and motivation. And they issue in actions such as confession, apology, and other direct and urgent effort to make amends, as well as in self-castigation – especially when restitution is impossible. Guilt is characteristically satisfied by indications that the injured party has accepted the apology, and that relations have been restored to something like the status quo ante. Hence, the goal of guilt seems best described as the *reparation* of some damaged relationship, either with a specific person or with the community at large.

Guilt exhibits the peculiarities characteristic of emotional motivation, despite its cognitive complexity. It can issue in acting without thinking, when it motivates overly direct and urgent means to meet its goal, or when it leads the guilt-ridden agent to sacrifice ends that are more important by his own lights. Actions performed in the throes of guilt are often insensitive to these other ends, and to some of the agent's information about how best to achieve the goal of reparation. Thus, people attempting to get away with wrongdoing can be undone by their guilt when it prioritizes the goal of reparation in ways they do not endorse on reflection. And even those who endorse reparation as their overriding goal can be prompted, by their guilt, to poor means of achieving it such as overapologizing, confessing too often or at too great length, and performing acts of contrition that predictably serve to discomfit the victim rather than repair the relationship. A hallmark of the emotions is their prioritization of a generic goal and narrowed attentional focus – that is, control precedence – and their

---

[12] An especially influential skeptic is Lisa Feldman Barrett (2017a). Her recent exchange with Ralph Adolphs illustrates some of the controversies within neuroscience (Adolphs, 2017a, 2017b; Barrett 2017b, 2017c). We address these issues at some length elsewhere (D'Arms and Jacobson, forthcoming) but will not pursue them here.

prejudice in favor of direct and urgent means to satisfy that goal. These similarities in what and how emotions motivate are common between so-called affect programs and some higher cognitive emotions, and this makes us skeptical about putting too much weight on that distinction.

Guilt is also susceptible to stable recalcitrance, in that you can feel strongly driven to apologize or make reparations for something you did, or even something that merely happened to you, despite your considered judgment that your guilt is unfitting. This can happen in cases of survivor guilt, for instance, when someone is convinced that he has done nothing wrong and yet continues to feel guilty. Recalcitrance is further evidence that guilt is a discrete source of motivation, despite its complexity, which can persist at odds with the agent's considered judgment. We think it plausible that guilt is an adaptation, which is part of normal human nature because it enabled our ancestors to respond to their own transgressions in ways that helped them maintain better relationships with others; but that claim is not essential to the theory or this chapter.

It thus appears that guilt, like fear and anger, is a distinctive kind of affect-laden motivational system that has a characteristic goal (of reparation) and motivates a distinctive way of pursuing that goal. That is, bouts of guilt prioritize the goal and direct cognitive resources toward its direct and urgent satisfaction, potentially at the cost of attending to its relative importance and whether the actions it urges are the best means of meeting its own goal. Its nature is a matter for empirical investigation, not for specification by conceptual analysis. It is not even partly constituted by a particular judgment or thought that can be given in response-independent terms, because the appraisal is an interpretation of the emotion as a whole, including its motivational aspects. The terms in which the gloss is given must therefore be understood in light of the emotion's goal, such that it appraises its object – in this case, one's own action – as giving one reason to act in reparation. How then should one interpret the generic appraisal of guilt, so as to understand the conditions under which it is fitting?

The procedure we previously outlined starts from an empirical characterization of guilt. While philosophers most often focus on guilt as a response to moral transgression, its paradigmatic elicitors actually fall into two broad kinds: not only actions involving moral violations, such as theft and murder, but also actions that constitute some sort of transgression against a personal relationship, like disappointing a loved one.[13] Its typical phenomenology involves feeling bad about what one has done, specifically

---

[13] Tangney and Dearing (2002) describe studies that support these commonsense observations.

for those it hurt, and the desire to express this feeling. In short, guilt is experienced as a felt desire to make amends. As noted, guilt motivates apology, confession, and efforts to compensate where possible; and it is most likely to be satisfied by sincere forgiveness or other signs that the relationship has been repaired. In light of these features, we suggest that someone in a bout of guilt can be interpreted roughly to appraise himself as having engaged either in some sort of *wrongdoing* or in a *personal betrayal*.[14]

If we are right that someone who feels guilty about something can be understood to take it as a wrongdoing or a personal betrayal, then those familiar with guilt should find this gloss plausible and agree that it sets the terms for assessing when guilt is fitting. But the gloss remains rough because of the point noted earlier: the way that you take something in the throes of an emotion is shaped by the character of the emotion itself. Hence, the relevant terms must be allowed enough semantic slack to accommodate the response-dependent evaluation they seek to articulate. In this case, they must be understood in a way that accommodates excuses. If someone was coerced into stealing in a way that you think renders guilt unfitting, for instance, then you think he has not really acted wrongly in the sense of that term that captures guilt's appraisal. One could say instead that guilt appraises what one has done as an *unexcused* wrongdoing or betrayal. Though this addition might avert certain misunderstandings, it creates others, since not everything that counts as an excuse in ordinary language, law, or social custom renders guilt unfitting. Instead, we will retain the simpler version, with the caveat that it is (inevitably) a rough-and-ready characterization of a response-dependent appraisal.

We consider some implications of this gloss in the final section. What is crucial for present purposes is that our account of guilt satisfies the success conditions previously given. We have argued that guilt satisfies the priority condition, because the motivational theory does not make it require any response-independent evaluative thought. Our gloss of its appraisal is not a constituent of the emotion but an articulation of what guilt concerns in light of its nature, which enables an account of when it is fitting. It is a further question whether guilt satisfies the rational assessment condition on an account of the blameworthy. This a matter of whether its nature

---

[14] Our account of guilt's appraisal is unconventional, and hence controversial, because it makes room for the possibility that guilt can be fitting over actions that are not morally wrong – and perhaps even obligatory. This will be the case for betrayals of an intimate for overriding impersonal reasons. We develop a case of this sort in D'Arms and Jacobson (1994) as part of an argument against Gibbard's (1990) neo-sentimentalist account of the blameworthy. In these cases, arguably *someone* has reason to blame you, namely the person whom you betrayed; but others have no such reason.

is such that it is appropriate, in the relevant respect, to feel guilty over just one's blameworthy actions. In order to assess this, we must offer an account of the relevant sense of appropriateness.

3 Appropriate Guilt: Fittingness, Not Desert

According to the Strawsonian dictum (*), for A to be blameworthy for x is for it to be appropriate for A to feel guilt for x. Clearly, the term "appropriate" is normative, in contrast to a dispositional view on which for A to be blameworthy for x is for A to be prone to guilt over x. Although there are more plausible forms of dispositionalism, we find them all inadequate. But "appropriate" is vague, and there are various ways to flesh it out that have disparate implications. If an attitude is said to be appropriate just in case it is optimal, for instance, then the dictum would be open to familiar counterexamples involving evil demons and eccentric millionaires who create incentives for having the attitude. Wallace (1994) has proposed that responsibility should be understood in terms of the *fairness* of the blaming emotions, but we agree with Carlsson (2017, p. 19) that certain considerations relevant to the fairness of blaming – like whether others have been blamed for similar actions – do not bear on whether an action is blameworthy (see also Vargas, 2004).[15] We will focus on what seem to us the two most promising ways to understand appropriateness in (*): as the claim that guilt is *fitting* and that it is *deserved*.

The cognitivist theory of emotion has a seemingly straightforward account of fittingness as the truth of an emotion's constitutive thought. We consider this a specious advantage of the theory, since cognitivists dispute exactly what is the constitutive thought of an emotion type, and their method affords them no good way to resolve such dispute. However that may be, we have now shown that the motivational theory of emotion can hold similarly that an emotion is fitting when its appraisal is correct. These appraisals are to be understood not as constitutive thoughts necessary for having the emotion, but as an overtly response-dependent interpretation of the emotional syndrome as a whole.[16] This allows us to hold that (*) should be given in terms of fittingness. Carlsson (2017) argues, to the contrary, that the relevant notion of appropriateness is that of desert.

---

[15] It may be that Wallace's view ultimately does not differ from that of Carlsson and Vargas, as Rosen (2015, p. 70) suggests, at least when it comes to guilt and self-blame.

[16] This means that both theories of emotion are compatible with what Rosen (2015) calls the *alethic* view. Rosen's terminology differs from ours, since he contrasts the alethic view of appropriateness with a view of appropriateness as fittingness. But Rosen uses "fittingness" for a different notion than that of correctness, specifically as a primitive normative notion.

The claim that someone deserves to feel guilt over what he has done is a moral assessment, but Carlsson's proposal is not simply the retributivist intuition that the blameworthy deserve to feel guilty. Although that claim is controversial, we find it plausible.[17] Rather, the question at hand concerns what it is to be blameworthy; specifically, whether the Strawsonian account is better off understanding appropriateness as fittingness or desert.

There is no tension involved in holding guilt to be both fitting and deserved in some circumstance, or even in thinking that guilt is deserved whenever it is fitting. Nevertheless, these are distinct notions that figure differently in an account of blameworthiness. We will argue that fittingness is the best way to understand appropriateness within a Strawsonian framework, on two grounds. First, this approach treats blameworthiness analogously to other sentimental values such as the funny, the shameful, and the disgusting. Second, it is plausible that guilt is deserved only when, and because, it is fitting.

We have argued elsewhere that a number of values are best understood in sentimentalist terms, as the appropriate object of some associated attitude (see D'Arms & Jacobson, forthcoming). Call these the *sentimental values*. What it is for something to be dangerous is for it to merit fear; to be shameful is to merit shame; and to be admirable is to be a fitting object of admiration. In each case, the relevant form of appropriateness is fittingness or merit, understood as a notational variant: for an emotion $F(x)$ to be fitting is for its object x to merit F. When something endangers a person sufficiently, it is fitting for her to fear it; however, she typically will not *deserve* to feel afraid, nor does the dangerous thing deserve her fear. If someone is especially graceful or beautiful, she may not deserve to feel proud of this trait, but pride is fitting simply because it reflects well on her. Similarly, for the other sentimental values, the relationship between sentiment and value is that of fittingness. Why should blameworthiness be different?[18] The proposal to understand appropriateness as fittingness gives a consistent theoretical treatment to an array of response-dependent values.

---

[17] It has been defended recently by Randolph Clarke (2016) and criticized by Dana Nelkin (2019). And, of course, it will be rejected by those who are skeptical of desert in general, such as Pereboom (2014).

[18] One might object that blameworthiness is different because to be blameworthy for some action is obviously tied up with being responsible for it, and being responsible for something bad makes you deserve your feelings of guilt. In contrast, one can have a shameful trait for which one is in no way responsible; while shame for such traits is fitting, one does not *deserve* to be ashamed. We accept this difference, but we think it is to be explained by the differences between guilt and shame that affect when they are fitting, not by a difference in the kind of emotional appropriateness involved in being blameworthy for something versus having a shameful trait.

Compare how each proposal explains why guilt is appropriate in those cases where it seems to be (such as for a robber), and inappropriate in other cases (as with survivor guilt). Our answer is that guilt over robbing someone is fitting – and therefore appropriate in the relevant sense – because it gets matters right. The robber's guilt appraises his action as wrong, and it is. The survivor's guilt appraises her survival in the same way, as a wrongdoing or betrayal, but it is not. The reason that survivor guilt is inappropriate is that she did nothing wrong and betrayed no one. The desert approach holds that guilt over having robbed someone is appropriate because the robber deserves to suffer for it – specifically to feel guilt over what he did – whereas the survivor did nothing to deserve that.

The general retributivist claim that the blameworthy deserve to suffer for what they have done is not tantamount to the claim that they deserve to feel guilt in particular. The thought that someone deserves to suffer does not differentiate between the suffering of a toothache and the suffering of feelings of compunction; all that matters for this basic retributivist intuition is that the suffering is proportionate to the degree of blameworthiness. A Strawsonian account of blameworthiness in terms of deserved guilt, on the other hand, is an attempt to explain blameworthiness in terms of that specific attitude. It therefore must explain why *guilt* is distinctively appropriate.

The answer must have to do with the nature of guilt, by virtue of which blameworthiness can be understood in terms of desert of this specific emotion. Carlsson characterizes guilt as a combination of painful affect and propositional content somehow held in mind – whether as a belief, thought, or seeming. Although the details are left somewhat vague, he proposes that guilt's propositional content is that the agent displayed an objectionable quality of will (2017, pp. 101–102). This suggests that what makes guilt the deserved form of suffering, which enables it to play a role in the analysis of blameworthiness, is that it involves being pained specifically at the thought that one displayed an objectionable quality of will.

But when does someone deserve this form of suffering in particular? The obvious answer is that one deserves this form of suffering just when that thought is correct. You do not deserve to suffer guilt in particular, as opposed to any other form of pain, unless the thought distinctive of guilt is true. If that is right, however, then the judgment that guilt is deserved is parasitic on the judgment that it is fitting. The point at hand does not depend on whether guilt takes its object as a wrongdoing or betrayal, simply as a wrongdoing, as an act of ill will, as all of those things, or some other thing. Nor does it matter if this content is to be found in a belief, thought, seeming, or appraisal. The point is simply that in order for guilt in particular to be deserved on the basis of what one has done and why one did it – as it must be to play the relevant role in an account of blameworthiness – its content must be correct. And that entails that in order for guilt to be deserved, it must be fitting.

Even so, defenders of the desert proposal might object that our argument shows only that it is necessary for guilt to be fitting in order for it to be deserved. It would still be possible for guilt to be fitting over some action but not deserved. According to this objection, such an action would not be blameworthy. It is unclear to us how best to make this argument, but perhaps a rationale can be found in Carlsson's claim that desert, unlike fittingness, accounts for the idea that in order for someone to be blameworthy, it must be noninstrumentally good that she suffers.[19] The idea that it is good for a wrongdoer to suffer is controversial, of course, even among those who accept that people can be blameworthy – not just that blame can be beneficial. It seems to us an advantage of fittingness that it can accommodate those who favor a Strawsonian account but are skeptical about the claim that it is noninstrumentally good for wrongdoers to suffer. And even those who grant the axiological claim can hope that the fittingness of guilt explains why that state in particular constitutes the sort of suffering that wrongdoers deserve.[20]

We conclude that fittingness best captures the appropriateness of guilt invoked in (*). Hence, a Strawsonian theory of blameworthiness that focuses only on self-blame should hold that for A to be blameworthy for x is for it to be fitting for A to feel guilty for x. We have offered an account of guilt and its fittingness that allows the theory to avoid the challenges of circularity and otioseness. Even if a full account of blameworthiness ought to appeal to other reactive attitudes as well, we think it plausible that the fittingness of guilt provides one central human mooring on which our concepts of blameworthiness and responsibility depend.

---

[19] The claim that deserved guilt is noninstrumentally good is defended by Clarke (2013), and Carlsson cites his arguments for this claim approvingly. In our view, some of those arguments apply equally to fittingness. But Clarke is not arguing for an account of blameworthiness in terms of appropriate guilt, nor for a preference for desert over fit within such an account.

[20] Judgments of fittingness are normative. They involve thinking that there are reasons to have the emotion and, moreover, reasons to act in some way that is relevant to satisfying its goal. This suffices to give at least partial endorsement to feelings and actions that would constitute costs to the blameworthy party. We think this captures what is correct in the elusive intuition, which – like all claims about noninstrumental goodness – is difficult to argue for directly.

CHAPTER 2

The Trials and Tribulations of Tom Brady
Self-Blame, Self-Talk, Self-Flagellation

David Shoemaker

Tom Brady was one of the greatest quarterbacks of all time. His ability for pinpoint passing, taking hits without fumbling, identifying weaknesses in defenses, and simply finding ways to win was unparalleled in the history of American football. And yet every once and a while he seemed very unhappy with himself. When he threw an interception, even in a meaningless game, he sometimes wailed and moaned, even falling to the ground and pounding his helmet with his hands. He was obviously blaming himself.

There are many other familiar examples: Serena Williams, behind in a tennis match, screams at herself, pounds her racket, and stomps her foot angrily; Tiger Woods stares in shock and then mutters to himself for missing what we nevertheless deem a ridiculously hard putt; Lindsay Vonn tosses her ski poles, shouting in disgust after seeing her third-place time. But this sort of response is not the exclusive purview of elite athletes. The weekend golf "duffer" who shanks her iron shot, the aging academic who misses an easy layup in a departmental basketball game, the bar denizen playing pool who scratches on the 8-ball: these regular folks also clearly blame themselves for their failures.

In the contemporary stampede of theorizing about blame, self-blame has been something of an afterthought, and athletic self-blame mostly a non-thought. Theorists instead have mostly just focused on articulating the nature of *other*-blame, going on to explain self-blame, if at all, in light of other-blame, as having the same core features, just directed reflexively. Drawn from the overt and dyadic paradigm, blame is thought to be a response, depending on the specific theory, to poor quality of will, a violation of the legitimate demands of one's fellows, a threat to someone's moral standing, and/or to some kind of moral wrongdoing.[1] It is thought to consist, again depending on the specific theory, of an interpersonal

---

[1] See, e.g., in order, McKenna (2012); Wallace (1994); Hieronymi (2004); and Clarke (2016).

conversational move, a communique of a demand or invitation for acknowledgment, a protest, and/or a kind of relationship modification.[2]

But while some of these overt, directed, interpersonal features might be present in some cases of self-blame, they are particularly hard to find in cases of athletic self-blame. These athletes haven't done anything *to* anyone else, let alone anything other-blamable.[3] They didn't manifest a poor quality of will, they didn't violate any of their fellows' demands, they didn't make any "threatening" claims, and they haven't engaged in any moral wrongdoing. And what does their self-blame consist of? Well, we know what it *isn't*: they aren't making conversational moves with themselves, they aren't communicating a demand for acknowledgment from themselves (they already know what they did!), they aren't protesting their threatening behavior, and they aren't modifying their relationships with themselves (what might that even mean?). Athletic self-blame constitutes a surprisingly serious *prima facie* counterexample to theories that take other-blame to be their paradigm.[4]

Recently, though, a few enterprising theorists have advanced and defended the idea that self-blame is actually more fundamental than other-blame, and that we can and should understand other-blame in light of it.[5] Understanding the athletic cases, then, should simply be a matter of applying the more general and fundamental notion of self-blame to that particular instantiation of it.

As I will show first in this chapter, though, such a move won't work, precisely because it relies on a crucial misunderstanding about the emotional

---

[2] See, e.g., in order, McKenna (2012); Watson (2004); Smith (2013); and Scanlon (2008).

[3] Perhaps the professional athletes at least have failed their fans or the team owner? Fans surely don't have a claim on an elite athlete's best performance. I myself don't think they have *any* kind of accountability claim on athletes except, perhaps, that the athletes put in a good faith effort in accordance with the rules, which might be the same claim the owners have on them. But I just can't see how one could think that Tom Brady violates any obligation to his fans when, in trying his hardest, he nevertheless throws an interception. This may *disappoint* his fans, but it can't fail or betray them. Of course, we can get rid of all the fans in the cases of the everyday golfer and pool player, and when it comes to the professionals we can focus just on cases of self-blame they engage in on the practice field or when working out alone to make the point. Thanks to Dana Nelkin, Randy Clarke, Angie Smith, Michael McKenna, and Sandy Reiter for discussion.

[4] Michael McKenna denies that self-blame for failures to live up to one's own ideals are counterexamples to his conversational theory of responsibility and blameworthiness, but he does "grant that accommodating them requires more attention to the topic than I have given it here" (McKenna, 2012, p. 73, n. 14). I'm not entirely sure how that accommodation project might go, especially as there could be no point to self-conversation in reflexive cases, as "both" sides are already aware of all the information and agent-meaning there is to be had.

[5] Carlsson (2017 and 2019) is the paradigm example; Duggan (2018) takes a somewhat similar tack; Clarke (2013, 2016) is a forerunner only in some respects; Graham (2014) is an ally, but again, only in some respects.

nature of self-blame that is, unfortunately, maintained widely in the literature. I will then go on to take a fresh look at self-blame (and other-blame) by *starting* with the athletic cases, arguing ultimately for the view that they have very different paradigmatic emotional cores, and as a result we cannot understand either form of emotional blame in terms of the other.

1   Guilt Mongers

Blame in our ordinary lives is ridiculously capacious, directed to all sorts of objects throughout space-time and having many different contents. Consequently, finding where to start theorizing about it can be difficult. Many theorists insist, though, that blame requires some sort of emotional content, and even those who reject this requirement don't deny that very often certain emotional responses are indeed *sufficient* for blame.[6] So we can start there.

The relevant blame emotions are what I will label the Holy Trinity: resentment, indignation, and guilt (see, e.g., Strawson, 1962/2003, pp. 77–89; Wallace, 1994, pp. 51–52; Fischer & Ravizza, 2000, pp. 5–8; McKenna, 2012, pp. 71–73; Franklin, 2013; Carlsson, 2017, p. 92). These are all "reactive attitudes," emotional responses to someone who is perceived to have violated legitimate demands or expectations.[7] Resentment is thought to be blame's second-personal emotion, a victim's response to the offender who injured or slighted her. Indignation is thought to be blame's third-personal emotion, someone else's response to that offender. And guilt is thought to be blame's first-personal emotion, the offender's response to him- or herself.

From the Holy Trinity, resentment and indignation are taken to be the paradigmatic emotional forms of "other-blame," whereas guilt is taken to be the paradigmatic emotional form of "self-blame." All three blame emotions are taken to mutually entail one another, differing essentially only in terms of their standpoints and targets. Their mutual entailment means that if it's appropriate for me to resent an offender for injuring or slighting me, it is also appropriate for you (and others) to be indignant toward this offender *and* for the offender to feel guilt for what he did (see, e.g., Carlsson, 2017, p. 102).

Given the presumed mutual entailment and symmetrical structures of their representative emotions, emotional self-blame and other-blame are

---

[6] Carlsson (2017, p. 91) says "blame *is* an emotion" (emphasis mine), and many others would agree (including, e.g., Hieronymi, 2004; Wallace, 2011; Wolf, 2011; Graham, 2014). Some others (like Sher, 2006; Scanlon, 2008; Smith, 2013) disagree with the identity claim, but they nevertheless agree that sometimes blame can be emotional.

[7] The phrase and characterization of course comes from Strawson (1962/2003, p. 76).

thought to be capturable under a single umbrella theory. As noted earlier, most people theorize first about other-blame, and then they simply apply their findings to self-blame, but this method leaves them vulnerable to the serious *prima facie* counterexample of athletic self-blame. Does the recent movement to start with self-blame thus do any better?

The movement has been spearheaded by Andreas Brekke Carlsson, in a few important papers (Carlsson, 2017; 2019). I will call him and those inclined to follow him the *Guilt Mongers*, because their fundamental claim is that emotional self-blame is just guilt, and "an agent is blameworthy in virtue of the fact and to the extent that he deserves to feel guilt" (Carlsson, 2017, p. 91), where guilt necessarily involves suffering, that is, "the pain of recognizing what you have done" in wronging someone (Carlsson, 2017, p. 91).

On Carlsson's view, resentment and indignation, even if they demand guilt, can be apt while remaining private, so they don't necessarily cause pain to anyone, and so they don't necessarily call for any moral defense. Guilt enjoys no such privacy, though: to feel guilt is to feel its pain. Guilt cannot be morally justified, then, unless it is *deserved* (Carlsson, 2017).[8] This suggests, then, that guilt requires different – more robust – agential *control* conditions than resentment or indignation do, seemingly implying a disanalogy between self- and other-blame. Carlsson, however, argues instead that we can preserve the analogy between self-blame and other-blame as long as we take deserved guilt to be "the basic notion in our conception of blameworthiness" (Carlsson, 2017, p. 103, drawing in part from Clarke, 2016). The more fundamental appeal to guilt then reveals what makes resentment and indignation appropriate, as follows: someone is other-blameworthy for X, that is, someone is an appropriate target of another's resentment and indignation for X, if and only if she deserves to feel guilt for X (Carlsson, 2017, p. 104). Consequently, when resentment and indignation are experienced and expressed, they count as other-*blame* in virtue of their guilt-mongering aims (Carlsson, 2017, p. 105).

But how would this approach apply to our athletes? It should be fairly obvious that most athletes who blame themselves for poor performance typically don't feel anything remotely like *guilt* about it.[9] Consider: if I am playing by myself and miss a two-foot putt for par, or if you scratch on the 8-ball in pool, we may likely both blame ourselves, but utterly without

---

[8] There are others who have run a line like this about guilt and desert, including McKenna (2012) and Clarke (2013, 2016).

[9] And again, to avoid complication, just eliminate fans, owners, teammates, and even professionalism from the equation and think about athletic self-blame on the practice field or all alone, say, on the golf course.

guilt. And this seems true as well in the high-profile athletic cases. When Serena Williams breaks her racket, she is surely not doing so out of guilt. Consequently, if the self-blame-first strategy is entirely a guilt-first strategy, it cannot account for many obvious cases of athletic self-blame.

What we might do, then, is tweak the account by following Douglas Portmore in expanding the relevant self-directed emotional repertoire to include *regret* and/or *remorse* (Portmore, this volume).[10] Now most of the athletes we are considering probably aren't feeling remorse either. But they are surely feeling *regret*, and regret is also painful. Consequently, we could construe the more expansive Guilt Mongering view to be that, to the extent that these athletes are blaming themselves aptly, they must be representing themselves as blameworthy and aiming to cause the blame-pain of regret in themselves, and insofar as aptly aiming at (self-)pain requires moral justification, they must deserve that pain.

With this tweak, the Guilt Mongers' general approach, and its application to athletic self-blame, initially looks promising. Unfortunately, it makes the mistake of many other accounts of blame by misunderstanding the relation between the self-directed emotions and blame more generally.

2   Blame and Guilt

The problem arises from the assumption that since the emotions of the Holy Trinity all mutually entail one another, they must also all have the same function, namely, that of being the paradigmatic emotional cores of blame. But while resentment and indignation are indeed plausible contenders for being the paradigmatic emotional core of other-blame, *guilt just isn't blame, let alone self-blame.*[11] Guilt is instead a *response* to blame, both self- and other-.

---

[10] I should stress that Portmore is not a Guilt Monger, for he thinks he is developing a conceptual account of blame proper that applies equally to self- and other-blame (and so he doesn't think one form of blame is more fundamental than the other).

[11] The conflation is everywhere. See, e.g., R. J. Wallace: "To hold myself responsible for a moral wrong [i.e., to blame myself], for example, it is sufficient that I should feel guilt about my violation of a moral obligation that I accept. ... [R]esentment, indignation, and guilt are backward-looking emotions, responses to the actions of a particular agent ...; they are essentially *about* such actions, in a way that exactly captures the backward-looking focus of moral blame. ... *Once blame is understood in terms of the reactive emotions* ..., we ... have a natural and appealing explanation to hand of what unifies the sanctioning responses to which the stance of holding people responsible disposes us ..." (Wallace, 1994, p. 67; second emphasis mine). See also McKenna (2012, p. 72): "In moral contexts, guilt is the self-reflexive emotion whereby one holds oneself morally responsible and blameworthy for doing wrong. In short, it constitutes self-blame." See also Carlsson (this volume): "To blame oneself in the accountability sense is to feel guilt." Scanlon also allows that guilt can be an element of self-blame (Scanlon, 2008, p. 143, pp. 154–155). Finally, see Portmore (this volume), who gives "fitting guilt" as one example of self-blame (the others being regret and remorse).

More carefully, guilt is a response to blam*ing*, to *being* blamed. But of course it isn't a response *only* to being blamed; it may also respond directly and exclusively merely to one's perception of one's own wrongdoing (or ill will, or failure to meet a legitimate demand, etc.), without having been spurred by blaming of any kind (including self-blaming). I can (aptly) come to feel guilt without having been blamed by anyone, including myself.[12]

This makes guilt an uneasy – or an unholy – member of the Trinity. Let's assume, as is plausible, that indignation and resentment are the paradigmatic emotional cores of (other-)blame. When deployed in active blam*ing*, they may best be described (especially by the Guilt Mongers) as *guilting* the wrongdoer, that is, as drawing her attention to what she did and aiming for her to feel guilt as a result. But that's explicitly to aim for an apt *response to the blame*. Guilt plays no analogous other-directed role, though: it's not as if in feeling guilt I aim for you to resent or be indignant with me *in response*![13] Instead, my guilt is simply a proper response to others blaming me. But my guilt isn't only a response to your other-blame of me; it may also in principle be a response to my self-blame (and so forestall or undercut your blame of me). And if and when it is, it's not like my guilt is a response to my *guilt*. It could only be a response to my (self-directed) guilt*ing*. So self-blame just isn't guilt.

What is it, then? If we are to have any chance at preserving a continuity or analogy between self-blame and other-blame, we have to think of self-blame's emotional core as somehow akin to that of resentment and indignation, which would have to make it a kind of *anger*.[14] And this should feel familiar and plausible: we get angry at ourselves for our screw-ups on a regular basis (or at least I do, as I screw up regularly), and we do so across all normative domains: moral, prudential, aesthetic, etiquettal, epistemological, and, yes, athletic. This means that in order to understand self-blame, we have to understand anger. And that's where we will start our positive case.

3　Anger(s)

Anger is a pancultural emotion that has certain characteristics in common with other pancultural emotions: it is irruptive, impulsive, urgent, and

---

[12] Of course, we do say things like "I blame myself – I just feel terrible for what I did." But this simply means that I take the blame, that is, I accept any blame there is for what I did by feeling the appropriate guilt.

[13] Except perhaps for self-flagellators, to be discussed below.

[14] I'm in full agreement with D'Arms and Jacobson (2003), as well as Pereboom (2014, p. 179) that indignation and resentment are just "cognitively sharpened" versions of anger.

flexible, and it involves involuntary bodily changes (see, e.g., Frijda, 1986; D'Arms, 2013, p. 3; Scarantino, 2014, pp. 157–159). Call such emotions, fol lowing D'Arms and Jacobson (forthcoming), *natural emotions*. These are best thought of as natural psychological kinds, and they are syndromes, typically constituted by some kind of (a) affective component, (b) appraisal, and (c) action tendency/motivational impulse (see Szigeti, 2015 for a nice overview and discussion). The last feature typically aims us toward a goal pertaining to what the emotional syndrome as a whole can best be interpreted as appraising (its "core relational theme," in the words of Lazarus, 1991; for this notion of interpretation and appraisal, see D'Arms & Jacobson forthcoming). The most straightforward illustration of an emotional syndrome comes from *fear*: its feelings involve trembling, dry mouth, heart pounding, and so forth. Its appraisal is of some perceived event's being a danger or threat. And its action tendencies – prototypically one of the famous three of fight, flight, or freeze – aim its bearer toward safety.

Disputes among emotion theorists are primarily over which of these three features of emotional syndromes serves to define and differentiate them. To that end, there have been feeling theorists, who prioritize the emotion's affective component (e.g., James, 1894; Prinz, 2005); appraisal theorists, who prioritize the emotions' evaluative component (e.g., Lazarus, 1982; Greenspan, 1988; Roberts, 1988; Solomon, 1988; Nussbaum, 2004); and motivational theorists, according to whom "the identity of an emotion is essentially tied to a prioritized tendency to action (or inaction) with the function of being elicited by a core relational theme," a theory which "replaces the primacy of the appraisal and feeling aspects of emotions with the primacy of their motivational dimension" (Frijda, 1986 is a forerunner; Scarantino, 2014, p. 168).

I favor the motivational theory, which implies that various natural emotions are identified and differentiated from other emotions in terms of their "action-readiness," what the emotions urgently urge us to *do*. I cannot here give a full explication and defense of this theory, but I will at least offer a few considerations in its favor. The strongest argument for it, I think, comes from considering emotion's role in both natural and cultural selection. We can best understand why we have the emotion of fear, for example, by considering how it must have enabled our ancestors to survive and reproduce (and thus pass the trait along), namely, by better enabling their safety in the presence of danger via its irruptive and urgent action tendencies. Fear was selected for as a result of its effects in achieving fear's goal (safety) in the presence of danger (Scarantino, 2014, p. 178). This etiological view has normative import as well. As Scarantino puts it, "[F]ear will be *defective* in the absence of danger. … In … such cases, emotions do not prioritize relational goals in the presence of those core relational themes that explain why prioritizing such goals in the past was selected for" (Scarantino, 2014, p. 178; emphasis in original).

Another argument in favor of the motivational theory is that there seems to be nothing special or necessary about the affect or appraisal aspects of emotions in and of themselves marking them out as distinctive or generating the kind of clamoring-for-attention-action-readiness we most associate with them. The affective features of different emotions are quite often indistinguishable. For example, shame and guilt feel phenomenologically similar (and are also close in terms of bodily changes), as do joy and amusement (both have a feeling of "levity"), grief and sadness, and disgust and contempt. And as for appraising thoughts, they too on their own don't necessarily or even typically generate the sustained attention, urgency, or action-readiness distinctive of emotions. Indeed, it is only the action tendencies that "tend to persist in the face of interruptions; they tend to interrupt other ongoing programs and actions; and they tend to preempt the information-processing facilities" (Frijda, 1986, p. 78). They produce what's called control precedence (Frijda, 1986, p. 78; Scarantino, 2014, p. 171).[15] But appraisals alone need not play any such role. Indeed, appraisals can be distinctly *un*emotional, as in a special forces soldier trained not to be afraid when he comes across scenarios he nevertheless properly appraises as dangerous or threatening (Scarantino, 2014, pp. 162–163).

For other-blame and self-blame to be analogous or continuous with one another, blame's paradigmatic emotional syndrome must be anger. But what is anger? Everyone agrees on its affect: a heated, aggressive feeling, sometimes accompanied by clenched fists, sweating, and shaking. Disagreement arises, however, over anger's appraisal and its associated action tendency. On one familiar side of the disagreement are those who follow Aristotle, maintaining that anger appraises *slights*, and its action tendency aims at *retaliation* (Aristotle, 1954).[16] This makes anger a response to a certain sophisticated kind of intentional agency.

There are some serious problems with this view, though. First, we don't feel anger exclusively toward (blameworthy) agents; we also feel anger at

---

[15] There are important qualifications to be made here. Obviously, one can process information in the meantime, and emotions may also be cool, and sometimes the tendency is for *in*action. See Scarantino (2014) for the nuances of the view.

[16] For retaliation as anger's aim, see, among philosophers, D'Arms & Jacobson (2003 and forthcoming); Nichols (2007, 2013); McGeer (2013). Among psychologists, see, e.g., Izard (1977); Shaver et al. (1987); Frijda (1994); Boehm (1999); Haidt (2003).

non-agential things, including the weather, computers, our chronic pain, and our physical disorders (see Craig & Brown, 1984, Trost et al., 2012). But none of these things can slight us, so retaliating against them would just be silly or impossible. Second, babies and some non-human animals also seem to feel anger, yet they surely lack the cognitive sophistication to be tracking and responding to agential slights or to be thinking about retaliation (see, e.g., Lewis et al., 1990; Lewis, 1993).

As a result of these problems, there is a different side of the disagreement that describes anger's appraisal instead to be of *goal-frustration*, and anger's action tendency to be toward *eliminating or bypassing the blockage* (see Haidt, 2003 for cites and discussion). This view easily accounts for the non-agential and baby cases, and it might also be able to encompass anger at slights, given that when you slight me you may also plausibly be construed as frustrating my goals.

However, the goal-frustration view of anger has its own problem, namely, it seems to lose anger's normal *blame and responsibility* feel. If all I am doing in being angry is looking for a way to get around the goal blockage, even if you (another agent) are its direct source, then it's unclear how this response could be an instance of, or connect up to, blame of you for causing the goal blockage qua agent. On this account, it makes sense to describe me as merely angered *that* there's a goal blockage, not angry *at you* (qua agent) for being its direct source, and this seems to lose a great deal of the intuitive power of the original Aristotelian view of anger.

I think there are good considerations in favor of both views of anger, though, so good that I have suggested in other work that we be *pluralists* about it, allowing that there are two distinct types (Shoemaker, 2018, pp. 72–74). There is, on the one hand, *goal-frustrated anger*, and there is, on the other hand, *slighted anger*.[17] They have very similar phenomenal feels, but they differ in their action tendencies, aims, and appraisals.[18]

Start with the action tendencies. Very often both types of anger co-occur. When you block the doorway out of a malicious desire to prevent

[17] I have also labeled the latter "agential anger" (Shoemaker, 2015: Chapter 3) and "blaming anger" (Shoemaker, 2018). Given what I go on to say in this chapter, I now think neither label captures the best way to think about the phenomenon.

[18] Why not, then, call them two different emotions, namely, frustration and anger? (D'Arms and Jacobson informally lean in this direction, I think.) I'm not crazy about that, but I won't fight it kicking and screaming, as I'm concerned fundamentally only with the emotional syndromes, not their labels. Still, I think it worthwhile to maintain some continuity here with the long literature in psychology and philosophy that calls both syndromes *anger*; the phenomenological feel of both responses is remarkably similar, and the only chance at continuity between self- and other-blame is if they both have anger as their paradigmatic emotions cores, so I will continue to label both as types of anger.

me from getting to work on time, I'll be angry, but I'll be motivated in two different directions: (a) to get around you somehow to get to work on time and (b) to confront or get back at you (likely later) for blocking my path. But there are cases in which we get only one or the other. If I'm driving to work and come across a rockslide preventing my getting there on time, again, I'll be angry, but I'll *only* be motivated to look for a way around the rockslide, not also to confront or retaliate against it later (Shoemaker, 2018, p. 73)! Alternatively, suppose someone stayed in my AirBnB spare room last weekend, and I find out after he's gone back to Estonia that he was secretly spying on me through a hole in the wall when I took showers. I will be angry, and aptly so, it seems, but there is simply no occurrent goal frustration in such a case to get around.[19] I merely want to confront or retaliate against him.

The different action tendencies of the different types of anger also differ in their aims. Slighted anger, on a story I have told and defended in detail elsewhere (Shoemaker, 2015, Chapter 3; 2018), aims at, demands, and is aptly resolved by the slighter's remorseful acknowledgment of how he made the slighted person feel, where what the slighter comes to recognize is how poor (or insufficiently good) his quality of will toward the other person had been. Goal-frustrated anger ultimately aims to get one back on track to achieving one's goals, and so, depending on the goal and source of its blockage, may or may not demand anything at all. This is why responsibility, guilt, and relationship repair are implicated in the former but irrelevant to the latter. Perhaps you have parked your car too close to mine for me to open my door and get out to make an important meeting, but you did so by accident (my car was camouflaged), or perhaps you were justified (it was the only place available to park quickly so you could help someone who'd collapsed in the street). In this case, my demanding remorseful acknowledgment from you would be inapt. But my merely goal-frustrated anger neither wants nor needs such things – it just wants your goddamn car out of the way! Excuses and justifications are relevant only to slighted anger. Your reasons why you did what you did matter insofar as they reveal to me what your quality of will was, that is, whether you had a slighting attitude toward me. They are irrelevant, however, in determining whether you frustrated my goals. That fact obtains or not independently of your quality of will.

---

[19] Unless it's the very artificial "goal" that I not have been spied upon while in the shower. I have a hard time thinking about this as an actual goal, though, given that goals are forward-looking, things one aims to achieve, and so things one thinks one *can* achieve. One can't change the past, though.

Relatedly and finally, there is a crucial difference between these two forms of anger in terms of what they are each appraising. When you mean to hurt me, my anger at you appraises what you did as a slight. Slighted anger is anger at psychologically sophisticated agents in virtue of their exercises of agency. But I don't actually get angry *at* "the weather" for ruining my long-planned July 4 military parade; rather, I get angry *that* it is raining on my parade. If it stops raining, I (should) stop being angry.[20] So in getting angry when it rains, I am in essence appraising that climatological state of affairs as *frustrating* (or, perhaps better, as *maddening*), and to the extent that the rain is indeed frustrating a goal of mine, I have appraised the situation correctly, and so in fact I have a reason to feel goal-frustrated anger (only) so long as that state of affairs obtains. When that reason is removed – when it stops raining – I no longer have a reason (of *fit*) to feel it (on reasons of fit and anger, see D'Arms & Jacobson, 2000 and forthcoming; Shoemaker, 2017, 2018).

Your goal-frustrated anger aims to get you back on track to getting what you want, and, as it turns out, it is really effective at doing so (Veling, Ruys, & Aarts, 2012). Angry people are, perhaps surprisingly, more optimistic, and so tend to have greater perseverance than the non-angry (Lerner & Keltner, 2001), and this makes them better at self-improvement in a variety of domains (Kassinove et al., 1997). Anger also produces psychological self-insight (Kassinove et al., 1997), and it is well-known for its effectiveness in business negotiations (Van Kleef, De Dreu, & Manstead, 2004). People who express anger are perceived as powerful, as leadership material (Duhigg, 2019). Anger unleashes creativity, as it helps us see previously unseen solutions, and it motivates people to take on tougher tasks than they might have otherwise done (Duhigg, 2019). Anger makes us feel like we are taking control, and the brain activity of people who are expressing anger looks extremely similar to the brain activity of those who are experiencing happiness (Duhigg, 2019).

In sum, those aiming to explicate self-blame have been mistaken to focus on guilt, which is instead a *response* to blame. For self-blame to have any plausible chance of being analogous or continuous with other-blame, its paradigmatic emotional core must be a kind of anger. But as we have just seen, there are two kinds of anger, slighted and goal-frustrated. Which kind(s) do other- and self-blame deploy? To answer that question, I will introduce a little oddity.

---

[20] Such anger may of course be recalcitrant.

Hypocritical Self-Blame[21]

If paradigmatic emotional self-blame and other-blame were to consist of the same form of anger, then a familiar complaint in other-blame cases should regularly be grounded and voiced in cases of self-blame too. But it just isn't. So paradigmatic emotional self-blame and other-blame don't consist of the same form of anger.

That, in a nutshell, is the argument I will now develop. Suppose that we are friends. I tend to lie to you on a regular basis about fairly trivial things (e.g., that I saw a concert I didn't really see), and I do so without remorse. While you know this about me and don't like it very much, you put up with it, as we have been friends for a long time. One day you lie to me in the same fashion I regularly lie to you, and when I find out, I self-righteously and angrily blame you for doing so. Your response will – and likely should – be: "Who are *you* to blame me?!"[22] I'm a hypocrite, and my hypocrisy renders my anger at you "off" in an important way, making it something you may permissibly ignore, even if what you did was blameworthy.

It seems clear that I am blaming you via slighted anger. On the account I spelled out earlier, if my slighted anger is apt, I am appraising what you did (lying to me) as a slight, and my action tendency is to confront you with a demand for remorseful acknowledgment, a demand for you to painfully appreciate from my perspective how you made me feel in slighting me this way (Shoemaker, 2018 and 2021). When I remain guilty of doing what I'm slighted angry at you now for doing, my blame is hypocritical, in the sense that I'm demanding remorseful acknowledgment from you for doing the very same thing which I myself have *not* remorsefully acknowledged. I thus lack some kind of standing, right, or authority to make such a demand of you until I do so.[23]

Here is the oddity: if paradigmatically emotional self-blame were fundamentally like other-blame, consisting of slighted anger, it should in every case ground a legitimate charge of hypocrisy. That's because if the blamer is one and the same person as the blamed, then the blamer himself is guilty of having done precisely what he is now blaming the blamed for.

---

[21] I received, and am grateful for, helpful feedback on the ideas in this section from the readers of PEA Soup in response to my post of August 2019 (http://peasoup.us/2019/08/the-puzzle-of-hypocritical-self-blame/). I'm also grateful to Kasper Lippert-Rasmussen and Thomas Pink for helpful discussion and pushback.

[22] For the "Who are you?" form of the objection to hypocrisy, see Tognazzini and Coates (2013). This is merely one way of dramatically putting the hypocrisy charge.

[23] There are many diagnoses of the "offness" of hypocritical blame in the literature. These are only some of them. I need not rely on any one in particular to make my point here, though.

For the self-blamer's demand for remorseful acknowledgment to have any point as blame, he must not have already remorsefully acknowledged his slight (i.e., there is simply no point in demanding something from somebody that you've already received). So were I to angrily blame myself for slighting someone, I-the-blamed ought to be able to challenge myself-the-blamer: "Who are *you* to blame *me*?" But this is just silly; such a charge neither arises nor seems warranted. And yet we obviously engage in lots of self-blame that seems perfectly legitimate. So the paradigmatic forms of anger in other-blame and self-blame must be different.

I don't think that this oddity has been pointed out before.[24] It resonates, in a way, with Plato's remark in the *Republic* that the notion of self-control, taken literally, is "ridiculous," as the "stronger self that does the controlling is the same as the weaker self that gets controlled, so that only one person is referred to in all such expressions" (430e–431a). Plato's solution was to render the phrase intelligible by distinguishing between different *parts* in the soul of a person, so that a self-controlled soul is one in which the naturally better part of the person (rationality) controls the naturally worse part of the person (appetite).

So too, in trying to explain why there is no hypocritical self-blame, we might try to distinguish between different parts of the soul, a (naturally better?) blaming part and a (naturally worse?) blamed part. And indeed, this is precisely how Adam Smith paints the picture:

> When I endeavor to examine my own conduct, when I endeavor to pass sentence upon it, and either to approve or condemn it, it is evident, in all such cases, I divide myself, as it were, into two persons; and that I, the examiner and judge, represent a different character from that other I, the person whose conduct is examined into and judged of. The first is the spectator, whose sentiments with regard to my own conduct I endeavor to enter into, by placing myself in his situation, and by considering how it would appear to me, when seen from that particular point of view. The second is the agent, the person whom I properly call myself, and of whose conduct, under the character of a spectator, I was endeavoring to form some opinion. The first is the judge; the second the person judged of: but that the judge should, in every respect, be the same with the person judged of, is as impossible, as that the cause should, in every respect, be the same with the effect. (Smith, *Theory of Moral Sentiments*, Part III, Chapter 1)

---

[24] I did learn from the PEA Soup discussion that Matt King, Patrick Todd, and Brian Rabern might each have made a similar point informally and independently, but none have published anything on it yet, and at any rate, none seemed to be thinking of it in terms of blame's angry emotional core in the way I am.

Regardless of Smith's final insistence, though, the judger and judged *are* one and the same person. Taking up one's behavior from different perspectives does not literally divide one.[25] Consequently, the "person judged" still ought to be able to legitimately demand of the "judge," "Who are *you* to blame me?!" Furthermore, while there is something phenomenologically plausible about Plato's picture of a wrestling match between reason and desire taking place in the face of temptation, there is no such phenomenological wrestling in self-blame. Indeed, when I blame myself for something, the thorough *unity* of blamer and blamed is what feels most striking.

Alternatively, then, we might appeal to Alfred Mele's explanation of self-deception, a phenomenon which on its face is also paradoxical: in self-deception, I have somehow brought myself to simultaneously believe both p and not-p (Mele, 1987, pp. 121–122). Mele's solution is that in such cases I might have caused myself to be deceived *unintentionally* and, further, that this can be a function of motivated irrationality, a desire to believe something against evidence that I might easily have absorbed and deployed in my belief-formation were it not for the desire in question (Mele, 1987, p. 136).

Nevertheless, self-blame isn't, or isn't necessarily, irrational, and it's not necessarily a function of motivated reasoning. If I have slighted someone, then I *do* have a reason to feel slighted anger at myself (as does anyone). Indeed, we often talk as if self-blame is both rational and appropriate. Yet surely we don't think the self-blamer is a hypocrite. So what gives?

The answer is that emotional other-blame and self-blame consist, at least paradigmatically, of different types of anger. The paradigmatic form of other-blame is clearly slighted anger. So if both types of blame deploy anger, and there are two forms of anger, the paradigmatic form of self-blame must be *goal-frustrated* anger. But what does this look like? And don't we nevertheless get slighted angry at ourselves? I aim to answer these questions in the next several sections by actually *starting* the investigation with cases of athletic self-blame.

4 Negative Self-Talk and Goal-Frustrated Anger

What I want to explore and develop is the idea that the most plausible construal of the paradigmatic emotional core of self-blame is that it is "talking angrily to oneself." In laying out this view, I draw from empirical findings

---

[25] Thanks to Richard Moran for discussion.

in the psychological literature about a phenomenon labeled self-talk, which has remarkable effects on athletes and has been studied widely in the athletic domain by theorists of sports psychology, competitive anxiety, exercise, and cognitive behavioral therapy.

Here is how the concept is operationalized in the literature: "Self-talk should be defined as: (a) verbalizations or statements addressed to the self; (b) multidimensional in nature; (c) having interpretive elements associated with the content of statements employed; (d) is somewhat dynamic; and (e) serving at least two functions; instructional and motivational ..." (Hardy, 2006, p. 84). This is meant to capture a phenomenon with which we should all be intimately familiar. Just think back to your last bout of exercise and the ways you might well have coaxed yourself to get through it (e.g., "Just ten more reps – you can do it!").

What are the effects of self-talk on the studied athletes? As demonstrated repeatedly, it can dramatically increase their motivation and mental toughness (Hardy, 2006, p. 88; Hatzigeorgiadis et al., 2008). Positive self-talk (as in "That's it!" or "You're doing great – keep it up!") can actually increase physical endurance, staving off exhaustion significantly longer than for those in non-self-talking control groups (Blanchfield et al., 2014). And, very importantly for our purposes, *negative* self-talk (e.g., "That was terrible!" or "What are you *doing*?") can increase both motivation and performance *equally as well* in some athletes (Van Raalte et al., 1994; Van Raalte et al., 1995; Hardy, 2006, p. 88).[26]

Self-talk has also begun to be studied outside of the athletic domain. In both its positive and negative expressions, it has been found to reduce shyness (Coplan & Armer, 2005), and even pain (Girodo & Wood, 1979), and there is a well-documented link between self-talk and the formation of various emotions (Lazarus, 1982; Hardy, Hall, & Alexander, 2001). One can, of course, talk oneself into emotions like anger and fear by repeatedly focusing one's attention on the anger- or fear-making properties. But one can also regulate one's emotions, and increase one's emotional intelligence generally, by deploying self-talk (Lane et al., 2009).

I believe that self-blame's paradigmatic emotional form is just *negative self-talk*, where the negativity is an expression of goal-frustrated anger. The action tendencies of goal-frustrated anger simply aim at eliminating or bypassing a blockage, caring not a whit for any agential *why* (i.e., quality

---

[26] For some athletes, however, negative self-talk correlates with decreased motivation and performance. Unfortunately, the phenomenon of negative self-talk remains understudied, and it seems that many psychologists view it, almost a priori, as dangerous or imprudent for athletes to engage in. I think the case of Serena Williams is a powerful counterexample to that thought, however.

of will), except as an epistemic aid to avoiding frustrating one's own goals in the future. And because the *why* doesn't matter, the reflexive nature of the anger does not generate the charge of hypocrisy, a charge that sticks on someone only in virtue of having expressed an insufficiently good quality of will: I am a hypocrite when I get slighted angry at you for manifesting the same poor quality of will that I myself have manifested, and so I demand remorseful acknowledgment from you for exactly what I myself have not remorsefully acknowledged. But quality of will just isn't what matters to goal-frustrated anger, which focuses instead simply on the *fact* of goal frustration and how to overcome it, not on any of the *reasons* someone may have had for frustrating that goal.

This is precisely the content and role of negative self-talk, according to the psychological literature: in angrily criticizing yourself for frustrating your own goals, you are motivating yourself to get around self-caused obstacles and to improve your performance. Self-talk is crucially forward-looking: it aims to keep your head in the game, to get you to try harder, and to expand your physical limits. These good consequences may be achieved, the empirical research tells us, by either positive or negative self-talk. When it is negative ("Why do you keep losing focus?!" or "Keep your stupid head still when putting!"), it's an extremely familiar form of what we can only describe as self-blame.[27] The anger involved isn't about accusing and guilting, though; rather, it is about *coaching* and *constructing*. But obviously this makes it a very different form of emotional blame than the paradigmatic versions of other-blame, which are thoroughly backward-looking, track the *why* of agential activities, respond to and appraise slights, motivate confrontation and/or retaliation, and aim at remorseful acknowledgment.

5 Self-Talk and Moral Self-Blame; or, The Tom Brady Fumblin' Blues

Self-directed anger is also distinctly non-moral. In some recent psychological work, subjects were directed to think back to times when they had been angry at themselves, and these responses were studied in comparison to memories subjects had about when they had felt anger at others, as well as when they had felt shame or guilt at something they had done. While shame, guilt, and other-directed anger all tended to have predominantly moral overtones for subjects, self-directed anger simply did not. That is to

[27] And while I won't talk about it here, it should be obvious that I think the best construal of self-*praise* is going to be positive self-talk.

say, people angry at others typically feel that they are in the right and that "what happened was unfair and morally wrong" (Ellsworth & Tong, 2006, p. 581), and people who feel shame or guilt also "feel that they were morally wrong" (Ellsworth & Tong, 2006, p. 582), whereas while people who feel angry at themselves do believe they did something wrong, they "do not see the situation as involving a *moral* violation" (Ellsworth & Tong, 2006, pp. 581–582). This point is borne out by the kinds of examples people repeatedly gave for what they remembered causing self-directed anger: "hitting one's head against a shelf, locking oneself out of the house …, losing keys, getting a bad grade" (Ellsworth & Tong, 2006, p. 579). This in fact explains why the overwhelming action tendency of self-directed anger in the psychological studies was "wanting to get out of the situation" (Ellsworth & Tong, 2006, p. 582). And the most natural response to this kind of self-directed anger, then, is not guilt or shame; it is, rather, *embarrassment*. This is why people often try to keep self-directed anger private, or to avoid being seen during such episodes: they want to hide their embarrassment (Ellsworth & Tong, 2006, p. 582). This is perhaps why Tom Brady hung his head low after fumbling.

6   Self-Effacing Moral Self-Blame

The most familiar form of self-blame, I have argued, is negative self-talk: non-moral, self-directed, goal-frustrated anger. This is how the elite athletes I've mentioned enjoin themselves to greater performance. But it is how we ordinary schlubs enjoin ourselves to greater performance too, across many normative domains. In recognizing our prudential, culinary, aesthetic, and athletic failings, we may angrily yell at ourselves in a forward-looking attempt to get us to undermine or bypass the blockages we have put in our own way.

But why is this a *non*-moral phenomenon? It's because there is something distinctive about the moral domain, the domain of slights and remorseful acknowledgment, that has a curious psychological upshot when we try to blame ourselves for slighting others. When anyone recognizes a slight, that person has a reason, no matter who he or she is, to feel slighted anger at the offender, on behalf of the slighted agent. Consequently, when you yourself slight someone else, you do have a reason to feel slighted anger at yourself. But it turns out to be very hard to *feel* it. That's because the moment you discover what you did was a slight, and so the moment you recognize a reason to be slighted angry at yourself, *that discovery is actually just the dawning of guilt*, the moment when you will typically begin feeling remorseful acknowledgment, which meets – and thus undercuts the point of – slighted anger's demand. Once you have recognized what you did to someone else *as a slight* (which you presumably didn't see as such when you did it, as people don't typically aim to slight others), there's nothing left for your self-directed slighted anger to fittingly *do*. It can't fittingly demand acknowledgment, for that demand is already being met, and it can't fittingly protest a threat, for that threat is already being removed. To have a reason to feel self-directed slighted anger *is just* to have a reason to remorsefully acknowledge one's slight in a way that, at least for those with functional emotional sensibilities, seems instantly to meet its aims by *replacing* slighted anger with guilt or remorse.[28] Rationally fitting moral self-blame is self-effacing.[29]

7 The Pathologies of Self-Directed Slighted Anger

But that's not to say that people can't or don't nevertheless feel self-directed slighted anger; of course they can (and do)! I can conceive two ways one might do so, only one of which seems very psychologically plausible. In the first, someone could be *fittingly* slighted angry at herself for slighting someone else, yet not feel any remorse or guilt, even though she's capable of doing so. She thus would be demanding acknowledgment from herself, *for reasons she recognizes as legitimate* (thus the "fit" of her slighted anger), without recognizing those simultaneously just to be reasons to feel the remorseful acknowledgment she herself is demanding that she feel. This seems psychologically bizarre to me, however. So maybe instead this person is *incapable* of guilt and remorse, while remaining capable of slighted anger? This might describe some psychopaths, who seem to get angry at others for what they take to be slights, but they don't respond with guilt or remorse when they slight others. But psychopaths also seem incapable of *slighted* anger at themselves. This is likely precisely because the reasons for self-directed slighted anger and guilt/remorse just are identical, so if they can't recognize reasons for the latter, they can't recognize reasons for the

---

[28] Sometimes, of course, it's not so instant. After all, if I have seriously slighted you, causing you lasting pain or damage, then there's no way I can instantly acknowledge the full extent of your harm. For me to fully appreciate what it was like for you to live with my foul deed, I may have to "feel your pain" for a long while. In the meantime, then, I may be angry at myself simultaneously with my remorsefully acknowledg*ing* what I did. However, in such cases, I am strongly inclined to believe that this ongoing self-directed anger actually turns into the *goal-frustrated* kind, as I'm prevented from fully appreciating what I put you through quickly, and so I'm coaching myself to keep working at it. This view is implicit in Shoemaker (2021). Many thanks to Andreas Brekke Carlsson for thinking about this point with me.

[29] Indeed, this is why I suspect that so many have conflated self-blame with guilt, as at least the *reasons* for slighted self-anger are essentially identical to the *reasons* for guilt.

former. So once again, it's hard to conceive of the psychological possibility of feeling fitting slighted angry at oneself without remorse or guilt.

The second way one might feel self-directed slighted anger is absolutely conceivable, though, as people do it all the time. It is to feel *unfitting* slighted anger in the form of self-beratement, self-flagellation, and self-punishment. Suppose you remain slighted angry at someone who slighted you in the past but who has since come to manifest sincere remorse and done everything possible to address and make up for the slight (e.g., apology, compensation, relationship-repair). She has effectively *eliminated* the slight, and so eliminated your reason for slighted anger. If you still feel it, though, your anger is unfitting and so is recalcitrant, that is, it is *irrational* (D'Arms & Jacobson, 2003). But if you nevertheless continue to feel and then especially to *express* it to your former slighter, you have moved from the irrational to the immoral, as you are flagellating the no-longer guilty: you could only be aiming at her pain at this point, as you've already gotten her acknowledgment.

Fortunately, with respect to unfitting and recalcitrant other-directed slighted anger, you can keep it to yourself. But if you yourself are the slighter, you can't. Suppose, then, that you are slighted angry at yourself despite already having fully recognized and acknowledged what it is that you put your victim through (from her perspective), and despite already having gone through whatever reparative or compensatory process anyone could reasonably be expected to undertake, and your victim has fully forgiven you as a result. Your reason for slighted self-anger has now been completely eliminated, so if it persists, you are simply carrying out a punishment on yourself – beating yourself up. This sort of irrational flagellating self-blame has three key features: (a) it highlights your helplessness – your lack of personal control – insofar as there's nothing (left) you can do to rectify, replace, or change what you did; (b) as a form of punishment, it carries with it the clear overtones of *desert* the Guilt Mongers think all self-blame has (as in "this is what you deserve, you miserable so-and-so"); and (c) coincident with the previous two features, it is directed to your *character*, attributing negative traits to you as a person as a result of what you've done.

This type of self-blame is what psychologists call *characterological*, as opposed to *behavioral*. Behavioral self-blame focuses simply on what one did, not on who one is, and it aims at getting one to do better in the future. That makes it most closely akin to the goal-frustrated angry self-talk already discussed. Characterological self-blame, though, is the provenance of all sorts of pathologies and disorders. It strongly correlates with depression, low self-esteem, non-suicidal self-harm, PTSD, maladaptive coping in victims of sexual assault, and suicide (Janoff-Bulmin, 1979;

Pagel, Becker, & Coppel, 1985; Baumeister, 1990; Ullman, 1996; Bryant & Guthrie, 2007; Swannell et al., 2012). It is destructive and unhealthy, and even if there were magically some right kinds of reasons in its favor, they would easily be outweighed, all things considered, by these "wrong" kinds of reasons against it.

The athletic arena again provides illustration. Leading three games to one in the 1986 American League Championship Series, and with one strike to go to seal a fourth victory and get his team to the World Series, Donnie Moore, a solid relief pitcher for the California Angels, gave up a go-ahead home run to Dave Henderson, of the Boston Red Sox. The Red Sox eventually won that game, and they went on to blow out the shell-shocked Angels over the next two games to make it to the World Series. After the game, Moore admitted he had made a bad pitch to Henderson. He said, "I was horseshit. … Somebody's got to take the blame, so I'll take it. … I threw that pitch. I lost that game." He was never the same. He struggled with injuries for two more years before he was finally released. Two months later, in July 1989, he killed himself. His agent, Mike Pinter, said the following: "I think insanity set in. He could not live with himself after Henderson hit the home run. He kept blaming himself. That home run killed him."[30] This is self-flagellation taken to the most unfitting and unhealthy extreme.

*****

The charge of hypocrisy would always arise for self-blame if its paradigmatic angry core were of the same type as other-blame. As this charge never arises, however, their emotional cores must consist in different *types* of anger. Other-blame consists paradigmatically of slighted anger, whereas self-blame consists paradigmatically of goal-frustrated anger. Indeed, psychologically possible self-directed slighted anger is either self-effacing or unfitting. This is also the most fundamental reason that those who aim to explain self- and other-blame in light of each other are likely to fail, for they are just two different emotional animals.[31]

---

[30] Taken from Baker (2011). There are many complications to the story that Baker's account fills in. In particular, right before he shot himself, Moore shot his wife multiple times. I should also note that in the Red Sox World Series that year against the New York Mets, there was another series-losing mistake, this time on the part of the Red Sox's own Bill Buckner. Buckner did *not* kill himself, and he seemed to move past the error, even parodying himself on an episode of *Curb Your Enthusiasm*.

[31] I'm very grateful to Andreas Brekke Carlsson for getting me to write this paper for a great conference he put together in Oslo (September 2019) on self-blame. I'm also grateful to all of the other philosophers at that conference, both for their own excellent papers and for their helpful comments on mine: Randy Clarke, Justin D'Arms, Christel Fricke, Dan Jacobson, Coleen Macnamara, Michelle Mason, Michael McKenna, Dana Nelkin, Derk Pereboom, Doug Portmore, Piers Rawling, and Krista Thomason.

CHAPTER 3

A Comprehensive Account of Blame
Self-Blame, Non-Moral Blame, and Blame for the Non-Voluntary

Douglas W. Portmore

Blame is multifarious. It can be heated or sedate. It can be expressed or kept private. We blame both the living and the dead. And we blame ourselves as well as others. What's more, we blame ourselves, not only for our moral failings but also for our non-moral failings: for our aesthetic bad taste, gustatory self-indulgence, or poor athletic performance. And we blame ourselves both for things over which we exerted voluntary control (e.g., our voluntary acts) and for things over which we lacked such control (e.g., our fallacious beliefs, malicious desires, and irrational intentions).

Unfortunately, though, many extant accounts of blame fail to do justice to the manifest diversity in our blaming practices. For instance, T. M. Scanlon holds that "to blame a person is … to take your relationship with him or her to be modified" (2008, pp. 128–129) and, as a consequence, "to alter or withhold intentions and expectations that that relationship would normally involve" (2013a, p. 89). Yet, it seems clear that we can blame the dead without either taking our relationship with them to have been modified or altering our intentions with respect to them. Others – for example, Miranda Fricker (2016) – acknowledge blame's manifest diversity but hold that, given this diversity, there can be no hope of providing illuminating necessary and sufficient conditions for blame. These philosophers hold that just as there's nothing common to all instances of the word "game," there's nothing common to all instances of the word "blame." They believe that the best that we can hope for is an account that specifies the extension of "blame" in terms of sufficient resemblance to some paradigm, or in terms of what Ludwig Wittgenstein (1953) called *family resemblances*. Still others – for example, Angela Smith (2013) – think that although the diversity in our blaming practices shouldn't lead us to give up on the prospect of providing illuminating necessary and sufficient conditions, we should give up on trying to specify those conditions in terms of what's *constitutive* of blame. For, as these functionalists see things, the only thing that unites all instances of blame is that they all play the same functional role.[1]

I'm more optimistic about the possibility of providing an illuminating set of necessary and sufficient conditions that specifies blame's extension in terms of its constitution as opposed to its function. In what follows, I'll propose just such an analysis. This proposal is stated and then clarified in Section 1. On this proposal, there are two conditions for blaming someone that are individually necessary and jointly sufficient. So, in Sections 2 and 3, I defend the necessity of each. And in Section 4, I defend their joint sufficiency. In Section 5, I go through all the disparate forms of blame and how my proposal can account for each of them. I then conclude in Section 6 with a summary of results along with an explanation of their importance.

1   My Proposal for a Comprehensive Account of Blame

To be blamed for something is, in part, to be held responsible for it. But there are at least two ways of being responsible for something. One is to be the cause of it. This is *causal responsibility*. Another is to be accountable for it. And if one is accountable for something, then one can appropriately be held liable to reward or sanction for it. The reward or sanction needn't come from the law, society, or common opinion, but it must at least come from the approval or disapproval of one's own conscience – see Mill (1991, chap. 5). And to distinguish this from causal responsibility, I'll call it *normative responsibility*.[2] It's important to distinguish these two, because one can be causally responsible for something without being normatively responsible for it. I can, for instance, be causally responsible for spreading a virus at work even if I'm not normatively responsible for doing so given that I had no reason to suspect that I was infected.

---

[1] Functionalists hold that blame is, in a certain respect, more like a mousetrap than a diamond (Polger, 2019). What makes something a mousetrap is not that it's constituted in a certain way but that it has a certain function: that of trapping a mouse. By contrast, what makes something a diamond is not that it has a certain function but that it is constituted by carbon crystals with a certain molecular lattice structure. On functionalist accounts, then, blame is just whatever has some particular function. But, like Dana Kay Nelkin (2017, p. 816), I doubt that our conception of blame is at bottom a functionalist one, though I don't have space here to adequately address the issue.

[2] The type of responsibility that contrasts with causal responsibility is typically called *moral responsibility*, but given that we can (or so I'll argue) have this sort of responsibility with respect to the violations of non-moral demands, the "moral" qualifier can be quite misleading. For this reason, I've chosen to borrow Rik Peels's more apt phrase "normative responsibility" (2016, p. 16). Also, as I see it, the relevant sort of responsibility is accountability as opposed to answerability or attributability – see Shoemaker (2015).

My aim in this chapter is to provide an account of *normative* as opposed to *causal* blame.[3] In the remainder, though, I'll leave the "normative" qualifier implicit.

> *My Proposal:* For any action φ, any subject S, and any potential target T (where T may or may not be identical to S), S blames T for having seemingly φ-ed if and only if both of the following conditions are met:
> - (Condition₁) S has some set of mental states that represents T (a) as having φ-ed; (b) as having violated a legitimate demand in φ-ing; and (c) as not having suffered all the guilt, regret, and remorse that she deserves to suffer in the recognition of having violated this legitimate demand, and
> - (Condition₂) S feels, as a result of these representations, disapproval of, or disappointment in, T.
>
> Additionally, the greater the amount of guilt, regret, and remorse that S represents T as deserving to suffer, the greater the intensity to which S blames T.[4]

This proposal is meant to be an account of what it is, in fact, to blame someone for having φ-ed. It isn't meant to be revisionary. I'm not trying to figure out what blame would need to be for our blaming practices to be justified. Indeed, I'm interested in the correct account of blame partly because I'm interested in exploring (in future work) whether our blaming practices are justified even if it turns out that all our actions are causally determined. And depending on what the correct account of blame is, it will be more or less plausible to think that people can be blameworthy for acts that they were causally determined to perform. For if, on the one hand, blaming people involves merely evaluating them, then, given that evaluations can be accurate – and, thus, appropriate – regardless of whether the people being evaluated had control over the properties that make those evaluations accurate, there would be nothing problematic about blaming people for actions that they were causally determined to perform. But if, on the other hand, blaming people entails deliberately causing them to suffer, then, given that no one deserves to suffer in virtue of things over which they lacked control, it would be problematic to blame

---

[3] Blaming a person for having φ-ed is just one way of holding her to account. Another way is to punish her for having φ-ed.

[4] Although I won't discuss the positive analogue of blame in detail, it's an advantage of my account that it suggests the following symmetrical view: For any action φ, any subject S, and any potential target T (where T may or may not be identical to S), S feels gratitude – or whatever the positive analogue of blame is – toward T for having seemingly φ-ed if and only if both of the following conditions are met: (Condition₁) S has some set of mental states that represents T (a) as having φ-ed, (b) as having done what she ought to have done in φ-ing, and (c) as not having felt all the pride that she deserves to feel in the recognition of having done what she ought to have done, and (Condition₂) S feels, as a result of these representations, approval of T.

people for acts that they were causally determined to perform – at least, it would on the assumption that causal determinism rules out the sort of control that's required for being deserving of suffering.

Fortunately, in my proposal, blame lies somewhere between these two extremes, such that blame goes beyond mere evaluative judgment but falls well short of necessitating the deliberate infliction of suffering.[5] In my proposal, blame must go beyond mere evaluative judgment in that it necessitates feeling disapproval of, or disappointment in, its target. Thus, it requires a change in one's attitude toward the target. And so there is, in my proposal, a distinction between blaming someone and merely making some set of judgments about her.[6]

But my proposal stops well short of insisting that blame must involve the deliberate infliction of suffering. Thus, there is, in my proposal, also a distinction between blaming someone and punishing her. Since my proposal denies that blame requires taking any deliberate action, and since the deliberate infliction of suffering necessitates deliberate action, my proposal allows that one can blame someone without punishing her. Indeed, in my proposal, blame essentially involves only two things: (1) a set of mental states that represent its target in various ways and (2) a feeling of disapproval of, or disappointment in, that target. And these are mental states, not deliberate actions.

Beyond the fact that my account lies between the extremes of mere evaluative judgment and punishment, there are several other aspects of my proposal that need clarifying.

First, the variable φ ranges over non-voluntary actions as well as voluntary actions. For I'm using the term "action" broadly to cover anything that's "done" directly in response to reasons. This includes not only those things that we do at will (e.g., raising one's hand to ask a question) but also some things that we do non-voluntarily, such as forming a belief, desire, or intention in response to reasons. Moreover, φ ranges over omissions as well as actions. Indeed, the only things that φ doesn't range over are those things that can't be done directly in response to reasons, for example, fainting, digesting, and perspiring. And this is important because it seems that we can be blamed for things that we do non-voluntarily. For instance, it seems that I can appropriately be blamed for non-voluntarily forming

---

[5] Most agree with me in thinking that the correct account of blame must lie somewhere between these two extremes. See, for instance, Coates and Tognazzini (2013), Darwall (2010), Scanlon (2008, 2013), Sher (2006), and Smith (2013).

[6] Thus, I concur with David Shoemaker in thinking that "blame involves attitude adjustment (and not mere deployment of judgments)" (2013, p. 101).

the belief that taking vitamins causes an increase in longevity if I do so in response merely to learning that there's a correlation between the two

Second, as I understand things, emotions such as guilt, regret, and remorse are inherently unpleasant. For in feeling these emotions, we represent ourselves as having violated a legitimate demand while painfully appreciating the awful significance of our having done so. So, if what we're feeling is not painful, it can't be guilt, regret, or remorse that we're feeling.

Third, when I speak of a "demand," I have a requirement as opposed to a mere expectation in mind. Technically, then, my account rules out the possibility of someone's being appropriately blamed for performing a "suberogatory act" (Driver, 1992) – that is, a permissible act that's worse than some permissible alternative.[7] Suberogatory acts violate expectations, but not requirements. To illustrate, my fellow test-taker may not be required to lend me her extra pencil, but it seems legitimate for me to expect her to do so. Now, some philosophers think that it's appropriate for me to resent (and, thus, to blame) my test-taker if she refuses to lend me her extra pencil even if she doesn't violate any requirement in so refusing.[8] Personally, I find this implausible, but there's little point in debating the matter here. So, those who think it's appropriate to blame people for performing suberogatory acts can just substitute "expectation" for "demand" throughout the above formulation.

Fourth, as I see it, what makes a demand (or expectation) *legitimate* is just that there is decisive, objective reason to comply with it. To illustrate, suppose that an agent has decisive, objective reason to maximize utility. It will, then, be legitimate to demand that she does so. Yet, she may fail to do so and not be blameworthy. For she may have been non-culpably mistaken about which of her options she needed to perform to maximize utility. And this means that there's nothing circular about my accounting for blame in terms of legitimate demands. For the sense of "legitimate" at issue is not one that necessitates being blameworthy for violating such a

---

[7] Another worry along these lines, suggested to me by Philip Swenson, is that someone can be blameworthy for always doing no more than the bare minimum. But I don't think that this is an instance of someone's being blameworthy for performing a suberogatory set of acts. Rather, I think that it's an instance of someone violating the legitimate demand to do more than just the bare minimum required to fulfill all of one's perfect duties. For it's legitimate to demand that people also fulfill their imperfect duties (e.g., the duty of beneficence), and these duties require us to do more than just the bare minimum needed to fulfill our perfect duties.

[8] See, for instance, Macnamara (2013, p. 45). Others are less sure about whether resentment is appropriate and are confident only that anger is appropriate – see, for instance, Shoemaker (2015, p. 95). I concede that anger can be an appropriate response to the suberogatory, but whereas I accept that resentment is sufficient for blame, I deny that generic anger (as opposed to resentment or indignation) is.

demand. Also, I should note that it's not just morality that can give rise to legitimate demands. For it seems that prudence can also give rise to demands that we have decisive, objective reason to comply with. And, perhaps, even athletic, aesthetic, and intellectual demands can be legitimate when we make these demands of ourselves.

Fifth, someone deserves something (say, X) if and only if, as a matter of justice and in virtue of her prior activities or possessed characteristics, she merits X in the sense that entails that the world in which she gets X and merits X in this sense is, other things being equal, non-instrumentally better than the world in which she gets X but doesn't merit X in this sense (cf. Feinberg, 1970, p. 58). Thus, one who claims, as I do, that the blameworthy deserve to suffer guilty feelings need not claim that it is *overall* non-instrumentally good that the blameworthy suffer guilty feelings. Rather, such a person need only claim that it is *in some respect* non-instrumentally good that the blameworthy suffer guilty feelings such that it is, other things being equal, non-instrumentally better that the blameworthy suffer such feelings than that the non-blameworthy do. Also, note that the relevant sense of "merit" here is not the one in which, say, Southwest Airlines merits a five-star customer-approval rating given its exceptional customer satisfaction. For even if Southwest Airlines does, in some sense, merit a five-star rating, it's not in the sense that entails that the world in which Southwest Airlines gets a five-star rating and merits such a rating in this sense is, other things being equal, non-instrumentally better than the world in which Southwest Airlines gets a five-star rating but doesn't merit such a rating in this sense. For if it's at all good that Southwest Airlines gets a five-star rating, it's only *instrumentally* good in that in helps customers find an airline with which they'll be satisfied. After all, there is nothing inherently good about Southwest Airlines getting a customer-approval rating that accurately reflects its degree of customer satisfaction. By contrast, there is something inherently good about someone getting what she deserves.

Sixth, to have a mental state that represents its object as having a certain feature, one need not have the occurrent belief or thought that it has (or even that it seems to have) this feature. For imagine that while walking through the woods I have the perception of something slithering underfoot and immediately fear it, reflexively jumping up and out of its way. In this case, my mental state – specifically, my fear – represents its object as a danger to me. And this is true even if there wasn't enough time for this thought to enter into my consciousness. In this regard, I'm in complete agreement with Justin D'Arms and Dan Jacobson (2017, forthcoming, and their chapter in this volume). For we agree that to determine how a mental state of a certain kind represents its object, we must first do some empirical work to discover such things as what typically elicits mental states of this kind, what normally attenuates them, what their phenomenology is like, what interpretation of their representational content rings true to those who possess them, and what sorts of act tendencies and patterns of attention are generally associated with them. Then, in light of this empirical data, we are to give an interpretation into natural language of how someone who possesses this kind of state represents its intentional object. This articulation of the representation will be propositional in its content such that a state of this kind will count as accurate in its representations if and only if the associated proposition is true. To illustrate, take fear. Fear is, I believe, best interpreted as the kind of mental state that represents its object as being a danger to its subject, for this is what makes most sense of the empirical data: (1) that those in the grip of fear dread what they fear, (2) that fear tends to focus one's attention both on its object and on the means of avoiding or getting away from it, (3) that fear is typically elicited by objects that are perceived to be a danger to its subject, (4) that fear tends to result in urgent action aimed at avoiding or getting away from its object – or, at the very least, it results in physiological changes that readies one to take such action, and (5) that those under the grip of fear – including self-aware phobics who know that what they fear isn't dangerous – accept the interpretation that fear represents its object as a danger to oneself.[9] And if we accept this interpretation of how fear represents its object, a given instance of fear will count as accurate in its representations if and only if its object does indeed constitute a danger to its subject.[10] So, in my proposal, a subject can count as blaming some target for having seemingly φ-ed even if she doesn't have the occurrent belief or thought that this target meets sub-conditions a–c of Condition$_1$. Rather, what needs to be true is only that the relevant empirical data suggests that the kinds of mental states that constitute blaming (e.g., guilt, resentment, and indignation) are best interpreted as representing their targets as meeting sub-conditions a–c.

---

[9] We should also appeal to such things in determining the intensity of the given mental state. Thus, one's fear counts as more intense the greater one's sense of dread, the more it tends to focus one's attention both on its object and on ways of getting away from it, the greater one's tendency toward urgent action aimed at getting away from its object, and the more dangerous that one takes that fear as representing its object as being.

[10] This account helps to explain why very young children can fear and blame even though they lack the sophisticated concepts that appear in our interpretations of their representational contents – interpretations such as "constitutes a danger to its subject" or "has violated a legitimate demand." Again, on this account, one needn't have such thoughts; one need only have the relevant affect along with its associated elicitors, attenuators, act tendencies, and patterns of attention.

Seventh, a subject's mental state can represent an object as having a certain feature even if she believes that it doesn't have this feature. In other words, a mental state can be *recalcitrant* in that it stubbornly persists even in the face of an occurrent belief that its representations are inaccurate. To illustrate, consider the recalcitrant fear of flying. This is where someone fears flying despite judging that it poses no significant danger to herself or others. This is possible because although the fear of flying necessitates representing flying as a danger to oneself, it is compatible with the occurrent belief that this is inaccurate. And given that a mental state can be compatible with the belief that its representations are inaccurate, it's also possible for blame to be recalcitrant.[11] That is, it's possible for a subject to blame someone while simultaneously believing that the mental states constituting this are inaccurate in their representations of the target. To illustrate, consider the following real-life example. One morning early in our marriage, I noticed that my wife's manner and behavior indicated that she was angry with me. Yet, when I pressed her, she denied it. But her strange manner continued and so my inquiries grew more insistent. Eventually, she admitted that she was feeling resentful toward me. As she explained, she had just woken up from a very vivid and seemingly real dream in which she had non-veridical perceptions of my cheating on her. And although she now realized that it was all just a dream, she still felt the same resentment that she had felt in her dream. For she still had the very vivid perceptual memories of my having seemingly cheated on her. And this made her feel like lashing out at me. Indeed, it seemed to her as if I deserved to suffer for what I had seemingly done. And this persisted despite her believing that I had done nothing to deserve to suffer. Thus, her mental states represented me as having violated a legitimate demand and as deserving to suffer guilt, regret, and remorse in the recognition of this despite her believing that none of these representations were accurate. Her blame of me was, then, recalcitrant in the same way that many people's fear of flying is recalcitrant.

2 The Necessity of Condition$_1$

Having both stated and clarified my proposal, I now need to defend it. For one, I need to defend the necessity of each of its two conditions. I'll start with Condition$_1$, which holds that a necessary condition for a subject's

---

[11] Proponents of the possibility of recalcitrant blame – or, at least, recalcitrant guilt, indignation, or resentment – include Brady (2009), Carlsson (2019), D'Arms and Jacobson (2003), Gibbard (1990), McKenna (2012, p. 67), Menges (2017b, p. 261), Pickard (2013), and Wallace (1994).

blaming a target for having seemingly φ-ed is that she has some set of mental states that represents that target (a) as having φ-ed, (b) as having violated a legitimate demand in φ-ing, and (c) as not having suffered all the guilt, regret, and remorse that she deserves to suffer in virtue of her having violated this legitimate demand.[12] There are, I believe, at least four reasons for thinking that this is a necessary condition for blame.

The Empirical Data

One reason to think that blame must consist of a set of mental states that represents its target as meeting sub-conditions a–c is that this seems to offer the best interpretation of the empirical data concerning the blaming emotions: guilt (where I blame myself), resentment (where I blame some other for transgressing me), and indignation (where I blame some other for transgressing a third party). I take these three emotions to be paradigm instances of blaming, so, I take what's true of them to be true of blaming in general.

Let's start, then, with the first of the three: guilt. According to the psychological literature, what typically elicits feelings of guilt are self-perceptions of responsibility for an act that constitutes a transgression (Ortony et al., 1988; Tangney & Dearing, 2002), or what I'm referring to as the violation of a legitimate demand. And people who feel guilty typically believe that they could and should have acted differently (Niedenthal et al., 1994). In this respect, guilt is unlike shame. For whereas guilt is typically elicited by unstable, controllable aspects of the self (i.e., transgressive acts), shame is typically elicited by stable, uncontrollable aspects of the self (specifically, those that fall below some standard and that could, consequently, result in a loss of honor, respect, or esteem) (see H. B. Lewis, 1971b, p. 30, Niedenthal et al., 1994; Lewis, 2000; Tangney & Dearing, 2002; and Tracy & Robins, 2006). Similarly, when it comes to resentment and indignation, we find that what typically elicits such emotions is the judgment that someone has been treated unjustly or otherwise wrongly (Mikula, 1986; Shaver et al., 1987; Prinz & Nichols, 2010, p. 125). So, given

---

[12] A close cousin to my view is Brendan Dill and Stephen Darwall's *accountability theory* (2014). In their view, blame represents its target (oneself or some other) as having violated a legitimate moral demand without excuse. Their view will be especially close to my own if we assume, as I believe we should, that all and only those who have violated a legitimate demand without excuse deserve to suffer guilt, regret, or remorse in the recognition of having violated that demand. But, unlike them, I don't think that the demand in question needs to be a moral one. And, unlike them, I think that blame represents its target not only as having violated a legitimate demand without excuse but also as deserving to suffer guilt, regret, or remorse in the recognition of having violated that demand.

that the blaming emotions are typically elicited by transgressive acts, my proposal interprets the blaming emotions as representing their targets as having performed an act that violates a legitimate demand.

Admittedly, some of the empirical data may initially seem problematic for my proposal. For, as Baumeister et al. (1994) point out, feelings of guilt can be elicited by the belief that one has undeservedly fared better than others, and these feelings arise even when one knows that one bears no responsibility for this unfairness. For instance, people often experience what's known as survivor's guilt when, by pure chance, they survive in a situation in which most others perished. But I think that we should understand survivor's guilt either (disjunct₁) as inaccurately representing surviving as something both that one "does" and that violates the seemingly legitimate demand not to enjoy inequitable benefits or (disjunct₂) as an entirely different form of guilt that has nothing to do with blame. Indeed, some suggest that there are two distinct types of guilt: one that isn't tied to blame and is elicited by the possession of inequitable benefits and another that is tied to blame and is elicited by feelings of responsibility for a transgressive act (see, e.g., Prinz & Nichols, 2010, p. 134). In either case, my proposal fits the data concerning the *blaming* emotions, which may or may not include survivor's guilt depending on which of the above two disjuncts is correct.

Of course, my proposal also requires that blame (and, thus, the blaming emotions) involves representing its target as not having suffered all the guilt, regret, and remorse that she deserves to suffer. But this too is supported by the empirical data – specifically, by the data concerning the act tendencies associated with the blaming emotions as well as their palliators. Again, let's start with guilt. Guilt is inherently unpleasant, yet we do not react to it as we do most other unpleasant experiences. When it comes to bodily aches, for instance, we're typically motivated to take a pill to get rid of them. Or if there's nothing we can do to get rid of them, we seek to distract ourselves from them. Yet, guilt typically motivates us to focus our attention on it and its source (i.e., on our transgression and those who were adversely affected by it) and to act in ways that will – at least, initially – aggravate it. Indeed, we're often motivated to wallow in our guilt. Additionally, guilt motivates us to seek out those who we've transgressed so as to express our guilt, regret, and remorse to them. And this, typically, only inflames these feelings – at least, initially. Thus, guilty feelings tend to motivate us to act in ways that will – at least, initially – aggravate them rather than alleviate them.[13]

---

[13] I admit, of course, that in the long run these expressions of guilt, regret, and remorse can lead to our being forgiven by the transgressed and that this will then help to alleviate our feelings of guilt, regret, and remorse.

What's more, we find the idea of just taking a pill to rid ourselves of our guilt morally problematic. Admittedly, some do turn to drugs or the bottle to palliate their guilt. But this is not, we think, the best way to deal with our guilt. For this doesn't so much rid us of our guilt as merely momentarily numb us to it. To get rid of it, we must atone, repent, apologize, and make amends. Of course, sometimes transgressors don't have the opportunity to make amends, express remorse, or even apologize. And, in such instances, the psychological research shows that those who feel guilty for a transgression are motivated to self-punish by inflicting physical pain or economic loss on themselves (Nelissen & Zeelenberg, 2009; Bastian et al., 2011; Watanabe & Ohtsubo, 2012; Ohtsubo et al., 2014; Tanaka et al., 2015).[14] As Herbert Morris puts it, "the man who feels guilty often seeks pain and somehow sees it as appropriate because of his guilt.... When we think of what it is to feel guilty then, we think ... of something that is owed; and pain is somehow connected with paying what one owes" (1976a, pp. 89–90). And it's been shown that the guiltier one feels, the more severe the punishment one is likely to inflict upon oneself (Gintis et al., 2001; Nelissen & Zeelenberg, 2009; Nelissen, 2012; Watanabe & Ohtsubo, 2012; Tanaka et al., 2015). Likewise, resentment and indignation over a transgression motivate people to punish the transgressor. Indeed, people are willing to pay to punish a transgressor even if they know that they will never again interact with her and so will never recoup the cost (Fehr & Gächter, 2002).[15] And, as Gollwitzer and Denzler (2009) have shown, people's aim in inflicting such punishment is not solely to ensure that the transgressor suffers, for their research shows that people also want the transgressor to recognize that she's been made to suffer *because* of her transgression. I believe that this is because they want the transgressor to recognize that they disapprove of what she has done and hope that she will come to share in their disapproval by feeling guilt, regret, and remorse. So, we find both that guilt motivates punishment of the self and that resentment and indignation motivate punishment of the relevant other: the transgressor. Given this and the fact that the ultimate aim seems to

---

[14] The tendency that people who feel guilty have to punish themselves when they don't have the opportunity to compensate the victims of their transgressions is what Nelissen and Zeelenberg (2009) have labeled the Dobby Effect. Also, Inbar et al. report that "a sizable experimental literature indicates that people often deal with their guilt over a bad deed by doing a good deed for someone else or for society in general" (2013, p. 17). And, arguably, doing good deeds can help atone for one's past bad deeds, making it such that one deserves to suffer less guilt, regret, and remorse than one once did.

[15] As Dill and Darwall point out, "several studies have shown that people are willing to punish at cost to themselves even in totally anonymous conditions, which offer no opportunity for reputational gain or loss" (2014, p. 47).

be to induce guilt, regret, and remorse, it makes sense to interpret the blaming emotions as representing their targets as not having suffered all the guilt, regret, and remorse that they deserve to suffer.

Further support for this interpretation comes from the fact that self-punishment palliates the blaming emotions. For instance, psychological research shows that self-punishment palliates feelings of guilt and that the more severe the self-punishment, the greater the palliative effect (Bastian et al., 2011; Inbar et al., 2013). As Morris observes, "feelings of guilt may disappear and the man [who used to feel guilty] may connect their disappearance with the pain he has experienced" (1976a, p. 90). Moreover, self-punishment palliates feelings of resentment and indignation in others, signaling to them that one is remorseful (Nelissen, 2012). And this in turn encourages them to forgive (Zhu et al., 2017). And the more painful the punishment that one inflicts upon oneself, the stronger the effect it has on the tendency of others to forgive (Zhu et al., 2017). In general, it seems that what best palliates feelings of resentment and indignation is the judgment the transgressor has got her comeuppance (Haidt et al., 2010; Prinz & Nichols, 2010, p. 126). Indeed, the psychological research suggests that what palliates these feelings is not rehabilitation or other good consequences, but only the transgressor's suffering what she deserves to suffer (Haidt et al., 2010; Prinz & Nichols, 2010, p. 128).[16] And, here, I strongly suspect that the reason that the transgressor's self-punishment palliates people's resentment and indignation toward her is because they see her self-punishment as a sign of her guilt, regret, and remorse. For in many of these experiments, the transgressor self-punishes by leaving her hand in an ice-water bath for a painfully long time. But I very much doubt that her doing so would palliate people's resentment and indignation toward her if they believed that she was doing so only to prove how tough she was rather than doing so as a result of her feelings of guilt, regret, and remorse. Indeed, as Brendan Dill and Stephen Darwall have pointed out, "one of the most robust findings from [the psychological] research on forgiveness is that forgiveness usually occurs when and only when the perpetrator has adequately demonstrated remorse by acknowledging guilt, apologizing, and/or offering compensation" (2014, p. 40).

---

[16] See Dill and Darwall (2014, pp. 46–52) for citations to numerous studies showing that what motivates us to reproach, sanction, or punish someone for violating a legitimate demand is not the hope that this will bring about some happy result such as deterrence or self-benefit. Rather, we reproach transgressors to get them to hold themselves accountable for their transgressions, and they do this by feeling guilt, regret, or remorse in the recognition that they have violated a legitimate demand.

Given all the empirical data showing that the blaming emotions motivate people to punish with the aim of getting the transgressor to hold
herself accountable and to punish in proportion to the felt intensity of
these emotions, and given all the empirical data suggesting that the transgressor's suffering guilt, regret, and remorse both palliates these blaming
emotions and promotes forgiveness, it seems best to interpret the blaming
emotions as representing their targets as not having suffered all the guilt,
regret, and remorse that they deserve to suffer. And this along with the
empirical data concerning the elicitors of these emotions suggests that
blame represents its target as meeting sub-conditions a–c of Condition$_1$.

The Pro Tanto Permissibility of Deliberately Guilting the Blameworthy

Another reason to think that Condition$_1$ is necessary for blame is that it
provides the most plausible explanation for why it is *pro tanto* morally permissible to express our blame of the blameworthy with the aim of getting
them to feel guilt, regret, or remorse. As A. P. Duggan (2018, p. 296) notes,
expressed "blame is a form of 'guilting' in that blamers intend their blame to
result in the blamed feeling guilty for doing wrong" (see also Carlsson, 2019;
Dill & Darwall, 2014, p. 43; Fricker, 2016, p. 167; Macnamara, 2015b, p. 559;
McKenna, 2012, pp. 139–140; and Wolf, 2011, p. 338). That is, we often
express our blame of transgressors in the hopes that they will both come
to recognize that we disapprove of what they've done and come to share in
our disapproval by feeling guilt, regret, and remorse for what they've done.[17]

Of course, we recognize that it will be unpleasant for them to feel this
way. So, in expressing our blame with the aim of getting them to feel guilt,
regret, and remorse, we are deliberately causing them to suffer.[18] And this

---

[17] As Hannah Tierney and others have pointed out, another reason we're often motivated to
express our blame to those who have transgressed us is as a means of standing up for ourselves by
expressing our sense of dignity and self-respect. See Tierney (2021a), Murphy (2005, p. 19), and
Reis-Dennis (2019).

[18] I concede that one can express one's blame with only the aim of getting the transgressor to rectify,
repent, or reconcile and that this needn't involve deliberately causing her to suffer. That is, the associated suffering could be merely a foreseen but unintended side effect of one's aim of getting her to
rectify, repent, or reconcile. But I don't see how one can express one's blame with the aim of getting
the transgressor to feel guilty (i.e., to feel the painful appreciation of the awful significance of what
she has done) without deliberately causing her to suffer. And this is often something we aim to do,
which is why we are appropriately frustrated when we express our blame with the aim of guilting
our target and our target responds with no hint of guilt or remorse but only an acknowledgment of
having done wrong and a sincere promise to do better in the future. We get frustrated because, as
Prinz and Nichols (2010, p. 126) point out, our goal is not merely to secure some happy result but
also to ensure that our target experiences feelings of guilt, regret, and remorse.

is potentially morally problematic, for it's wrong to deliberately cause suffering unless either those thereby made to suffer deserve to so suffer or our causing them to so suffer is the only way to ensure a fair distribution of undeserved burdens overall. But despite this, expressions of blame actually seem to be *pro tanto* morally permissible – at least, when the targets are blameworthy (Carlsson, 2017, p. 95).[19] This means that either the blameworthy must deserve to suffer guilt, regret, and remorse or having them so suffer must be the only way for us to ensure a fair distribution of undeserved burdens overall. Yet, it's unclear why either would be the case. After all, to be blameworthy is just to be someone whom it is fitting to blame, where its fittingness is purely a matter of the accuracy of its representations.[20] In this respect, the blaming emotions seem to be no different from other intentional attitudes – such as fear, envy, belief, desire, shame, grief, and admiration. In each case, the attitude is fitting just in case it is accurate in its representations of the intentional object.[21] For instance, belief is fitting just in case it's correct in representing its object as being true. Envy is fitting just in case it's correct in representing its object as something good that one's rival possesses but that one lacks. And shame is fitting just in case it's correct in representing its object as some sub-standard aspect of oneself that could potentially lead to a loss of honor, respect, or esteem. So, someone is fittingly blamed – that is, blameworthy – if and only if that blame is accurate in its representations. But why think that the accuracy of these representations depends either on its target deserving to suffer or on it being fair to make her suffer? After all, it's fitting to distrust those who are untrustworthy regardless of whether they deserve to suffer the burden of being distrusted, and regardless of whether inflicting this suffering upon them would result in a fair distribution of undeserved burdens overall.

The problem arises because blameworthiness concerns the fittingness of blame, and it can be fitting for you to adopt an attitude toward someone even if she doesn't deserve to suffer the burdens associated with your adopting that attitude toward her. For instance, it is, as Pamela Hieronymi

---

[19] To say that it is *pro tanto* morally permissible for us to express our blame of the blameworthy is not to say that it is always morally permissible to do so. It's just to say that there is a significant moral reason to do so such that, absent countervailing reasons or undermining considerations, it will be permissible to do so.

[20] The idea that to be blameworthy is just to be fittingly blamed is not entirely uncontroversial, but I'll address the relevant controversy below. Also, it may be that not everyone uses the term "fitting" to mean "accurate in its representations," but this is how I'll use the term.

[21] For my purposes, an intentional attitude is to be understood as any mental state that has an intentional object that it represents as being a certain way. Thus, examples of intentional attitudes include hope, fear, envy, guilt, shame, desire, belief, intention, and resentment. But they exclude mental states such as pain and hunger, which don't have intentional objects.

(2004, pp. 119–120) has pointed out, fitting to distrust the untrustworthy even if they don't deserve to suffer the burdens associated with being distrusted, and even if there's nothing fair about their having to suffer these burdens. But we can solve this (merely apparent?) puzzle so long as we keep separate the issue of whether it's unjust to distrust the untrustworthy (or to blame the blameworthy) and the issue of whether it's unjust to *express* distrust of the untrustworthy (or to *express* blame of the blameworthy) with *the aim* of making them feel some inherently unpleasant emotion. These are importantly different issues because, for one, the burdens associated with *expressing* distrust (or blame) can go far beyond those associated with merely distrusting (or blaming) in private. For another, one can distrust (or blame) someone without deliberately causing them to suffer, but one cannot express one's distrust (or blame) of someone with *the aim* of making her feel, say, shame (or guilt) without deliberately causing her to suffer. Thus, although it's unproblematic for us to distrust the untrustworthy, it is – at least, potentially – problematic for us to express our distrust of some untrustworthy person with the aim of, say, shaming her. For she won't deserve to suffer for her untrustworthiness if she came to be this way due entirely to formative circumstances outside of her control. So, we still need to explain why it is *pro tanto* morally *permissible* to express our blame of the blameworthy with the aim of guilting them when it is *pro tanto* morally *impermissible* to express our distrust of the untrustworthy with the aim of shaming them.

Fortunately, my proposal explains this, for my account entails that, even though the untrustworthy don't necessarily deserve to suffer shame, the blameworthy do necessarily deserve to suffer guilt.[22] In my account, blaming a target for having φ-ed entails representing her as deserving to

---

[22] Many philosophers agree that the blameworthy deserve to suffer guilt, regret, or remorse – see, for instance, Carlsson (2017, p. 89) and Duggan (2018, p. 297). But, of course, some disagree. For instance, Nelkin (2019) has argued that there is no *pro tanto* reason to induce feelings of guilt in the blameworthy. To convince us, she poses the following thought experiment. Imagine that someone has culpably wronged another and that you have the power of "The Look," whereby you can, simply by giving this someone a certain look, induce her to feel guilty in the recognition that what she has done is wrong. But we are to imagine that she is already reformed, so will never do this sort of thing again. Moreover, we're to imagine either that her relationship with the relevant others has been irreparably damaged or that all has been forgiven. Thus, we're to imagine that inducing her to feel guilt isn't a means to any good. Nevertheless, Nelkin maintains that you would not be "making a mistake, or leaving a reason on the table, so to speak, by taking a pass on inducing this painful feeling." I disagree. You may not be required to give her "The Look," but you certainly have a reason to do so. Randy Clarke and Piers Rawling agree with me (this volume), and much of the psychological research cited above suggests that most people want the blameworthy to feel guilty, not as a means to reform or any other instrumental good, but simply because they think that the blameworthy deserve to suffer guilty feelings.

suffer guilt, regret, or remorse in the recognition that she has violated a legitimate demand in φ-ing. Thus, she is worthy of being blamed if and only if this representation is accurate. And it's accurate if and only if she deserves to suffer these unpleasant feelings. Thus, in my account, the blameworthy are just those who have the normative property of deserving to suffer guilt, regret, or remorse. By contrast, Hieronymi (2004) holds that the blameworthy are simply those who have the descriptive property of having acted out of ill will. So, she thinks that a subject is blameworthy just in case she has, in fact, acted out of ill will. But given that someone can act out of ill will without deserving to suffer (for she may have come to possess this ill will due entirely to formative circumstances outside of her control), Hieronymi can't explain why it is *pro tanto* morally permissible to express blame with the aim of getting the target to suffer guilt, regret, and remorse.[23] So, my account has an advantage over accounts such as Hieronymi's in that it explains why we expect even morally good people to be motivated to express their blame of the blameworthy with the aim of getting them to suffer guilt, regret, and remorse in the recognition that they've violated a legitimate demand.

Now, the only other way to account both for this expectation and for the *pro tanto* moral permissibility of deliberately guilting the blameworthy is to adopt Andreas Brekke Carlsson's view (2017). In his view, the blameworthy are not, as in my view, those for whom it is *fitting* to feel guilty, but rather are those who *deserve* to feel guilty. His view, like mine, ensures that the blameworthy necessarily deserve to suffer guilty feelings, which is what we must hold if we're to account for the *pro tanto* moral permissibility of deliberately guilting the blameworthy. But I believe that we should reject Carlsson's view for the following two reasons. First, it leaves unexplained why the blaming emotions (e.g., guilt, resentment, and indignation) are unlike all other intentional attitudes (e.g., pride, fear, belief, shame, disgust, and admiration), which are all appropriate just in case they are fitting – that is, accurate in their representations (for more on this point, see Portmore, 2019c and D'Arms & Jacobson, 2019). Second, it faces the following unattractive dilemma.[24] Carlsson must either accept or reject what I'll call the Deserves-Only-Fitting-Guilt Claim: someone deserves to suffer guilt only if that guilt would be fitting. And it seems that either way his view will be problematic. If, on the one hand, he accepts the Deserves-Only-Fitting-Guilt Claim, then he must, it seems, hold that what makes someone deserve to suffer fitting

---

[23] I borrow this point from Carlsson (2017, p. 96).
[24] This objection comes from D'Arms and Jacobson (2019), but I put a slightly different spin on it.

guilt is simply the fact that it's fitting. After all, in his view (2019), what makes it fitting for one to feel guilt for having φ-ed is not whether it represents one as deserving to suffer in this way, but rather something such as whether guilt represents one as having manifested ill will in φ-ing. So, what makes fitting guilt deserved is not the nature of guilt's representations, but simply its fittingness.[25] The problem, though, is that it's implausible to suppose that what, in general, makes someone deserve to suffer some unpleasant emotion is simply that it's fitting. After all, it can be fitting for someone to feel fear (or grief) without her deserving to suffer it. So, on this horn of the dilemma, Carlsson needs to explain why it's only guilt (and not also fear and grief) that's deserved simply in virtue of its fittingness. And there just doesn't seem to be any plausible way for him to account for this.

On the other hand, if Carlsson rejects the Deserves-Only-Fitting-Guilt Claim, then his view will imply that someone could deserve to suffer unfitting guilt. But this is implausible. I can see how someone might deserve to suffer in general, and I can see how someone might deserve to suffer the specific sort of unpleasantness associated with a fittingly felt emotion. But I can't see how someone could deserve to suffer the specific unpleasantness associated with an unfittingly felt emotion. To illustrate the problem, let's suppose that, contrary to what I've suggested and in accordance with what Carlsson has himself suggested (2017, p. 107), guilt for having φ-ed represents one as having manifested ill will in φ-ing. Now, if we thought it possible for someone to deserve to feel unfitting guilt, then we would have to hold that it's possible for someone to deserve to feel the unpleasantness in recognizing that her actions manifested ill will even though, in fact, her actions didn't manifest ill will (which is what accounts for its unfittingness). But it's just implausible to suppose that someone who didn't manifest ill will could deserve to suffer the specific unpleasantness associated with representing oneself as having manifested ill will.

So, for these two reasons, I think that we should reject Carlsson's explanation for why the blameworthy necessarily deserve to suffer. Instead, we should take the explanation to be, as I've supposed, both that the blameworthy are those who are fittingly blamed and that it's fitting to blame

---

[25] Carlsson might resist this by claiming that he can account for the Deserves-Only-Fitting-Guilt Claim by holding that one's manifesting ill will necessitates one's deserving to suffer. But in that case, he should just admit that, given both that guilt represents one as manifesting ill will and that one's manifesting ill will necessitates one's deserving to suffer guilt, guilt for φ-ing represents one as deserving to suffer guilt; it's just that it does so via representing one as having a feature that necessitates one's deserving to suffer guilt. And in that case, Carlsson's view would be a version of, not an alternative to, my own. For his view would then be one that holds that the blameworthy are those for whom it is fitting to feel guilty.

someone only if she deserves to suffer the unpleasantness of guilt, regret, or remorse given the nature of blame's representations.

The Conditions for Blameworthiness

Another merit of my proposal is that it can account for the fact that there are certain necessary conditions for being blameworthy (e.g., the control condition and the epistemic condition) as well as certain necessary conditions for being blameworthy to a certain degree (e.g., the proportionality condition). Take, for instance, the control condition (sometimes called *the freedom condition*). It holds that someone can be blameworthy for having φ-ed only if she had the relevant sort of control over whether she was to φ. My proposal can explain this so long as we assume, as seems plausible, that someone deserves to suffer some inherently unpleasant emotion for having φ-ed only if she had the relevant sort of control over whether she was to φ. Thus, we get the following argument for the control condition.

(P1) Someone is blameworthy for having φ-ed if and only if blaming her for having φ-ed is accurate in its representations. [Assumption]

(P2) Blaming someone for having φ-ed is accurate in its representations only if she deserves to suffer guilt, regret, or remorse for having φ-ed. [From Condition₁ of my proposal]

(C1) Thus, someone is blameworthy for having φ-ed only if she deserves to suffer guilt, regret, or remorse for having φ-ed. [From P1–P2]

(P3) Someone deserves to suffer guilt, regret, or remorse for having φ-ed only if she had the relevant sort of control over whether she was to φ. [Assumption]

(C2) Therefore, someone is blameworthy for having φ-ed only if she had the relevant sort of control over whether she was to φ. [From C1 and P3]

We can similarly argue for the epistemic condition (sometimes called *the knowledge condition*). It holds that someone is blameworthy for having φ-ed only if she could have reasonably been expected to have known that her φ-ing would entail violating a legitimate demand. To get this argument, we simply need to replace "she had the relevant sort of control over whether she was to φ" with "she could have reasonably been expected to have known that her φ-ing would entail violating a legitimate demand" throughout the above argument, while replacing "control condition" with "epistemic condition" in C2.

What's more, we can offer the following argument for the proportionality condition, which holds that someone is worthy of being blamed to extent E for having φ-ed only if E is proportionate to the stringency of the demand that she violated in φ-ing (see, e.g., Fricker, 2016, p. 168).

(P1*) Someone is worthy of being blamed to extent E for having φ-ed if and only if blaming her to extent E for having φ-ed is accurate in its representations. [Assumption]

(P2*) Blaming someone to extent E for having φ-ed is accurate in its representations only if the amount of guilt, regret, and remorse that she deserves to suffer for having φ-ed is proportionate to E. [From my proposal]

(C1*) Thus, someone is worthy of being blamed to extent E for having φ-ed only if the amount of guilt, regret, and remorse that she deserves to suffer for having φ-ed is proportionate to E. [From P1*–P2*]

(P3*) The amount of guilt, regret, and remorse that she deserves to suffer for having φ-ed must be proportionate to the stringency of the demand that she violated in φ-ing. [Assumption]

(C2*) Therefore, someone is worthy of being blamed to extent E for having φ-ed only if E is proportionate to the stringency of the demand that she violated in φ-ing. [From C1* and P3*]

We need to appeal to all three conditions in order to account for our judgments about when it is appropriate to blame people and in what degree.[26] And accounting for such judgments is, I believe, crucial. As Scanlon has pointed out, "a satisfactory account of blame should be as faithful as possible to the phenomenology of blaming and to our judgments about when it is appropriate to blame people and in what degree" (2013a, p. 84). So, consider that without the proportionality condition we have no way of accounting for the fact that it would, other things being equal, be inappropriate for us to blame someone who has violated a less stringent demand more harshly than we blame someone who has violated a more stringent

---

[26] I readily concede that there may be other conditions for being blameworthy. For instance, it may be that the person-stage who is now to be blamed must be, in certain relevant ways, psychologically similar to (or contiguous with) the person-stage who committed the given transgression. But I won't explore the possibility of such other conditions here. In any case, it seems that these other proposed conditions will be plausible only insofar as they're plausible conditions for a target's deserving to suffer guilt, regret, or remorse in virtue of something that some earlier person-stage did.

demand. For instance, it would, other things being equal, be inappropriate for us to blame someone who has told a self-serving but relatively harmless lie more harshly than we blame someone who has committed murder.

We need the epistemic condition to explain why non-culpable ignorance can excuse one from being blameworthy for having violated a legitimate demand. For instance, even if it's legitimate to demand that I not come into the office while contagious, it's inappropriate to blame me for doing so if I couldn't have been reasonably expected to have known that I was infected, let alone contagious.

Lastly, we need to appeal to the control condition to explain both why the only subjects that we can appropriately blame are those who possess the relevant sort of control over the things that we blame them for and why the only things that we can appropriately *directly* blame them for are those things over which they directly exerted such control.[27] Thus, the control condition explains why newborns and primitive animals – both of which lack the relevant sort of control – are exempt from blame. And it explains why normal adult human beings cannot appropriately be blamed for their reflex actions, muscle twitches, or heart palpitations. After all, they lack the relevant sort of control over these bodily movements. What's more, it explains why a drunk driver can be held directly responsible, not for her impaired motor skills but only for that which led to her impaired motor skills – assuming that that was something over which she did exert the relevant sort of control. Perhaps, then, the only thing that we can appropriately hold her directly responsible for is her having started to drink without having first arranged for a designated driver.

Of course, some cite the fact that we often take ourselves to be (normatively) responsible for our non-voluntary "actions" – for example, for desiring what's bad, believing what's contrary to the evidence, and intending to do what's incompatible with our ultimate ends – as reason for being skeptical of the control condition. But the fact that we can be responsible for such things doesn't give us any reason to doubt the control condition, but only reason to doubt that the relevant sort of control is as narrow as voluntary control. To understand why, we must understand what

---

[27] Note, then, that I deny what's known as resultant moral luck (Zimmerman, 1987): the idea that one's degree of accountability for φ-ing can be affected by the uncontrolled events that determine the results of one's φ-ing. For some compelling arguments against resultant moral luck, see Khoury (2018). And for some experimental evidence suggesting that what most affects our judgments about an agent's degree of accountability for some act is not whether, by luck, the act had a bad result but whether we judge that the agent was unjustified in believing that her act had little chance of having that bad result, see Young, Nichols, and Saxe (2010). Also, some take Frankfurt-style cases as evidence against the control condition, but see Portmore (2019a, 2019b) for a rebuttal.

voluntary control consists of and why we must exert it over our actions to be responsible for them.

For a subject to have *voluntary control* over whether she performs an action is for her to have volitional control over whether she performs it while having rational control over whether she forms the volitions that would result in her performing it. She has *volitional control* over whether she performs the act so long as, holding everything else fixed, whether she performs it just depends on whether she forms the relevant volitions (e.g., the intention to perform it), and she has *rational control* over whether she forms the relevant volitions so long as, holding everything else fixed, whether she forms them just depends on whether and how she responds to the relevant reasons. Note, then, that volitional control over our actions is insufficient to ground responsibility for them. After all, just as I have volitional control over whether I raise my hand, a cat presumably has volitional control over whether it will swat at the mouse that scurries by. Yet, presumably, a cat is not responsible for swatting at the mouse because whether it forms the volition to swat isn't under its rational control. That is, whether it forms this volition is just a matter of some non-reasons-responsive mechanism, such as pure instinct – or so I'll assume. By contrast, I can be responsible for raising my hand given that (or insofar as) whether I form the volition to do so is reasons-responsive and, thus, under my rational control. This, as I've argued elsewhere (Portmore, 2019b), suggests that what really matters for responsibility is rational control. Indeed, it seems that the only reason that we need to have volitional control over our actions to be responsible for them is that it's only by having volitional control over our actions that we come to have rational control over them (see also McHugh, 2017, p. 2749). For we cannot *act* directly in response to our reasons. Indeed, we act in response to our reasons only by being guided by our reasons to form the volitions that will, if the world cooperates, result in our performing the act in question.

It seems, then, that we need the control condition in conjunction with the idea that the relevant sort of control is rational control to adequately distinguish between those things for which we can be held responsible – e.g., our beliefs, intentions, and voluntary actions – and those things for which we can't be held responsible – e.g., our sensations, pangs of hunger, and involuntary actions. The former are those things over which we exert rational control and the latter are those things over which we lack such control. So, I admit that many of the things that we hold each other responsible for are non-voluntary and, thus, are things over which we lack voluntary control. But this shows not that we should reject the control condition but only that we should accept that the relevant sort of control is rational control. So, it's a merit of my proposal that it allows us to account for the fact that we can be blameworthy for the non-voluntary.[28]

How What a Transgressor Has Done and Experienced Subsequent to Her Wrongdoing Can Affect the Extent to Which She Is Presently Blameworthy for That Wrongdoing

A fourth and final reason to accept the necessity of Condition$_1$ is that it allows us to plausibly account for the fact that what a transgressor has done and experienced subsequent to her violating a legitimate demand can affect the extent to which she is presently blameworthy for that violation. I'm not saying that it affects the extent to which she is responsible for having committed that violation in the first place, but it does, I believe, affect the extent to which she should continue to feel guilt, regret, and remorse as well as the extent to which others should continue to feel resentment and indignation toward her. To illustrate, suppose that Alexa has wrongly harmed Alex and that Berta has wrongly harmed Bert. And assume that everything else is equal but for the following two facts. First, whereas Alexa has subsequently experienced much guilt, regret, and remorse for what she has done, Berta has experienced none.[29] Second, whereas Alexa has done much to make amends (apologizing profusely and even paying

---

[28] Of course, many will concede that we can be blameworthy for the non-voluntary but claim that this responsibility for the non-voluntary must be indirect. That is, they'll appeal to the well-known tracing strategy (i.e., the strategy of claiming that our responsibility for something non-voluntary must ultimately trace back to something that was under our voluntary control) to account for our responsibility for our forming the relevant beliefs and volitions. There are several problems with this strategy when it comes to accounting for our responsibility for such attitudes – not the least of which is that it can lead to an infinite regress. For more on the problems with tracing, see Smith (2015a), Vargas (2005), McKenna (2008), and Portmore (2019a).

[29] This is relevant, for feelings of guilt are *self-consuming* (Na'aman, 2021) with respect to their fittingness such that it becomes unfitting to continue to have such feelings – or, at least, to continue to have them with the same intensity – if you've already experienced them quite a bit. In this respect, guilt differs from grief. For no matter how much grief you have already experienced, it never ceases to be fitting to feel further grief, nor does it cease to be fitting to grieve with the same intensity as before. After all, grief over X represents X as a significant loss, and the more intense your grief, the more significant a loss it represents it as being. Yet, a loss doesn't become any less significant just because you've already grieved a lot over it. So, if your present circumstances make vivid to you the true significance of your loss, it will be entirely fitting for you to feel the same intense grief that you initially felt when you first came to grips with that loss. By contrast, guilt for having φ-ed represents you as someone who has not suffered all that you deserve to suffer in virtue of your having φ-ed, and the more intense your guilt, the greater the amount of guilt it represents you as still deserving to suffer. So, guilt, unlike grief, is self-consuming with respect to its fittingness given that you can come to deserve to suffer less (and, perhaps, even not at all) as a result of your having already suffered a lot. (I acknowledge that it can be inappropriate to regularly feel the same intense

reparations to Alex), Berta has done nothing to atone for her wrongdoing. It seems, then, that the extent to which it is appropriate for Alexa to continue to feel guilty and for Alex to continue to feel resentment is much less than that to which it is appropriate for Berta to continue to feel guilty and for Bert to continue to feel resentment (for more on this, see Carlsson, this volume, and Portmore, 2019c).

My proposal explains why Alex and Berta differ in their degrees of blameworthiness. Given that Alexa, unlike Berta, has done much to atone for her wrongdoing and has already suffered a tremendous amount of guilt, regret, and remorse, she doesn't deserve to suffer as much further guilt, regret, and remorse as Berta does. In my proposal, those who deserve to suffer less guilt, regret, and remorse are less blameworthy because, in my proposal, the greater the amount of guilt, regret, and remorse that one represents some target as still deserving to suffer, the greater the extent to which one blames that target. Thus, it is fitting to blame someone to extent E if and only if E is proportionate to the amount of guilt, regret, and remorse that she still deserves to suffer. So, Alexa is less blameworthy than Berta given that the amount of guilt, regret, and remorse that Alexa still deserves to suffer is less than the amount of guilt, regret, and remorse that Berta still deserves to suffer.

This gives my proposal a distinct advantage over most other views of blame, for most other views of blame are unable to account for the fact that what a transgressor has done and experienced subsequent to her wrongdoing can affect the extent to which she is presently blameworthy for that wrongdoing. For although what someone has done and experienced subsequent to her wrongdoing can affect the extent to which she still deserves to suffer guilt, regret, and remorse for that wrongdoing, most other views about blame deny that blaming someone for having φ-ed represents her as not having suffered all that she deserves to suffer for having φ-ed. Instead, they hold that this represents her as having "violated a moral requirement of respect" in φ-ing (Graham, 2014, p. 408) or as having manifested ill will in φ-ing (Hieronymi, 2004), or as presently possessing the same flaw that led her to φ (Khoury & Matheson, 2018). And the correctness of these representations does not depend on what she has done or experienced subsequent to her φ-ing. So, unlike my proposal, these views cannot account for the fact that what a transgressor has done or experienced subsequent to

grief that you initially felt over some loss when it's now been several years since that loss occurred. But I think that it's inappropriate, not in the sense of being unfitting, but in some other sense and that we can, therefore, account for this without thinking that grief is self-consuming with respect to its fittingness – see Portmore [2019c].)

her transgression can affect the extent to which she is presently blamewor-thy for that transgression.[30]

Indeed, the only view of blame besides my own that can account for this fact is Carlsson's view. For like my view, his view implies that the extent to which someone is presently blameworthy for having φ-ed depends on the extent to which she still deserves to suffer guilt, regret, and remorse for having φ-ed. But, as we saw above, Carlsson's view faces an unattractive dilemma. So, it seems that the only plausible way to account for this fact is to accept my proposal.

3 The Necessity of Condition$_2$

In my proposal, Condition$_2$ is also necessary for blame. That is, a subject blames someone for having seemingly φ-ed only if she feels disapproval of, or disappointment in, that someone for having seemingly φ-ed. We should accept this because, as everyone seems to agree, blame requires more than mere representations (see, for instance, Coates & Tognazzini, 2013; Darwall, 2010; Scanlon, 2008, 2013; Sher, 2006; Shoemaker, 2013: 101, and Smith, 2013). To blame someone, you must do more than simply represent her as having violated a legitimate demand in having φ-ed. You must feel disapproval of, or disappointment in, her as a result. This, I take it, is uncontroversial. The controversy is not about whether such disap-proval is required but is only about what, if anything, beyond this and certain representations is required. And, as I'll now argue, nothing else is. I'll argue, that is, that Condition$_1$ and Condition$_2$ are jointly sufficient.

4 The Joint Sufficiency of These Two Conditions

In defense of their joint sufficiency, I hope to show that no other proposed condition is necessary. Take, first, the proposal that blame must involve resentment, indignation, or some other kind of hostile emotion (Wallace, 1994, p. 75). We should reject this proposal, for, as George Sher (2006) and several others have noted, blame need not involve any anger or hostility (see Brown, 2020; Smith, 2013, p. 32, and Shoemaker & Vargas, 2019). As Sher notes, "we may, for example, feel no hostility toward the loved one whom we blame for failing to tell a sensitive acquaintance a hard

---

[30] My view implies that if one has suffered sufficiently, one may have thereby ceased to be blame-worthy. That said, there may be some transgressions that are "unforgiveable" such that it never ceases to be appropriate (no matter how much one has already suffered) to continue to feel guilty about them.

truth, the criminal whom we blame for a burglary we read about in the newspaper, or the historical figure whom we blame for the misdeeds he performed long ago" (Sher, 2006, p. 88). Of course, in my proposal, blame must involve a feeling of disapproval or disappointment, but neither need be heated or hostile; these attitudes can, instead, be quite calm and sedate.

Second, Scanlon has proposed that blaming someone involves taking "your relationship with him or her to be modified" (2008, pp. 128–129). But, as Susan Wolf has noted, this isn't a necessary condition for blame. Sometimes when we blame someone there is a lot of screaming and remonstration but no relationship modification (2011, p. 334). Indeed, when it comes to certain close family members, we are often resigned to continuing on with the relationship as always despite everything. Of course, this doesn't prevent us from blaming them by both disapproving of their behavior and representing them as deserving of guilt, regret, or remorse. Indeed, this may just be part of our relationship's normal pattern in which they wrong us and then we blame them, but, despite this, we both just continue on with the relationship as always.

Third, some propose that blaming someone necessitates some belief or judgment about her, such as that she is blameworthy (Sher, 2006) or has displayed ill will (Hieronymi, 2004), or has been diminished in her moral standing (Zimmerman, 1988). But not only do we not need to assent to such things, we can even deny such things while blaming. For, as I noted above, blame can be recalcitrant. My wife can blame me for having seemingly cheated on her while denying that I am blameworthy or that I have cheated on her, or even that I have manifested ill will toward her. Indeed, it seems that if there are any beliefs or judgments that are necessitated in blaming someone, it is only those that are constitutive of disapproving of, or being disappointed in, her.

Fourth, someone might claim that blame must involve some overt act – perhaps, one that communicates some protest or a demand for respect. But even those who hold that blame's function is communicative allow that blame need not actually be communicated. For they hold that one's blame, like one's unsent email, can count as communicative in nature even if it is never in fact communicated (e.g., Macnamara, 2015b). Therefore, we should deny that blame must involve some overt act. Indeed, blame seems to be something that one can do in the privacy of one's own study (Coates & Tognazzini, 2013, p. 8).

Of course, these four don't exhaust the possibilities for potential necessary conditions for blame. But I believe that they constitute the most plausible candidates, and, what's more, they're the ones that have been most central in the existing literature. So, I think we should – at least, tentatively – conclude that there are no other necessary conditions besides Condition$_1$ and Condition$_2$.

5 How My Proposal Accounts for All the Disparate Forms of Blame

Another advantage of my proposal is that it can account for blame in all its disparate forms. First, as we've already seen, it allows that blame can be recalcitrant.

Second, it allows that blame can be either intrapersonal or interpersonal. For in my proposal the target of blame may or may not be identical to the one doing the blaming. Thus, the target of blame can be either oneself (and, thus, intrapersonal) or some other (and, thus, interpersonal).

Third, it allows that the target of blame can be alive or dead. For in my proposal, blaming need involve only both a feeling of disapproval and a representation of desert. And we can have both attitudes toward the dead as well as the living. For just as we can disapprove of what the living have done, we can disapprove of what the dead have done. And just as we can represent the living as not having suffered all the guilt, regret, and remorse that they deserve to suffer, we can represent the dead as not having suffered all the guilt, regret, and remorse that they deserve to suffer. Or if you think that it makes no sense to talk of the dead *deserving* (present tense) to suffer, we can just add the following parenthetical remark to the relevant portion of *My Proposal* to get the following: "not having suffered all that she deserves *(or deserved)* to suffer."

Fourth, it allows that blame need not be heated or hostile. Although it is quite common for us to feel anger and hostility toward those we blame, my proposal allows that blame need not involve such hostility, for we can feel disapproval without feeling any anger or hostility. Thus, when we blame some historical figure for some long past misdeed, we may be quite calm and sedate. For we may just calmly disapprove of what that figure has done while believing both that she did thereby violate a legitimate demand and that she did not suffer all the guilt, regret, and remorse that she deserved to suffer for having done so.

Fifth, my proposal allows that blame can be either expressed and made public or unexpressed and kept private. For, again, my proposal holds that blame need only involve both a feeling of disapproval and a representation of desert. And one can possess such attitudes without expressing them.

Sixth, my proposal allows that we can be blamed both for the voluntary and for the non-voluntary. In my proposal, the variable φ ranges over all the things that a target can do in response to reasons and not just those things that are under her voluntary control. And I've concluded, therefore, that φ ranges over such things as the formation of a reasons-responsive attitude (e.g., a belief, a desire, or an intention). Thus, we can, in my proposal, be accountable for such things as desiring what's bad, believing what's contrary to the evidence, and intending to do what's incompatible with our ultimate ends – and this is so despite the fact that we don't (at least, not typically) have voluntary control over whether we form such attitudes.

Seventh, my proposal allows that blame need not be specifically moral. For, in my proposal, blame requires representing the target as having violated a legitimate demand, but that demand needn't be a moral one. And this is important because we often blame ourselves for our non-moral failings: for our aesthetic bad taste, gustatory self-indulgence, or poor athletic or intellectual performance. As David Shoemaker and Manuel Vargas (2019) have noted, we often blame ourselves for failing to live up to the ideals that we set for ourselves. And, as J. David Velleman (2003) notes, we routinely blame ourselves for failing to fulfill our commitments to ourselves – for example, our commitment to maintain a certain diet or exercise regimen. What's more, we even blame *others* for their non-moral failings. For instance, "a Mafioso can be said to blame an associate for violating the code of omertà" (by, say, ratting him out to the FBI) even if he admits that his associate hasn't thereby violated any moral demand and has, in fact, done what he was morally required to do (Scanlon, 2013, p. 88).[31]

My proposal accounts for such non-moral blame, both because the demands that my proposal refers to need not be moral demands and because my proposal allows that in blaming someone we need not represent her as deserving to suffer some unpleasant *moral* emotion (such as *moral* guilt) but could instead represent her as deserving to suffer some unpleasant *non-moral* emotion (such as regret or *non-moral* guilt).[32] Of course, you may question whether there is such a thing as non-moral guilt. But consider that we feel guilty for such things as skipping the gym, drinking too much, overindulging at the buffet, and making some impulsive and ill-advised purchase. We even have special names for some of these kinds of guilt, for example, food guilt and consumer guilt. And these kinds of guilt don't seem to be particularly moral.

---

[31] Other proponents of the view that we can be blamed for our perceived non-moral failings include Björnsson (2017c) and Matheson and Milam (2021).

[32] Also, the demands need not be legitimate ones. In my proposal, blaming the Mafioso requires only representing him as having violated a legitimate demand. And one can make this representation without the code of omertà actually being a legitimate demand.

But even if you insist that guilt must concern morality, my account allows that when we blame someone, we may represent her as deserving only regret, and regret needn't concern morality. To illustrate, consider the sorts of objections that I get during the Q&A of one of my talks. Sometimes, it's an objection that I've anticipated. Other times, it's an objection that I never would have thought of myself. But, occasionally, it's an obvious objection that I should have, but failed to, anticipate. In these instances, I blame myself for not having anticipated the obvious objection. I get angry with myself. Indeed, I could just kick myself. Perhaps, what I'm feeling is better characterized as regret rather than as guilt. But such regret seems to share with guilt what are, for our purposes, the same relevant features. My regret, like my guilt, is elicited by a transgression. It's just that, in this case, the standards that I've transgressed are the intellectual standards to which I've committed myself. My regret, like my guilt, is unpleasant in its affect. And yet, like my guilt, my regret focuses my attention on the mistake and its adverse effects, thereby inflaming its unpleasantness. Thus, like my guilt, my regret motivates me to self-punish. Instead of trying to distract myself from it by focusing my attention elsewhere, I wallow in its associated pain. Indeed, it strikes me as if I deserve to suffer in this way. For it's not that I'm thinking that it's instrumentally good for me to suffer in this way. That is, I'm not thinking that I need to suffer like this so that I'll remember next time to think long and hard about such possible objections. After all, I did think long and hard this time around. And this is what makes my failure all the more infuriating: this objection should have occurred to me because it should have occurred to anyone who had dedicated even a quarter of the time that I did to thinking of possible objections.

Perhaps, you might think that I'm idiosyncratic in my propensity for self-flagellation. But athletes react in the same way to their failures (Shoemaker, 2019). Some will even pound their heads or pull their hair. What's more, psychological research suggests that guilt and regret are very similar in the ways that I'm suggesting. As Zeelenberg and Breugelmans (2008, p. 594) found in their research, "both emotions involved thoughts about having done something wrong, having done damage to oneself, and being responsible for what happened, feeling angry with yourself, feeling like kicking yourself, wanting to undo what happened, and wanting to improve yourself" (Zeelenberg & Breugelmans, 2008, p. 594). So, I believe that it's a merit of my proposal that it allows that there can be non-moral blame and that such blame may involve representing its target as deserving to suffer only regret or non-moral guilt (and not some moral emotion) in the recognition that one has, say, failed to live up to the non-moral ideals that one is committed to.

6 Conclusion

I've argued that there are two individually necessary and jointly sufficient conditions for one's blaming someone for having seemingly φ-ed:
(Condition₁) one has some set of mental states that represents that target (a) as having φ-ed, (b) as having violated a legitimate demand in φ-
ing, and (c) as not having suffered all the guilt, regret, and remorse that
she deserves to suffer in the recognition of having violated this legitimate
demand and (Condition₂) one feels, as a result of these representations,
disapproval of, or disappointment in, that someone.

This proposal accounts for: (1) the empirical data concerning both what
elicits and what palliates the blaming emotions as well as the empirical data
concerning what sorts of act-tendencies are typically associated with these
emotions; (2) the fact that it's *pro tanto* morally *permissible* to express one's
blame of the blameworthy with the aim of guilting them even though it is
pro tanto morally *impermissible* to express one's distrust of the untrustworthy
with the aim of shaming them; (3) the fact that there are certain necessary
conditions both for being blameworthy (e.g., the control condition and the
epistemic condition) and for being blameworthy to a certain extent (e.g.,
the proportionality condition); and (4) the fact that what a transgressor has
done and experienced subsequent to her transgression can affect the extent
to which she is presently blameworthy for it. And I've shown that this proposal allows us to account for blame in all its disparate forms.

Given all that this proposal accounts for, I believe that we should accept
it. And whether we should accept it is important, not only because the
current literature seems to lack a comprehensive account of blame but also
because it tells us something very important about the nature of blame: it
represents its target as being someone who deserves to suffer guilt, regret,
or remorse in the recognition that she has violated a legitimate demand.
This is important because it may turn out both that all our actions are
causally determined and that no one ever deserves to suffer in virtue of an
action that she was causally determined to perform.[33]

---

[33] For helpful comments and criticisms on earlier drafts, I thank Vuko Andrić, Robert Audi,
Michael Bukoski, Cheshire Calhoun, Andreas Brekke Carlsson, Randy Clarke, Brad Cokelet,
Christian Coons, Justin D'Arms, Austin P. Duggan, Christel Fricke, Richard Alonzo Fyfe, Dan
Jacobson, Andrew Khoury, Eden Lin, Michelle Mason, Michael McKenna, Coleen McNamara,
Dana Nelkin, Derk Pereboom, Caleb Perl, Theron Pummer, George Sher, David Shoemaker,
Philip Swenson, Krista Thomason, Hannah Tierney, Travis Timmerman, Alec Walen, an anony-
mous reviewer, and audiences at both the twelfth annual Rocky Mountain Ethics Congress and
the University of Oslo's Workshop on Self-Blame and Moral Responsibility.

CHAPTER 4

A Forward-Looking Account of Self-Blame

Derk Pereboom

1 Introduction

Morality is shaped in part by our emotional attitudes, some of which introduce features of the practice of holding morally responsible that threaten to make demands that exceed our capacities, given how we are situated in the world of natural causes. These emotions include resentment and indignation, which, I argue, presuppose moral desert (Pereboom, 2001, 2014; McKenna, 2012). However, such desert is put at risk by the prospect of the causal determination of action and by the absence of control that indeterminism would introduce. In addition, the place of moral desert within general ethical frameworks such as consequentialism or Kantian universalizability theory is fraught. Here I continue the project of exploring the viability holding morally responsible absent desert, with a specific focus on self-blame and the related emotional attitude of regret (Pereboom, 2014, 2017).

The conception of holding morally responsible and of blame in particular that I endorse is largely forward-looking. While on this view blame has a backward-looking element, since it is a matter of conceptual fact that appropriately blaming someone for an action requires that the action has already been performed and was in fact wrong, blame's purposes are forward-looking, with objectives such as the moral formation of the wrongdoer and reconciliation with those who have been wronged. To blame is to adopt a stance of moral protest (Hieronymi, 2001; Talbert, 2012; Smith, 2013), whose aim is in part to be communicated (McKenna, 2012), while this aim may not in be realized in every case (Macnamara, 2015b; Chislenko, 2019). Moral protest itself need not presuppose desert (Pereboom, 2017), and emotions such as disappointment and sorrow, which also do not presuppose desert, may accompany blame as moral protest. Here I advocate a parallel account of self-blame. To blame oneself is to take on a stance of moral protest toward oneself in virtue of an action one regards as morally wrong. The reasons one has for doing so are forward-looking, and include one's moral formation and one's reconcilia tion in a relationship that has been impaired as a result of one's wrongdo ing. Regret, distinguished from guilt, may accompany self-blame, and this attitude does not presuppose desert, or so I will argue.

2   Moral Responsibility and Its Various Senses

Our practice of holding morally responsible is complex. It involves a num ber of different aims, and a range of responses justified by those aims. A number of theorists have argued that this complexity can be regimented, and that there is ultimately a single notion of moral responsibility that uni fies the practice. Proponents of such a unitary view include R. J. Wallace (1994) and George Sher (2006). I believe that a view of this sort misrep resents the practice, and here my potential allies include Gary Watson (1996), Dana Nelkin (2011), and David Shoemaker (2011, 2015). With them I contend that a certain kind of pluralism about the practice is true.

Consider, specifically, the blaming part of the practice. One might argue that blaming essentially involves a supposition of morally deserved feeling of guilt, which it's blame's function to produce. Often blame does have the aim of inducing a feeling of guilt conceived as deserved due to the wrong done (e.g., Clarke, 2013; Carlsson, 2017; Duggan, 2018). But a mother may blame her child just for the reason that it is her duty to see to his moral formation, specifically to moderate or extinguish the disposition to wrongdoing manifested in his action by presenting him with moral reasons to alter his behavior. What she does is to blame him for what he has done, but a supposition of a deserved feeling of guilt need not have a role in her calling him to account.

The advocate of a single sense has several options. One is to argue that what might seem to be different senses have a common essence. For instance, one might contend, perhaps despite apparent counterindica tions, that each sense of blameworthiness features, at its core, the supposi tion that the wrongdoer deserves to be blamed (McKenna, 2012), or to feel guilty (Clarke, 2013; Carlsson, 2017; Duggan, 2018), or that the wrong doer is an appropriate target of reactive attitudes (Strawson, 1962; Wallace, 1994). A second is to weed out all but one sense on the ground that the others are not notions of genuine moral responsibility, or on the theoreti cal ground that simplicity in theory is preferable. I resist these strategies, partly because I think that they don't withstand scrutiny in their own right. But I also believe that some of the senses are best eliminated from the practice while others are legitimate and remain in place. This proposal requires distinct senses. Reasons for holding that some are best eliminated are twofold. The first is that they can successfully be criticized on moral grounds, and the second is that they can be challenged because they presuppose a sort of freedom we do not have.

It's typically agreed that one aspect of the practice of holding morally responsible indeed features the notion of desert. In the basic form of desert, agents deserve to be blamed or punished just because they have knowingly acted wrongly, and agents deserves credit or praise just because they have knowingly acted rightly (Feinberg, 1970; Pereboom, 2001, 2014; Scanlon, 2013). Here is a more formal characterization of basic desert:

> For an agent to be *morally responsible for an action in the basic desert sense* is for the action to be hers in such a way that she would deserve to be blamed if she understood that it was morally wrong, and she would deserve to be praised if she understood that it was morally exemplary. The desert at issue here is basic in the sense that the agent, to be morally responsible, would deserve to be blamed or praised just because she has performed the action, given sensitivity to its moral status; and not, for example, by virtue of consequentialist or contractualist considerations (cf. Feinberg, 1970; Pereboom, 2001, 2014).

This characterization can be extended to include basically deserved punishment and reward.

There may in addition be senses of moral responsibility that involve a non-basic variety of desert. Essentially forward-looking notions of holding agents to be deserving of blame and punishment have been defended on consequentialist grounds (Dennett, 1984, 2003; Vargas, 2013; Dennett & Caruso, 2020) or for contractualist reasons (Lenman, 2006; Vilhauer, 2004). In one such account, our practice of holding agents morally responsible in a desert-involving sense should be retained because doing so would have the best overall consequences relative to alternative practices. Daniel Dennett (1984, 2003; Dennett & Caruso, 2020) advocates a version of this position, as does Manuel Vargas (2013). Such options must be considered seriously, but the proposal I envision involves a more resolutely forward-looking approach on the part of practitioners.

There are reasons to be skeptical of any notion of moral responsibility that involves basic desert. One concern for the basic desert sense is that for an agent to basically deserve a harmful response she must have a kind of free will that is unavailable to us, and the free will skeptic contends that this concern can't be successfully countered (Strawson, 1986; Waller, 1990, 2011; Pereboom, 1995, 2001, 2014; Caruso, 2021). As just noted, one might argue that some desert sense of moral responsibility can or should be retained because doing so stands to bring about good consequences, but such desert is not basic. Another concern is that for a number of contending general normative ethical theories the notion of desert seems to have the role of an awkward supplement (Pereboom, 2014). A place for desert in typical consequentialist views is arguably uncomfortable, and despite Kant's well-known invocation of desert in justifying criminal punishment (Kant, 1797/1963), that appeal is not plausibly justified by any formulation of the Categorical Imperative, which he held to be the supreme and comprehensive moral principle. An additional issue is that the conception of deserved pain or harm that is imposed in blaming or punishing would at least in its basic form seem to involve the idea of harm as a non-instrumental good (McKenna, 2019), an idea that might well be contested. Motivated by these considerations, I've proposed a view that rejects desert-involving senses of moral responsibility altogether.

3   Moral Responsibility without Desert

The notion of moral responsibility, and blame in particular, that I develop and endorse (Pereboom, 2014, 2017) is largely forward-looking. Blaming is, in its paradigm cases, a kind of calling to account, and is justified by forward-looking elements, including the following:

1. The right of those wronged or threatened by wrongdoing to protect themselves and to be protected from immoral behavior and its consequences
2. The good of reconciliation with the wrongdoer
3. The good of the moral formation of the wrongdoer
4. The retention of the integrity of victims of wrongdoing

Immoral actions are often harmful, and we have a right to protect ourselves and others from those who are disposed to behave harmfully. Immoral actions can also impair relationships, and we have a moral interest in undoing such impairment through reconciliation. Because we value morally good character and action that results from it, we have a stake in the moral formation of character when it is beset by dispositions to misconduct. For those whose sense of integrity has been undermined by having been victims of wrongdoing, blaming can be instrumental to restoring that integrity.

There is an account of praise that is parallel to this conception of blame. Of the forward-looking aims just cited, the one most clearly amenable to praise is moral formation. We may praise an agent for a morally exemplary action to strengthen the disposition that produced it. Praise can also have a protective function, since strengthening dispositions to act rightly stands to have the effect of reducing the incidence of harmful behavior. Corresponding to reconciliation is the notion of celebrating success in a relationship, and praising may have this objective as well.

Michael McKenna has proposed a conversational account of moral responsibility that, with a few revisions, is amenable to the forward-looking view I advocate (McKenna, 2012, 2019; Fricker, 2016). The actions of a morally responsible agent are potential bearers of a type of meaning by virtue of indicating the quality of will that resulted in the action (2012, pp. 92–94; see also Arpaly, 2006). Blaming an agent who manifests an immoral quality of will in acting expresses an attitude such as resentment or indignation, and its aim is to communicate to him a moral response to the indicated quality of will. Morally responsible agents understand that members of the moral community might attribute such a meaning to their actions. When they address actions that are morally charged, they understand themselves to be initiating a meaningful interaction in such a conversational exchange. McKenna labels this initial stage of the conversation *moral contribution*. In the case of an ostensibly immoral action, in the second stage the agent is blamed by an interlocutor; McKenna calls this stage *moral address*. In the third stage, *moral account*, the blamed agent offers an excuse, a justification, or an apology. The interlocutor might at this point carry on the conversation by forgiving or punishing the wrongdoer. In a subsequent stage of the interaction the blamed agent may be restored by other participants to full status in the moral community. McKenna points out that not all blaming conforms to this model; blaming the dead, for instance, does not. At this point he invokes a paradigm-similarity model for the meaning and extension of a concept (Rosch, 1972, 1973). A conversation with a living and present participant is a paradigm case of blaming, while blaming the dead, for instance, qualifies as a case of blaming in virtue of its similarity to paradigm cases.

I can and do endorse such an account, on the supposition that the objectives of blaming are forward-looking goals such as protection, reconciliation, moral formation, and retention of integrity, and that deserved blame is excised (Pereboom, 2014, 2017). As in McKenna's account, on the forward-looking view blame may be painful for the wrongdoer who is blamed. It may be painful to be called out for having done wrong, and the pain of regret (to be discussed) may result. But by contrast with blame conceived as involving basically deserved pain, the pain on the forward looking conception is not conceived as a non-instrumental good imposed by blaming, but rather as an instrumental good that serves the forward-looking goals to be achieved by blaming. This rejection of this pain as a non-instrumental good is significant, and lies at the core of what motivates the forward-looking account.

On the forward-looking conversational model, as in McKenna's, it's the agent's responsiveness to reasons that is engaged in the envisioned process for both blame and praise. For blame, at the stage of moral address, which in the case of wrongdoing is the blaming stage, one may request an explanation with the intent of having the agent acknowledge a disposition to act wrongly, and then, if he has in fact acted wrongly and is without excuse, one may intend for him to come to see that the disposition issuing in the action is best modified or extinguished. In the paradigm case, such dispositional change is effected by way of the agent's recognition of moral reasons to make it. More generally, it is an agent's responsiveness to reasons, together with forward-looking objectives, that explains why he is an appropriate recipient of blame in this forward-looking conversational sense.

Reasons-responsiveness is often advanced as the key necessary condition for basic desert responsibility by philosophers who maintain that this sort of responsibility is compatible with the action's causal determination by factors beyond the agent's control, and that it isn't explained by her ability to do otherwise (Fischer, 2007, p. 82; McKenna, 2012; Sartorio, 2016). The largely forward-looking conception of moral responsibility I advocate is also compatible with an agent's being causally determined to act by factors beyond her control, and in an appropriately constructed deterministic manipulation argument the manipulated agent will be morally responsible in this way (Pereboom, 2014; Pereboom & McKenna, 2022). In my view, agents can also be morally responsible in the forward-looking sense in Frankfurt examples (Frankfurt, 1969; Pereboom, 2001, 2014), and thus, just as in the compatibilist position that John Fischer (1994, 2007), Michael McKenna (2012), and Carolina Sartorio (2016) develop, the kind of freedom or control required for basic desert moral responsibility for an action will be a matter of its actual causal history. The compatibilists just mentioned are all committed to responsiveness to reasons as the central condition on basic-desert or reactive-attitudes-involving moral responsibility, while I view it as the most significant condition for a notion of responsibility that instead focuses on goals such as protection, reconciliation, moral formation, and retention of integrity.

4 Against Anger as the Core Blaming Attitude

Pamela Hieronymi (2001), Matt Talbert (2012), and Angela Smith (2013) have proposed that blame should be understood as moral protest, and I endorse a position of this kind (Pereboom, 2017). Mine differs in that for these other proponents the negative reactive attitudes of resentment and indignation are central to blame, while in my view they are not. As I see it, moral protest is a psychological stance, a posture of mind that has certain aims that are manifest as dispositions to act (Schwitzgebel, 2013). It is a stance of opposition to specific wrongful actions and their general type, whose aims include moral engagement with the wrongdoer by communication of this opposition to such wrongdoing together with reasons to refrain from it. Hieronymi (2001) connects moral protest to the negative reactive attitudes; in her account moral protest in fact is a reactive attitude such as resentment, which is commonly understood as a second-person attitude I have toward someone who has wronged me (Darwall, 2006; Shabo, 2012). By extension, one might include indignation, understood as a third-person attitude one has toward someone who has wronged someone else. I deny this connection.

David Brink and Dana Nelkin (2013) view blame as having a "core and syndrome structure," and they argue that there is a core to blame present in all cases of blame. So far I agree. In their view, that core is an aversive attitude toward the target that is predicated on the belief or judgment that the target is blameworthy. The syndrome features the disposition to manifest this aversive attitude in various ways. I contend, by contrast that the core is the stance of moral protest, which does not essentially involve resentment or indignation, both forms of moral anger (Pereboom, 2001, pp. 208–213; D'Arms & Jacobson, 2003).

David Shoemaker (2017) maintains that moral anger is essential to blame in the accountability sense (more on this later), and he develops and defends a Strawsonian response-dependence account of such blame in which the designated response is anger:

> **Fitting Response-Dependence about the Blameworthy**: The blameworthy (in the realm of accountability) just is whatever merits anger (the anger-worthy); that is, someone is blameworthy (and so accountable) for X if and only if, and in virtue of the fact that, she merits anger for X.

Shoemaker argues that what unifies all of the properties that make anger an appropriate response to wrongdoing is just that it merits anger, and this is what makes the account truly a response-dependent one. Here I don't wish to focus on the response-dependence feature of the account, but rather on the choice of anger as the response. As Shoemaker points out, there is a response-*in*dependent account that also features anger, but as a response which is independent of the property in which blameworthiness consists, while anger is made appropriate in virtue of that property:

> **Response-Independence about the Blameworthy**: The blameworthy consists of a property (or properties) of agents that makes anger at them appropriate, a property (or properties) whose value-making is ultimately independent of our angry responses. Anger at someone for X is appropriate if and only if, and in virtue of the fact that, she is antecedently blameworthy (and so accountable) for X. What makes her blameworthy is thus ultimately response-independent.

In this account, blameworthiness is not essentially dependent on the response of anger. But moral anger, in the form of reactive attitudes such as resentment and indignation, is the property that fixes the referent of the term "blameworthy." The blameworthy consists of properties that in fact actually merit such anger, even if blameworthiness doesn't consist of just whatever merits anger.

I have raised two concerns about the choice of anger in each of these accounts (cf. Nussbaum, 2016; Pereboom, 2020). First, there are cases of blameworthiness that are plausibly not cases of angerworthiness. Melanie is a high school teacher, whose students respect her but misbehave in ways typical for this age group in that context. They come unprepared not having done the assigned reading, or talk about non-class-related matters in distracting ways, or surf the internet instead of participating and paying attention. However, Melanie responds with firm protest but not with anger, understanding the level of moral and social development for late adolescents. Here the angry response stands to be counterproductive and to undermine her effectiveness and the respect students have for her. Or take Nicole, a parent whose teenage children misbehave in typical ways; they squabble, text their friends when they should be sleeping, and fail to expedite household chores. Nicole responds from the sense of a duty to correct and educate, combined with care, but not with anger. Here an angry response would tend to engender resistance, and is generally less effective for moral education than the approach Nicole adopts. For such cases of teachers and parents, evidence for an angry response actually being inappropriate is that those who become angry are routinely criticized and are not respected to the degree enjoyed by those who forgo anger.

The second concern is that anger has a strong tendency to distort judgments of blameworthiness, and that it's questionable whether being blameworthy is being worthy of a reactive attitude that systematically distorts judgments of blameworthiness. Surveys conducted by Mark Alicke and his associates indicate that subjects who spontaneously evaluate agents' behavior unfavorably are apt to exaggerate their causal control and any evidence that might favor it while deemphasizing counterevidence (Alicke, Davis, & Pezzo, 1994; Alicke, 2000; Alicke, Rose, & Bloom, 2012). Alicke calls this tendency *blame validation*. In addition, experimental evidence that blaming behavior is subject to problems of these kinds has been mounting (e.g., Nadelhoffer, 2006).

There is reason to believe that the anger that accompanies blame is what leads to these problems (Duggan, n.d.). Psychological research indicates that anger, once activated, degrades subsequent reasoning processes in various ways (e.g., Lerner et al., 1998; Goldberg et al., 1999; Litvak et al., 2010). Anger increases tendencies to overlook mitigating features of the circumstances before blaming, to perceive ambiguous behavior as hostile, to rely on stereotypes, concerning, for example, ethnicity in blaming, and to discount the role of uncontrollable factors when attributing causality. Anger makes subjects slower to associate positive traits than negative traits with an out-group. Julie Goldberg and her associates find in one of their studies that when the retributive desire to harm is not satisfied, anger "activate[s] an indiscriminate tendency to punish others in unrelated situations without regard for whether their actions were intentional" (Goldberg et al., 1999).

This second concern may be less decisive than the first, since even if anger has the distorting propensities cited, it may yet be the best candidate for a general emotional attitude to accompany blame. However, I contend that moral protest, as a psychological stance, is a better fit. This is especially true in virtue of the first problem, since, as the examples indicate, in relationships between teachers and students, and parents and children, for common sorts of wrongdoing anger is actually inappropriate.

One might respond by arguing that these are not paradigm cases of blame-involving relationships, since they are not relationships of mutual regard, but rather relationships in which there is a relevant discrepancy in maturity. But consider relationships between faculty members at a university, or relationships between administrators and faculty, which are relationships of mutual regard. Non-major yet significant wrongdoing in such relationships is not infrequent and is to be expected. For example, university faculty are partial to their close colleagues and political allies when it comes to appointments and honors, and often the resulting advocacy is wrong. Suppose Olivia is a university administrator who often faces these sorts of issues with faculty in her purview. Imagine that she responds not with anger, but calmly with arguments that invoke the rules that best govern the situations at issue. In such cases, angry responses typically reduce an administrator's effectiveness, and tend to cause false judgments which in turn motivate defective solutions. Here too, anger is arguably an inappropriate response.

5 A Moral Protest Account of Blame

These observations call for a general characterization of blame and blameworthiness in which anger is not the core attitude. I've proposed a conception of blame as moral protest that does not essentially involve moral anger as the designated attitude. When Melanie, Nicole, and Olivia morally protest the wrongful behavior at issue, they are morally concerned, but not resentful or indignant. Again, I conceive moral protest as a psychological stance, one that features a disposition to engage in overt protest against an agent for having performed an action that the protester perceives to be morally wrong. I've endorsed the following simple version of a moral protest view of blame, in which moral anger does not appear (Pereboom, 2017):

> **Moral Protest Account of Blame:** For B to blame A is for B to adopt a stance of moral protest against A for immoral conduct that B attributes (however accurately) to A.

The immoral conduct will typically be a wrongful action, but there are cases in which the action considered separately from the reasons for which it's performed is not wrong, but the reasons make the overall conduct wrong (e.g., Haji, 1998; Hanser, 2005; Markovits, 2010), and worthy of protest. Sometimes blame is misplaced, since no immoral actions have been performed, but the protest can still count as blame. This may happen when B believes A to have acted wrongly but the belief is false, perhaps due to misinformation or improper consideration of evidence. This can also happen when B does not believe that A acted wrongly but nonetheless represents A as having acted wrongly, as in cases of false accusation motivated by anger, envy, or fear. It's often the case that blame has the goal, as in Hieronymi's (2001) proposal, of moral protest against an agent for a past action that persists as a present threat, and this is one highly important objective for blame. But not all blame has this point, as when we blame the dead, or blame an agent who is alive but lacks a persisting disposition to act badly – someone, for instance, who has already undergone moral reform. In such cases protest may yet have the aim of explicitly noting immoral behavior in order to encourage moral improvement on the part of an audience. In the example of the already-reformed wrongdoer, blame might still be intended as a step in the process of reconciliation. Or the aim may be that the victim of wrongdoing reassert and retain her integrity.

An objection to the protest account of blame is that while unexpressed blame is possible, the idea of unexpressed protest is incoherent, and thus blame cannot be identified with moral protest. The objection is that protest is essentially communicative, and unexpressed protest is not communicative. Eugene Chislenko (2019) has recently provided a reply to this concern, citing the distinction Coleen Macnamara draws between the activity of communicating – of which mental states kept private are not instances – and the idea of a communicative entity (Macnamara, 2015b, p. 217). An unsent email, even though it does not actually perform the function of communicating, nevertheless has the function of evoking uptake of representational content in a recipient (Macnamara, 2015a, p. 548). An unsent email is thus communicative in nature; and similarly, unexpressed protest is communicative in nature. For a salient case in point, an unsent email might be an unexpressed message of protest. Chislenko writes: "We can even say, as [Angela] Smith does of blame, that the email 'expresses protest, and … seeks some kind of moral reply' (2013, p. 39), even when the email is unsent" (Chislenko, 2019). We can add that the email can express moral protest even if its author never intends to send it. Similarly, someone who privately blames may never intend to communicate it, even if that blame has the function of moral protest.

Thus in my proposal, moral protest is fundamentally a psychological stance one takes, one that is apt for being communicated, and has that aim, but that aim may not be implemented in specific instances. An entity having an aim or function that it does not actually implement in certain instances is familiar from biology – for example, a heart that fails to pump blood – and should not be regarded as unusual.

In accord with the protest account of blame, I would propose the following amended version of Shoemaker's response-dependent view about the blameworthy:

> **Fitting Response-Dependence about the Blameworthy**: The blameworthy (in the realm of accountability) just is whatever merits moral protest (the protestworthy); that is, someone is blameworthy (and so accountable) for X if and only if, and in virtue of the fact that, she merits moral protest for X.

This account has a response-independent correlate, which also invokes moral protestworthiness but claims that there are properties that make wrongdoing protestworthy that are independent of our protest responses, while appropriate moral protest can serve to fix properties which "blame-worthiness" picks out:

> **Fitting Protest-Response-Independence about the Blameworthy:** The blameworthy (in the realm of accountability) consists of a property (or properties) of agents that makes morally protesting their wrongdoing appropriate, a property (or properties) whose value-making is ultimately independent of our responses of moral protest.

Following Shoemaker, in these formulations I've retained the idea that the notion to be characterized is blameworthiness in the realm of *accountability*. He provides the following characterization of accountability he provides:

> To be accountable for something is to be liable to being appropriately *held* to account for it, which is to be eligible for a range of fitting responsibility responses with a built-in confrontational element. (2015, p. 87)

Moral protest, as I conceive it, is essentially confrontational, at least to some degree. But being confrontational is compatible with not involving anger. One's attitude toward the wrongdoer might be exclusively compassionate, while believing that in this case compassion requires confrontation. There are other characterizations of accountability on which blaming someone in this sense essentially involves the supposition that the wrongdoer deserves or basically deserves to be the target of blame. Given that notion of accountability, I reject it, and would want to frame the discussion in terms of a different notion of blame.

On the proposed account of blame, blame does not essentially involve anger, while it does essentially involve taking on the stance of moral protest. But despite moral anger involving a presupposition of desert, and indeed basic desert, which I claim is a false presupposition, angry blame may still be *practically* rational for the desert-denier. It may be, for instance, that in certain cases opposition to violence and abuse is most effective if it is motivated partly by moral anger. Then the putative epistemic irrationality of having the false supposition may be overridden. In this sort of case, moral progress needn't be held hostage to epistemic rationality.

6   Self-Blame and Regret

Just as one might take on a stance of moral protest against another for his having done wrong, one might also adopt such a stance in response to one's own immoral behavior. One might, by virtue of one's general moral commitment, view an action one has performed as wrong and the disposition that issues in it as morally defective, and as a result take on a stance of opposition against one's action and the disposition. In adopting this stance, one may, for instance, aim at one's own moral formation or at reconciliation with someone one has wronged. If one has mocked and embarrassed someone, and the relationship with him has been impaired as a result, one might assume a stance of protest against that action and one's disposition to act badly in this way. One might do so in order to extinguish this disposition and to reconcile with the person one has wronged.

Which emotional attitudes aptly accompany self-directed moral protest? Just as in the case of one's child having done wrong, one might feel disappointment or sorrow, without desert being invoked. But in accord with Randolph Clarke's (2013) suggestion, it's valuable to consider whether a wrongdoer deserves or basically deserves to feel guilty and the pain that it features (cf. Carlsson, 2017; Duggan, 2018). Clarke proposes, first, that there is value in the recognition by an agent who is blameworthy that he is blameworthy, and a further response, the feeling of guilt, provides an intuitively fitting addition to this acknowledgment. This response would intuitively have value insofar as it expresses moral concern for having done wrong and for those wronged.

Let's adopt the convention that "guilt" refers to an attitude that presupposes basic desert, that is, one's basically deserving to feel pain accompanying the recognition that one has done wrong, and that "regret" refers to a similar attitude, which also involves feeling pain that accompanies the recognition that one has done wrong, but which does not presuppose that this pain is basically deserved. Given this conception, I can agree that regret is a morally fitting additional reaction to one's own wrongdoing without committing to desert.

Two of my allies on this point, Bruce Waller (1990) and Hilary Bok (1998), argue that the fittingness of a pained feeling can be accounted for by a recognition that one has not lived up to one's standards for morality and self-control without the need to invoke desert. Bok sets out an example in which one has done something wrong, on account of which one suffers a painful response, which she compares to heartbreak (1998, pp. 168–169). She calls this response guilt, but I'd like to substitute "regret" for Bok's "guilt," reserving "guilt" for a desert-involving feeling:

> The relation between the recognition that one has done something wrong and the guilt one suffers as a result … is like the relation between the recognition that one's relationship with someone one truly loves has collapsed and the pain of heartbreak. Heartbreak is not a pain one inflicts on oneself as a punishment for loss of love; it is not something we undergo

because we deserve it … Similarly, the recognition that one has done something wrong causes pain. But this pain is not a form of suffering that we
inflict on ourselves as a punishment but an entirely appropriate response to
the recognition of what we have done, for two reasons. First, our standards
define the kind of life we think we should lead and what we regard as valuable in the world, in our lives, and in the lives of others. They articulate
what matters to us and living by them is therefore by definition of concern
to us. If we have indeed violated them, we have slighted what we take to
be of value, disregarded principles we sincerely think we should live by, and
failed to be the sorts of people we think we should be. The knowledge that
we have done these things must be painful to us.

I think Bok is right to contend that feeling pain on account of a recognition that one has not lived up to one's moral standards or standards for
self-control need not involve desert.

Here are several additional analogies. One might appropriately feel
pained that one failed to meet one's own standards for playing chess when
one understands that one's substandard performance is due to factors
beyond one's control, while this pain is not deserved. A similar example is
due to Shoemaker (this volume), one in which a baseball player feels pain
upon making a mistake, yet he doesn't deserve to feel this pain. A different
kind of example is due to McKenna: it would appropriate, and basically
so, to feel the pain of grief upon the death of a loved one, while this pain
is not deserved (McKenna, 2012, 2019). Saliently, these cases feature the
appropriateness of feeling pain without its being deserved.

In accord with these analogies, I contend that it's appropriate that
wrongdoers feel regret for what they've done, where regret, unlike guilt,
does not involve deserved or basically deserved pain. How can the feeling
of pain upon recognition of wrongdoing be appropriate – and even basically so – but not be basically deserved? What's required is an indicator for
distinguishing basically deserved pain from merely basically appropriate
pain. Both Andreas Carlsson (2017) and I (Pereboom, 2017) have suggested
that the pain of guilt, given its desert presupposition, would be (prima
facie) appropriately *imposed* while the pain of grief is not. Let me try to
make the suggestion more precise. If pain is basically deserved on account
of wrongdoing, this gives rise to a prima facie moral permission for appropriately situated agents to intentionally impose it on the wrongdoer for a
non-instrumental reason and thus for its own sake. If a wrongdoer basically deserves to be punished, there is then a prima facie presumption that
the right sorts of authorities, perhaps parents or state officials, are permitted to intentionally impose it on him for a non-instrumental reason and
thus for its own sake. Guilt, given that it presupposes basic desert, would

then involve pain that one regards as appropriately intentionally imposed by oneself or by suitably situated others for its own sake. The pain of grief lacks this feature. Despite grief and the pain that it involves being basically appropriate for those who have experienced loss of a loved one, no one is permitted to intentionally impose the pain of grief in such circumstances for its own sake. One may inform the bereaved that she has undergone the loss of a loved one, as a result of which it's evident that she will feel the pain of grief, but this is not a case of intentionally imposing the pain of grief for its own sake. The pain of grief is never basically deserved despite at times being basically appropriate, and so here we have a potential indicator for distinguishing basically deserved from non-basically deserved appropriate pain.

In the passage from Hilary Bok, she makes two claims regarding her analogy of the pain of regret to the pain of heartbreak. The first is that the pain of regret is not a pain that one inflicts on oneself as a punishment. The second is that it is not a pain that we undergo because we deserve it. This suggests that she conceives of the claims as linked: the pain of heartbreak's not being appropriately imposed is connected with its not being deserved. My related proposal is that it is impermissible to intentionally impose the pain of regret non-instrumentally and for its own sake, and this is what distinguishes it from the putative basically deserved pain of guilt (cf. McKenna, 2012, 2019). This allows that one may issue a moral protest against a wrongdoer for the reason that it stands to result in moral formation, foreseeing that it will result in the pain of regret. Here it is not the case that pain is imposed for a non-instrumental reason. It may be intuitive that in certain circumstances it is permissible to intentionally impose the pain connected with recognition of wrongdoing on others and on oneself for its own sake. But the retraction of basic desert has its costs, and this is one of them.

Dana Nelkin (2019, p. 186) provides a thought experiment that in her view supports the conclusion that the pain of guilt/regret is not appropriately imposed for its own sake:

> Imagine that you have a special power (call it "The Look"). By looking at another person in the right way, you can bring about feelings of guilt. The other person culpably wrongs another – it is not a trivial offense, but neither is it the worst possible. Imagine that she betrays the confidence of a friend and as a result the friend has a bad day. You now have the chance, by looking at the offender in that way you have mastered so well, to bring about guilt feelings in her. It would be the easiest thing, requiring nothing in the way of effort or sacrifice. But now also imagine that there is no further good to come from your exercising this power you have. The offender

has already resolved not to do the same sort of thing again, no one else is around to experience the results, the relationship is either already irreparably damaged no matter what, or all has been forgiven, so that there is no benefit to the relationship to be had, and so on. Would you be making a mistake, or leaving a reason on the table, so to speak, by taking a pass on inducing this painful feeling? Would there be a (non-instrumental) moral good that would have been costless to achieve that you failed to promote? I do not have the intuition here that you would be making this kind of mistake. That suggests to me that there is not a pro tanto reason to induce guilt that stems from blameworthy action alone.

I agree with Nelkin; the thought experiment provides intuitive reason, independent of the arguments for free will skepticism and the general concerns about basic desert, to deny the value of what I'm calling guilt. But it does not yield a challenge to regret.[1]

There are other justifications for regret on the supposition that it doesn't presuppose basic desert. Ben Vilhauer (2004) advocates an account of a pained response upon wrongdoing that grounds it in sympathy with those one has wronged, and according to which such regret is fitting because the sympathy is morally appropriate. It's credible that such sympathy-based regret can motivate repentance and moral reform, for reconciliation with those one has wronged, and restoration of integrity. Vilhauer argues that because such sympathy-based remorse is also other-directed rather than merely self-directed, it is morally preferable to guilt or remorse grounded in basic desert. Guilt on a basic desert conception has no essentially forward-looking moral objective. By contrast, sympathy-based remorse involves taking on the perspective of the agent one has wronged, which has morally beneficial consequences.

7 Final Words

I've proposed a conception on which to blame others is to take on a stance of moral protest toward them in virtue of an action one regards as morally wrong. The reasons for doing so are forward-looking, such as the wrongdoer's moral formation or reconciliation in a relationship that has been impaired as a result of the wrongdoing. By extension, to blame oneself is to take on a stance of moral protest toward oneself in virtue of an action one has performed and regards as morally wrong, and to do so for similar

---

[1] Here see McKenna's (2019) discussion according to which the pain of guilt and the value of guilt as an expression of moral concern make up an organic unity whose whole has a value that is not analytically decomposable, and Nelkin's (2019) response to McKenna.

forward-looking reasons. Regret, a painful response to one's own wrong-doing that does not presuppose basic desert, may appropriately accompany self-blame. Guilt and regret can both be classified as basically appropriate pained responses to one's own wrongdoing. But the pain of guilt, and not that of regret, counts as basically deserved because it is prima facie permissible for those who are appropriately situated to intentionally impose it on a wrongdoer for non-instrumental reasons.[2]

---

[2] For excellent comments and discussion I'm grateful to the participants at a workshop at the University of Oslo in September 2019, organized by Andreas Carlsson. Special thanks are due to Dana Nelkin for valuable comments on several drafts.

PART II

The Ethics of Self-Blame

CHAPTER 5

How Much to Blame?
An Asymmetry between the Norms of
Self-Blame and Other-Blame[1]

Dana Kay Nelkin

1 Introduction

There are cases in which it appears that it is appropriate for a person to blame herself more than for others to blame her. Consider two cases. The first, *Brakes*, was originally designed to test our intuitions about moral luck.[2] Two equally busy people put off getting their brakes checked by a week after their notices, they drive the same route, and both of their brakes fail. But in the case of the first person, she hits and kills a dog while trying to steer her car to an incline, and in the case of the second, no dog appears and she manages to steer her car to the incline without causing any harm. The first person, we can imagine, feels guilt-stricken and blames herself intensely, while the second feels shaken and blames herself, but not nearly to the degree as the first. At the same time, we can imagine a third party who has witnessed the striking of the dog and its aftermath blaming the driver less than the driver blames herself. Looking at the situation from the outside, it seems that if the driver *doesn't* blame herself more than the third party does, the omission would be morally problematic on the part of the driver for not blaming

[1] An earlier version of this chapter was presented at a workshop on *Who Are We to Blame?* at the University of Edinburgh, and I am very grateful for their excellent feedback to the organizers and participants, including Ellie Mason, Patrick Todd, Jessica Brown, Justin Coates, Maggie O'Brien, Brian Raburn, Sam Rickless, and Matt Talbert. Likewise, I am very grateful to the other authors of this volume and those who attended a workshop on *Self-Blame* at the University of Oslo, including Andreas Brekke Carlsson, Gunnar Björnsson, Randy Clarke, Justin D'Arms, Christel Fricke, Daniel Jacobson, Coleen Macnamara, Michelle Mason, Michael McKenna, Derk Pereboom, Piers Rawling, and Krista Thomason. I received many incisive questions at a meeting of the Agency and Responsibility Group at UC San Diego that helped me significantly improve the chapter still further. Many thanks in particular to Lucy Allais, Saba Bazargan-Forward, Emily Bingeman, David Brink, Kathleen Connelly, Cory Davia, Matthew Fulkerson, Jonathan Knutzen, Dylan Murray, Jacob Sparks, Andy Sin, Manuel Vargas, Monique Wonderly, and Keyao Yang, and also to two referees for this volume. Finally, special thanks to Andreas Brekke Carlsson for prompting many fruitful discussions and for bringing this volume together.
[2] See Williams (1981) for inspiration.

herself enough, or else on the part of the third party for blaming her too much.

In another case, *Friends*, two friends, Aida and Pablo, meet after a long and stressful day at work, and Aida says something hurtful to Pablo. Thinking about the moment later, Aida blames herself quite a bit, despite the fact that a stressful day had led up to the moment, and her self-blame seems appropriate. But it also seems that it would be inappropriate for a third party, even one close to the two friends, to blame Aida to the same high degree that Aida blames herself. The case is under-described, of course, but I hope that it will strike us as familiar in shape.

At the risk of over-sharing, I find the case of fairly deep self-blame *very* familiar. And yet while I take my own blame to be perfectly appropriate in many situations, I can also recognize that it might be odd, and even inappropriate, if others were to blame me to the same degree. One way of seeing this is via a thought experiment: if a friend had done the same thing, I would not blame them as much as I blame myself. Reflection on such cases suggests the following claim:

> The Blame Asymmetry Claim: In a wide variety of cases, it is appropriate for an agent, A, to blame herself to a certain degree, n, at the same time that it would be appropriate for others to blame her to a degree less than n, and there is a systematic explanation for this fact.[3]

Now a couple of points need to be noted immediately. First, the claim is limited. It does not entail that it is always the case that it is appropriate to blame oneself more than for others to blame one. There might be some circumstances in which the appropriate blame in each case is equal, or even in which it is appropriate for others to blame a person more than she herself should. But it does suggest that there is a systematic reason why more self-blame is often appropriate than other-blame in the absence of other overriding reasons.

Second, I have assumed so far that there is a common currency of self-blame and other-blame by which we can make a comparison. We have already seen some intuitive reason to believe this assumption is true: the thought experiment where one asks oneself whether one would blame a friend as much as one would blame oneself seems perfectly coherent, for example. But it will be helpful if we can say more about the nature of blame so that we can have an idea of just what the common currency is, and I will attempt to do just that later in the chapter.

---

[3] I take this claim to entail that in a wide variety of cases it is appropriate to blame oneself more than it would be appropriate for one to blame others in similar circumstances to oneself.

Third, I am assuming that a fairly robust form of blame is sometimes apt. At the same time, for present purposes, I hope to be quite ecumenical about what exactly this form of blame commits us to. I do assume here that the kind of blame in question is at least partly "backward-looking," and in my view such blame presupposes that the offender deserves a negative response. But I am interested in exploring whether a similar line of reasoning could work for other forms of backward-looking blame or even purely forward-looking forms of blame. (See Pereboom [2017] for a discussion of different forms of blame and moral address.)

Fourth, the Blame Asymmetry Claim distinguishes between self-blame and other-blame, while it does not distinguish among different sub-types of other-blame. For example, it does not distinguish between blaming someone who has harmed one directly and someone who has harmed others; nor does it distinguish between blaming someone with whom one is in a personal relationship and blaming strangers. It might be that there are additional principles that include appeal to these distinctions, but the Blame Asymmetry Claim is simply neutral about this possibility.

With these clarifications of the Blame Asymmetry Claim on the table, I turn in Section 2 to reasons that might first come to mind for why one might debunk or simply reject the claim. I then argue that they either fail or should await a further search for a positive grounding explanation before we draw a conclusion. In Section 3, I set out some accounts of blame that allow us to see self-blame and other-blame as comparable on a single dimension of degree, highlighting one that I favor. Then in Section 4, I set out a framework for the ethics of blame in which we should be able to locate explanations of the Blame Asymmetry Claim. In Section 5, I consider some attractive hypotheses that might explain and ground the Blame Asymmetry Claim, arguing that while they are on the right track, they do not ultimately succeed, and I offer my own proposal that appeals to a very general ethical principle distinguishing the ways we are permitted to treat ourselves and others. In Section 6, I consider objections, and address the debunking claims mentioned earlier with a positive proposal in hand. Finally, in Section 7, I explore the implications of a potential self-other blame asymmetry for moral theorizing, including in the area of moral luck.

2 Initial Reasons to Reject the Blame Asymmetry Claim

Let us begin with some reasons one might initially be tempted to reject or debunk the Blame Asymmetry Claim, as well as some reasons for thinking it might be true.

First, focusing on Brakes, one might object to the Blame Asymmetry Claim by arguing that the self-blaming driver is not really *blaming* herself more than the other driver, but is rather feeling a mixture of blame and agent regret, or a negative feeling whose constitutive thought is regret at having been causally implicated in harm (see Wolf, 2001 for this suggestion). One might think, then, that it is not the Blame Asymmetry Claim that is supported by our intuitions and phenomenological experience, but rather this related, but quite different, claim:

> Negative Attitudes Asymmetry Claim: In a wide variety of cases, it is appropriate for an agent, A, to feel negative feelings, including blame and agent regret, to a certain degree, n, at the same time that it would be appropriate for others to feel negative feelings, including blame and agent regret, to a degree less than n, and there is a systematic explanation for this fact.

This claim is interesting in its own right, but it is importantly different from the Blame Asymmetry Claim.

It is possible that this is what is going on in the Brakes case. There might be confusion of some sort on the part of the driver, and it might be hard to distinguish different negative emotions with different constitutive thoughts, but in the end, it seems psychologically realistic that the agent in the end truly *blames* herself a great deal, and more than a third party would appropriately blame her. Further, this way out of the Blame Asymmetry Claim looks even less plausible in other sorts of cases, such as Friends. Imagine a variant of that case in which one's friend didn't actually hear the hurtful thing one said because of the loud noise in the bar, so no harm was done. It is still natural that one blame oneself for having said it and thereby having imposed a serious risk of harm. And it seems appropriate for one to blame oneself more than for a third party to do so. The debunking explanation in terms of agent regret for being causally involved in harm simply won't get started in cases in which no harm is actually caused.

A second reaction that also seeks to undermine the Blame Asymmetry Claim is to propose that while some people *do* systematically blame themselves more than others blame them, they are not rational or right to do so, and the differential degrees of blame are not in the end appropriate. I will return to this debunking claim later. For now, note that the intuitions are powerful, and it is important to explore whether a plausible explanation for the Blame Asymmetry Claim can be found before rejecting it.

3 Common Currency and Theories of Blame

In this section, I briefly lay out several accounts of the nature of blame and argue that in each of them it makes sense to compare self-blame and other-blame on a single scale. I will be far from exhaustive here, but my aim is simply to make plausible the idea that blame is commensurable across self and others.

First, there is a simple emotion theory. To blame is to have a set of reactive attitudes toward the one whom one blames. These attitudes could be different in kind – guilt, for example, in one's own case, and resentment in the case of another. But fundamentally, blame is a set of emotions.[4]

This view has advantages that I will not rehearse here. A notable criticism is that it does not capture various interpersonal aspects of blame. This has caused some to adopt a communicative or conversational theory of blame.[5] Consider the theory defended by Michael McKenna (2012, 2013), who sees blame fundamentally as a move in a moral conversation. In his view, paradigms of blame are instances of expression and essentially communicative, while instances of unexpressed blame are non-paradigmatic and can be understood as derivative. According to McKenna, blame cannot be understood independently of the conversational moves that come before and after. He offers the following example of a moral exchange:

Moral Contribution: Leslie makes a moral contribution by telling a prejudicial joke.
Moral Address: By engaging in blaming practices, Daphne morally addresses Leslie.
Moral Account: Suppose Leslie offers Daphne an account of her behavior and in doing so acknowledges the offense, apologizes, and asks for forgiveness. (McKenna 2012, p. 89)

Since there are many ways of expressing the same thing, and since there are many different expressions that would be felicitous in response to an opening of a conversation, this view can accommodate the idea that a number of responses to wrongdoing count as blame, without requiring that any particular kind of response is necessary. For example, in McKenna's view, taking up a reactive attitude like indignation

---

[4] For a recent defense of such a view, see Menges (2017b), and see Shoemaker (2018) for the view that blame of an important kind is best understood as anger.
[5] See, for example, Watson (2011), McKenna (2012), and Macnamara (2015b). Importantly, conversational views can include as one element a role for reactive emotions.

is unnecessary. Blame on this view is a response to ill will as expressed in action in the first stage of the conversation, and *can* convey anger, shunning, and alienation as expressions of morally reactive attitudes (McKenna 2013, p. 132). For example, in the case at hand, this can include Daphne's failure to issue an expected invitation to lunch where this has a negative meaning for Leslie. This view thus has the advantage of being able to accommodate insights from a number of traditional accounts.

Note that it puts expressed blame front and center and sees unexpressed blame as derivative. While a full assessment of this view is outside the scope of this paper, one might hope for a view that does not leave unexpressed blame to the side. And one might aim for more in the way of unity than a paradigm view can provide. With this in mind, consider what I call a Core and Syndrome account of blame (for more detail, see Brink and Nelkin in press). Our approach begins by seeing that there is a *core* to blame that is present in all cases, even purely private instances of blame. The core, which is both necessary and sufficient for blame, is an aversive attitude toward the target that is predicated on the belief or judgment that the target is blameworthy. From the core, we can work outward to expressions, manifestations, and functions of blame. Because blame involves the belief that the target is blameworthy, which involves wrongdoing for which the agent was responsible, it is natural for appraisers not just to register private mental acts of blame but to be disposed to manifest this blame in various private and public ways in suitable circumstances – in particular, blamers are disposed to express their blame to the target and others, to protest the target's behavior or attitudes, to engage the target in a normative exchange that acknowledges breached relations and can provide the target with an opportunity to express remorse and make amends, and to reaffirm and enforce the norms that have been breached. These are all normal expressions of blame that constitute a non-accidental *syndrome*, but they lie *downstream* from the core of blame. As with any psychological disposition, blame's dispositions may not manifest themselves in particular circumstances due to the operation of other dispositions and other forms of psychological interference. For instance, if the target holds significant power over the appraiser, fear or prudence might reasonably inhibit manifestation of the disposition to express blame and protest publicly. So, although elements of the syndrome non-accidentally co-occur with the core of blame, it is quite possible for there to be blame without one or more of these downstream expressions of blame.

The tricky part in this account is specifying the core of blame. What exactly does it involve? Blame involves a cognitive element insofar as an attitude won't count as blame unless the appraiser regards the target as blameworthy, which involves two components – the belief that the target acted wrongly or poorly and that the target was responsible for her wrong-doing or failing. There are different ways to proceed from here and still retain the general framework of core and syndrome.

On the variation I favor, the core of blame is an attitude of "holding against" which is *sui generis* in one important sense, namely, that it is not simply reducible to two separate attitudes, such as a judgment and an affective attitude. But this does not mean that it is unanalyzable or that there is not more to be said about its nature. It is to say that it is a kind of stance, or, to borrow a phrase from Eric Schwitzgebel (2013), a "posture of the mind" or a (possibly) temporary way of living. It will be helpful to consider other examples of stances or attitudes that do not appear to simply reduce to an aggregate of familiar ones of belief, desire, or affect. To take an example of Schwitzgebel's, "to love baseball, too, is to live a certain way. It is to enjoy watching and participating in baseball games, to leave room for baseball in one's plans, to talk baseball with other afi-cionados, to relish the onset of the season, to care intensely about the outcome of certain games, and so forth – or at least to be disposed in most of these directions, ceteris paribus" (p. 13). Similarly, an influential set of views about the nature of caring takes it that to care about something is to possess a number of dispositions of various kinds – emotional, cognitive, motivational, and deliberative, and one might see this proposal as based on a similar sort of model, although I favor identifying the attitude with the posture itself as distinct from the dispositions to which it gives rise. For example, on Agnieszka Jaworska's account, "the carer is disposed to worry when the object of care is in danger, to be relieved when the object escapes danger, to be sad when the object of care suffers a setback, to hope that things will go well for the object, to be happy when the object is flourishing, and so on. The carer's emotions and emotional dispositions form a systematic pattern focused on the object and having some ele-ments of this pattern normatively commits the person to having the other elements. For example, if you worry when a certain object is in danger, you should be relieved when this danger passes. The motivational dispo-sitions parallel the emotional ones: a carer is disposed to act to promote and protect the flourishing of the object of care." (Jaworska, n.d.; see also Helm, 2001; Jaworska, 2007). In Seidman's (2016) view, what unifies these dispositions is that the carer takes the object to be reason-giving in a variety of ways. In this way, caring can also be seen as a kind of stance that implicates a variety of dispositions.

On Schwitzgebel's (2013) particular account of attitudes (or postures of mind), to have any attitude is to have a dispositional profile and meet additional conditions specific to the attitude-type. Adapting this model to apply to the core and syndrome account of blame, we can identify the core of blame with a stance of holding against that is partly constituted by a distinctive set of dispositions and that depends on the belief that the object of blame is blameworthy.

Note that there is *some* similarity with some emotion accounts, and that the Core and Syndrome view accounts for much of the variation that conversational theories also accommodate. And we can see that there can be unexpressed blame, but also that expression is a natural downstream effect of blame.

Though I think which theory of blame to adopt is an important question, I believe that each of these has the resources to compare self-blame and other-blame on the dimension of degree. The story in each account is subtle, and getting the details right in each case is a project of its own. For now, note that in the emotion theory, we can compare the intensity of emotion. (Here a full story of what "intensity" comes to will depend on one's theory of emotion and on which dimension of emotion, e.g., affective quality or motivational profile, intensity should be measured.) In conversational and other communicative views, things are tricky because we have to assume that conversations and communication with oneself are possible. But once we do so, we can compare how serious the apt conversational responses are in terms of possible harm to the offender, or to the level of moral concern. And in the Core and Syndrome view, we can compare both the content of the core belief – how blameworthy the offender is believed to be – and the scalar nature of dispositions. There is a common currency in the content of the relevant judgment and in the scalarity of the dispositions to feel, act, communicate, and judge, among others.[6]

Finally, the fact that we find the comparative question so natural and so coherent is itself a datum for us in selecting among theories of blame. A good theory of blame should be able to either accommodate a

---

[6] Other accounts of blame can also vindicate a common currency between self-blame and blame of others. For example, the "signaling" theory of blame recently defended by Shoemaker and Vargas (2021) also accommodates a common currency, and it is notable that the authors take being able to accommodate self-blame within a general theory of blame to be a *desideratum* for any good theory of blame.

comparison along a single scale, or explain away our sense that self-blame and other-blame can be compared in magnitude. Fortunately, it seems that a number of theories are in a good position to account for such a comparison.[7]

4 The Ethics of Blame

With an account(s) of blame in hand, we can turn to the question of what could explain and vindicate the Blame Asymmetry Claim. And to do this, we must engage in a framework for the ethics of blame. Consider that whether one ought, *all things considered*, to blame someone depends on whether that person is blameworthy, of course. But whether that person is blameworthy does not fully settle the question of whether any given person ought to blame her. For there are many possible morally relevant factors that go into deciding how much we ought, all things considered, to blame others, both privately and overtly. It is widely accepted that even if someone is seriously blameworthy, there might be a number of different reasons for any particular person not to blame her *overtly*, including but not limited to "she's suffered enough," "one was complicit in the crime," "it's none of your business," and so on. (Some of these factors are commonly known as considerations of "standing.") And there might be reasons not to blame even *privately*, despite the fact that the candidate blame is seriously blameworthy, as I'll discuss in what follows. We can easily make sense of the utterance "She is blameworthy, but I don't – and shouldn't – blame her." (See Beardsley [1970], for example.) The fact that one is blameworthy, or that blame is in some important sense fitting, simply does not exhaust the reasons for or against blaming in any given context.

This distinction between overt and private blame is crucial in assessing ethical principles. It seems clear that there can be some circumstances in which there is nothing at all morally objectionable about blaming someone who has hurt you, but in which it would be wrong to express that blame to the offender. For example, perhaps he has suffered greatly, and the expression would send him over the edge without any good consequences coming from it. Or perhaps it could be counterproductive, resulting in his becoming enraged and harming others. In fact, it is tempting to think that the ethics of blame is exclusively about the expression of blame or about other downstream manifestations of it, because it is only these things that we

---

[7] I believe that a detailed exploration of how a variety of theories of blame would actually carry out the comparison is important, and here I leave that for future work.

directly control, and, if ought implies can, then principles of obligation and permissibility govern only these things. But I think that there is a notion of moral appropriateness that can still find purchase when it comes to attitudes (or "postures"). We can have obligations to foster or eliminate or counteract them. Particularly in cases in which the attitudes are themselves so closely connected to actions as downstream consequences, this can be very important. So it is worth asking the question about both blame's overt manifestations, and the attitude of blame itself.

Once we are in the realm of ethics, we can see that considerations fall into a variety of categories, including consequences (harm vs. benefit); rights (violation vs. respect); duties (some that correspond to rights, and some that don't); distributive principles of equality or fairness; or the expression of virtue or vice. When we are assessing whether it is permissible or obligatory to blame to a certain degree for any reason and we have settled the question of *blameworthiness*, we ought to be able to locate the reasons in one or more of these categories.

5   The Ethics of Blame: Self and Other

Turning now to possible avenues of vindication for the Blame Asymmetry Claim, we can again borrow an idea from the moral luck literature: as is often pointed out, our intuitions of appropriate blame might be (reasonably) affected by our differential epistemic access from case to case. Where many have suggested that there is in fact no difference in blameworthiness between the two drivers in Brakes, people naturally *take* the different outcomes to indicate a real difference in negligence.[8] Thus, there is a rational explanation for why people judge the cases differently, even when there is no actual difference.

Transposing this insight relating to the lucky-unlucky contrast cases to the self-other contrast cases, we have the proposal that in our own case we simply have better epistemic access to our own morally salient inner states and capacities than other people. And this asymmetry in epistemic access might explain why we are typically in a better epistemically justified position to blame ourselves than others, who can only guess at things, such as the quality of our earlier opportunities to have had our brakes checked or whether we freely passed up easy opportunities to censor our hurtful words.

---

[8] See Richards (1986), Thomson (1993), Latus (2001), and Enoch and Marmor (2007), and for some support from empirical psychology, Kneer and Machery (2018).

Because we have greater justification in our belief that we are blame-worthy to a particular degree than do others, we are entitled to blame ourselves more than others as a result. This is an instance of a more general principle. We should require significant justification to expose anyone to harm, and blaming overtly, while not necessarily harmful, often risks harm to others.[9] And indeed, if we move to the legal case, we can note that criminal trials require a higher degree of justification for conviction than do civil ones. Depending on what is at stake, we require more justification. If in our own case we are more likely to meet higher levels of justification, this can explain an asymmetry in appropriate blame.[10]

I believe that this can explain some cases in which we find an asymmetry of appropriate levels of blame, but it does not exhaust the explanation. There are at least three reasons for this. First, we can imagine cases in which there is no epistemic asymmetry, for example, but the intuition remains. Variants of the cases with which we began can serve this purpose. We can suppose that third parties are given all relevant information and *still* blame less where this seems appropriate. Second, it is an interesting empirical question whether people *are* typically more accurate about themselves in the relevant respects than others are. I note that in entirely *blameless* cases – in which one has checked one's brakes and is driving perfectly cautiously toward one's job at a non-profit agency, say – it is a plausible empirical bet that many people blame themselves. This suggests that at least in some cases it is *other*-blame that rests on more accurate judgments. And of course, there are some people who appear to under-blame themselves, including the well-studied group of hypocrites, and one might think that in their case a lack of appropriate blame rests on a mistaken or unjustified judgment about their own capacities and faults. In any case, I take it to be an open empirical question whether we have better epistemic access to those aspects of ourselves that are relevant to responsibility. Third, even if we grant that we have greater epistemic

---

[9] For arguments that blame of others is not necessarily harmful (and can even be beneficial to the target), see Nelkin (2013a) and Carlsson (2017). Note that what the argument of the text depends on is the claim that blame risks harm, or even the weaker claim that blame often harms.

[10] Note that the talk of stakes and belief might suggest the phenomenon of moral encroachment on the justification of belief – the idea that depending on what is at stake we are more or less justified in our belief. (See, e.g., Stroud, 2006). To clarify, I do not mean to suggest this at all. To the contrary, the idea is simply that *given* a particular level of justification for a belief, we might be constrained in how we are permitted to act on its basis. And extending this idea, a given level of justification for a belief might constrain how we should cultivate dispositions to act in certain ways on its basis.

access in our own case, such access might in some cases lead to *lesser* self-blame, since we might also sometimes have better access to excusing conditions. Thus, epistemic access might work in both directions and thus there is no generalization like the Blame Asymmetry Claim that it could support.

Suppose, then, that an asymmetry remains in our judgments of appropriate levels of blame even after we keep fixed epistemic access. Because we've just raised a special question in "luck" cases, let's focus on the Friends case, and others like it. Are there *other* factors that could account for the asymmetry?

An intriguing suggestion is that there is a virtue (or set of virtues) related to *over*-blame of the self. Margaret Urban Walker writes of a set of qualities as the "virtues of impure agency," which includes one's acknowledgment that one's responsibilities outrun one's control (1991, p. 19). Susan Wolf picks up on this theme, arguing that there is a kind of nameless virtue for the trait of taking more responsibility than one actually has simply in virtue of having acted. She suggests that "one ought to take responsibility for more than what, from a bystander's point of view, would be justly impersonally assigned" (2001, p. 13). And she takes it that this is best thought of as a virtue:

> Perhaps the more obvious reason for regarding it as a virtue is that, when applied to harmful actions, this trait is a species of, or at least akin to, the well-established virtue of generosity. Generosity generally involves a willingness to give more – more time, more money, more love, more lenience, more, in one way or another, of oneself than justice requires. In offering to pay for the broken vase, in trying to ease the pain or provide comfort to the grieving family beyond what a rationalist assignment of liability would demand, an agent voluntarily benefits or tries to benefit others at cost to herself. That this should be seen as virtuous is not hard to understand. (p. 14)

The idea here is that one ought to blame oneself more than the degree to which one is *deserving* of blame, and that there is a kind of virtue in so doing. If this is right, it would explain and vindicate the Blame Asymmetry Claim.

Before assessing this suggestion (call it the Virtue of Self Over-Blame account), it is important to note that Wolf seems to equate self-blame in the relevant sense with feeling bad, and suggests that one ought to feel bad to a degree greater than one's *judgment* of blameworthiness would itself warrant. At this point, I note that it is not clear that the "feeling bad" part of blame can come apart from its constitutive thought in this way. The excess bad feeling might not be blame so much as another negative attitude (as Wolf herself notes is a possibility). Or such over-blamers might just make incompatible judgments – on the one hand, they judge rightly that they are only blameworthy to a certain degree, but can't help also judging that they are much more blameworthy than that, and it is the latter judgment that underwrites the greater self-blame.[11]

But what I would like to focus on here is that while both Urban Walker and Wolf speak about feeling bad, and self-reproach, and guilt, and self-blame, they also notably employ the locutions of "taking responsibility" and "one's responsibilities." Arguably, these are importantly distinct. And I suggest that insofar as there is a virtue in the ballpark, it concerns the latter and not the former. That is, it is plausible that it is a virtue to err on side of *taking responsibility* for more, rather than fewer, things. But this is quite distinct from blaming oneself.

To claim that it is a virtue to judge that one is blameworthy to degree n, but to blame oneself to degree n + x, is odd, even if coherent. Particularly if we view blame in terms of emotions (and, at least in Urban Walker's case, liability to punishment and more), it is unclear why this should be virtuous. It seems to build in a kind of irrationality (at least if we think of blaming emotions as having constitutive thoughts about blameworthiness). Why should that be virtuous? A better candidate for virtue is the acceptance of *liability* for more than one is blameworthy for. One ought to accept that one is on the hook for compensation and apology and more. But this is not to say that one ought to engage in more self-blame.

While I do not think this suggestion of the Virtue of Self Over-Blame is correct, there is something appealing to it, and I'll try to capture that shortly. But first, let us look at a suggestion that is the flip side of this one, namely the Virtue of Other Under-Blame.

Appealing to the way Gary Watson (2013) puts it, one might see what he calls judgmentalism as a vice. It is problematic to judge others – in a way that goes beyond simply making a judgment. As Watson points out, it is a staple of current therapeutic prescriptions to avoid being judgmental, and perhaps that norm has the status of a virtue. He gives four examples, three of whom are parents – including two mothers; a fundamentalist mother who judges her son for getting a divorce, and a proper mother-in-law who judges her daughter-in-law for being not proper enough, but also

---

[11] See Moore (2009) for an interesting reply to Wolf that in a different way takes issue with her distinguishing between degree of blameworthiness and degree of self-blame one should feel.

a salesperson who doesn't help his tattooed customers with as much respect and care as his non-tattooed customers, and a pacifist father who judges his daughter who has joined the military. The vice, or vices, as Watson sees them, are failures of interpretative generosity and failures of acceptance. Perhaps these considerations should lead us to see under-blame of others as a virtue. This would counteract tendencies to over-blame, and to err on the side of under-blame as an expression of a kind of generosity.

Here I will be brief and make just a few points in response. First, though the relevant article of Watson's appears in a collection called *Blame: Its Nature and Norms,* Watson himself does not see "judging" as the same as "blaming," and this seems right. The examples are not obviously ones that are best described as blaming (except, interestingly, the father?), or to the extent that they are, it isn't obviously the blaming that is problematic. Second, it is not at all clear that, once these are clearly distinguished, the vices really attach to blaming that is *not* a matter of "judging." Why should mere blaming to the degree that matches a person's blameworthiness amount to the exhibition of either sort of vice? And, finally, even if it were the manifestation of a vice of judgmentalism to blame to such a degree, we might ask why these vices should only manifest in the third-person case. Being interpretatively generous and accepting seem like virtues we should manifest to everyone, ourselves included, insofar as they are virtues. Or at least we would need an argument for why there should be an asymmetry.

At this point, then, neither the proposed virtues of Self Over-Blame or of Other Under-Blame seem like they can do the work asked of them. A different hypothesis might seem to jump out at this point: self-blame is essentially harmful or painful where other-blame isn't, or, at least, self-blame is more directly connected to something essentially painful than is other-blame. Call this the Direct/Indirect Harm Asymmetry hypothesis. Andreas Brekke Carlsson (2017), for one, argues that blameworthiness itself should really be understood in terms of desert of guilt feelings, because only these are essentially harmful to those who experience them.[12] This is certainly a very important asymmetry between self- and other-blame – or, at least, on the Core and Syndrome view – of an important part of the syndrome of self-blame and an important part of the syndrome of other-blame. Can it explain the Blame Asymmetry Claim?

As important as it is, it is not clear why it should make *higher* degrees of self-blame called for compared to other-blame. If anything, it seems that since the potential harm of self-blame is more direct than that of

---

[12] See Clarke (2013, 2016) for the claims that guilt is essentially painful, and that the guilty deserve to feel guilt.

other-blame, *less* rather than more might be called for if we are focused on the consequences of blame. Perhaps there is another category of moral considerations for which this point is relevant and through which it can support the Blame Asymmetry Claim, but I am not sure what it is.

The idea that blame can pose a risk of harm, though, seems an insightful one, and I suggest that it points the way to a new idea for explaining a systematic asymmetry between self- and other-blame. First, begin by noting that one motivation for attending to the Direct/Indirect Harm Asymmetry in the first place is that other-blame might not harm its target at all. Depending on how exactly we understand the core of blame in the Core and Syndrome view, it is possible that self-blame does not harm either. But either self-blame is essentially painful, or it is very likely to lead to painful feelings. Still, in both cases, blame poses a risk of harm. And this suggests a final hypothesis that aims to vindicate the Blame Asymmetry Claim.

Suppose that we keep epistemic access to the relevant facts fixed, so that judgments of blameworthiness on the part of the offender and on the part of a third party are the same, and equally justified. Still, there is a risk of error in each of two directions: under-blame or over-blame. Over-blame more typically poses a risk of undue harm. (Under-blame might, too, in some cases, and I return to this in the next section.) Thus, one reason to avoid the risk of over-blame in the case of others to a greater extent than in the case of oneself could be that it is subsumed under a more general ethical principle:

> All other things equal, it is harder to justify risking harm to others than to ourselves.[13]

Familiar instances of this asymmetrical risk principle abound. It is one thing for someone to quit his well-paying job to travel the world and find himself; it is another for a parent of a small child to do so. It is one thing for a person to set off firecrackers in the middle of his expansive private property and another to do so very near their neighbor's. Similarly, it is one thing to risk over-blame and, more importantly, its downstream consequences when it comes to oneself; it is another to risk over-blame and its downstream consequences when it comes to others. It seems that one has rights against others that are by default not waived, where this is not so in one's own case. (Either one doesn't have rights against oneself, or, if one does, then one can clearly waive them without needing to communicate them).

---

[13] Or perhaps even a weaker principle can do the work: all other things equal, it is harder to justify engaging in activities that very often harm others than engaging in those that very often harm ourselves (when it is difficult to discern when such engagement will be harmful).

Now this principle by itself provides grounds for an important moral asymmetry between self-blame and other-blame. It explains why it can be permissible to blame oneself more than it is permissible to blame others, all other things equal. But this does not yet fully justify the intuition that there seems to be a systematic positive reason for it being the case that we ought to blame ourselves more than others. I believe that there are two ways we might add to the picture to capture that stronger intuition.

The first is that we have good reason in general to blame the blameworthy to the right degree, and so where the permission to take greater risk is provided, this reason provides a reason why we ought, all things considered, to risk over-blaming in pursuit of accuracy when it comes to ourselves. In other words, once we are permitted to take this risk, we ought to do so in virtue of standing reasons to blame the blameworthy to the right degree. This is to add a symmetrical principle to the asymmetrical risk principle. It is a principle that enjoins us to (defeasibly) take blameworthy wrongdoing seriously where we find it, whether in ourselves or others, and reflect it accurately in our mental economy. This introduces a *pro tanto* duty of accuracy in blaming.

The second way of adding to the picture appeals not to a general principle providing reasons to blame accurately, but to special positive reasons to blame ourselves more. That is, it suggests that we have a special duty to get it right when it comes to ourselves. This would be to add a further asymmetrical positive duty principle to the asymmetrical risk principle. And here we face a further choice point: we could take that duty to be forward-looking in the sense that we have a duty to make ourselves better beings going forward that is stronger than we have to do so when it comes to others; or we could take that duty to be backward-looking insofar as it is a duty of justice that is stronger when it comes to ourselves.[14]

I believe that there are challenges facing both of these versions of an additional asymmetrical duty principle. When it comes to the forward-looking duty, it seems that it can be disassociated from blaming oneself (at least in the ways I have so far focused on). A duty of self-improvement can be fulfilled in many ways. When it comes to duties of justice, I am not sure exactly what is meant. But if what it means is something like a duty to take wrongdoing seriously, it is not obvious that this is always stronger

---

[14] See Clarke (2016) for a defense of the idea that feeling guilt (if a form of self-blame) is a kind of just state.

when it comes to oneself. Perhaps we owe it to others to take their wrong-doing as seriously as we do in our own case, and it would make an exception of ourselves to see our own as more important.[15] However, I am happy to take either of these suggestions on board if these challenges can be met. But even if not, I think that the symmetrical accuracy principle, combined with the asymmetrical risk principle, can together do the work of explaining and justifying an asymmetry in the Blame Asymmetry Claim.

Finally, it is very important to emphasize that additional principles might apply in the case of blame itself (the core) and its manifestations in action and expression. If one cannot blame less, say, then one can take steps to limit its manifestations. And concerns about potential harm seem – at least often – to be most salient in interpersonal cases compared to more distant cases. When we compare blaming the likes of Donald Trump or Boris Johnson to blaming our partners or children or colleagues or friends, it seems that the potential for harm is at least more salient in the latter cases than in the former. Thus, there may be a number of nuanced principles differentiating how much to blame different categories of others, but these are consistent with the Blame Asymmetry Claim.

6   Objections, Replies, and Limitations

A systematic countervailing reason. There is an important argument that failures to blame others in some cases exhibit a lack of respect, and this in itself is a harm. (See, for example, Kathleen Connelly [in preparation].) A first reply is that the Blame Asymmetry Claim is about relative *degrees* of blame, and not the claim that other-blame is appropriate to degree zero. But that is too quick. It is possible that such arguments for the conclusion that blame carries the good of respect can incorporate claims about a failure to blame to a *sufficient degree*, and, if these are sound, then they would provide a counterweight to the argument in support of the Blame Asymmetry Claim. If someone you know blames herself much more than you even though your transgressions are similar, you might think that there is a lack of respect and that her under-blame is morally problematic. She should blame you more!

Thus, a stronger reply is needed. It is to take on board the idea that blame to a sufficient degree carries the good of respect, such that there is a danger of under-blame of others, but that this, too, is consistent with

---

[15] I return to an argument along these lines below.

the Blame Asymmetry Claim. The idea that we ought to blame enough to embody respect is perfectly consistent with the idea that we ought not to take inappropriate risks of over-blame, and that what is an appropriate or sufficient degree of other-blame that carries respect can still be less than an appropriate degree of self-blame in a particular case.

A violation of a principle of equality. Closely related to the previous objection is the idea that differential blaming violates a "principle of equality." Interestingly, this is typically invoked in discussions of what might seem to be the opposite case to the one at hand, namely, that of hypocrisy – cases in which one blames *others* without blaming oneself for the same transgressions (see Wallace, 2010). If one violates such a principle in those cases by placing more importance on one's own interests than on others' interests, then it might seem that in the reverse case in which one blames oneself more than one blames others, one also violates the very same principle of equality. But here, too, I believe that the best response is to appeal to the asymmetrical risk principle. Once we appeal to that principle, together with the idea that we ought to take wrongdoing seriously in general, we have an explanation for why great self-blame can be justified that does not fall afoul of differential respect. Respect for people's interests can be equal in both cases, while the asymmetrical risk principle explains the fact that one can be justified in taking greater risk with oneself.[16]

Over-generalization. One might think that much of the force of the Blame Asymmetry Claim comes from over-generalization from a few cases, notably including my own. But many people let themselves off the hook. So the intuitive appeal of the Blame Asymmetry Claim is just not as strong as it might have seemed. I take this point, and there is an interesting empirical question about the frequency and magnitude of self-blame compared to other-blame. At the same time, the claim is ultimately a normative one. So the cases like Brakes or Friends are ultimately meant to generate the intuition about what is *appropriate*. While the over-generalization point is one to take seriously, if we can explain normative intuitions in independently compelling ways, appealing to attractive

---

[16] Interestingly, Wallace notes that the principle that he takes to explain the moral objectionability of hypocritical moral blame may pose a *prima facie* challenge to the idea that blaming oneself more is permissible, a claim he seems to endorse. His response is to point to the fact that people in this situation (as opposed to hypocrites) might reasonably think they are in better epistemic positions when it comes to themselves, and also to invoke a virtue of generosity (2010, p. 337). As argued above, however, the epistemic point does not seem to fully vindicate the Blame Asymmetry Claim, and it is not clear why a virtue of generosity should apply to others and not oneself.

general ethical principles, then we can provide an answer to the objection even without a full empirical account of blaming behavior.

Back to a debunking claim. Next, return to the debunking idea that even if we do tend to blame ourselves more, we just make a mistake in doing so. After all, we get it wrong in the blameless cases described earlier. And we even recognize a phenomenon called survivor guilt which is obviously not properly tracking the facts. I'm not sure that survivor guilt is really self-blame – it would depend on whether one really believes oneself to be blameworthy. The first kinds of cases seem more challenging for the Blame Asymmetry Claim. My reply here is to take the point that we are very fallible when it comes to ourselves, but we are also very fallible when it comes to others. And note that the intuitions backing the Blame Asymmetry Claim are normative ones.[17] And in any case, given that the Blame Asymmetry Claim is not an all-things-considered in-all-circumstances claim, it can still be true insofar as there is a systematic reason supporting an asymmetry, even if there are other reasons on the other side in a great variety of cases.

Acknowledging a (welcome) limitation. As mentioned at the outset, I restricted the discussion to a particular backward-looking form of blame (though I tried to be ecumenical within that category). However, one might argue that it is hard to separate this form of blame from others that could be purely forward-looking, and this requires its own exploration. But even if we focus on a particular backward-looking form of blame that risks harm, it is important to note that there may be other aspects of such blame, including some that may be forward-looking, such that focusing on these might give additional, but quite distinct, rationales for the Blame Asymmetry Claim. One might, for example, take it that one has greater responsibility for one's own moral character, so insofar as blame involves a kind of protest that can motivate better behavior in the future, one has reason for self-blame to be more intense.[18]

---

[17] One further strategy in support of the robustness of the normative intuitions would be to note that there seems to be a special problem accounting for circumstances in which self-forgiveness is justified as compared to forgiveness of others. Insofar as forgiveness has been thought to be one way of ceasing to blame, this could provide mutual support for the idea that self-blame has a different status than blame of others. I believe that the relationship between blame and forgiveness is complicated, however, and do not rely on this point here, though I hope to return to the relationship between these two debates.

[18] Interestingly, however, there is reason to think that these forward-looking reasons cannot be all there is to the story, in addition to the positive account given earlier. One reason is that, as we saw earlier, the forward-looking reasons would seem to favor comparatively more praise of oneself when one acts well, as well, given this duty. And this is somewhat counterintuitive.

7   Implications for Moral Theorizing

Interestingly, when it comes to the existing debate, one prominent position is to privilege blame intuitions about self over those about others (e.g., Moore). And we do often gain insight when faced with moral dilemmas from thinking about how we would feel in given situations. But if I've been on the right track here, then the story is more complicated. Perhaps rather than focusing on how much blame is appropriate all things equal from anyone in particular, we should focus on intuitions of blame*worthiness* to the extent we can do so. Or perhaps the best thing to do is to be aware of the various factors – level of justification of core beliefs of blameworthiness, self vs. other related to risk, fallibility, and so on that affect our intuitions about how much blame is apt. I am not yet sure which of these directions (or both) it is best to move in, but one thing that is clear is that knowledge of a systematic difference in the appropriateness of self- and other-blame, even if often washed out by other factors, is important when assessing different methodological claims like which blame intuitions to privilege in our theorizing.

CHAPTER 6

Don't Suffer in Silence
A Self-Help Guide for Self-Blame

Hannah Tierney

1 Introduction

There are better and worse ways to blame others. Likewise, there are better and worse ways to blame yourself. And though there is an ever-expanding literature on the norms that govern our blaming practices, relatively little attention has been paid to the norms that govern expressions of self-blame. But the conditions under which other-directed blame is appropriate are very different from the conditions under which self-blame is appropriate. Take, for example, work on the standing conditions to blame. Much of this research focuses on articulating the kinds of relationships potential blamers ought to have with wrongdoers, as well as their wrongs, in order for their blame to be appropriate.[1] But in the case of self-blame, the potential blamer and wrongdoer are one in the same, and the relationships we have with ourselves and our actions are very different than the relationships we bear to others and their actions. Given these differences, it should not be surprising that asymmetries can be found between the norms that govern self-blame and other-directed blame.[2]

Because it is not possible to read off the ethics of self-blame from the ethics of other-directed blame, it will be important to explore the norms that are unique to self-blame. In this chapter, I explore one dimension along which self-blame can be better and worse. Of course, what follows is far from a complete ethics of self-blame, and in focusing on one set of factors that are relevant to the appropriateness of self-blame, I've failed to attend to others. But even this truncated discussion can improve our

---

[1] Though I use the terminology of "wrongdoer" and "wrong" in this chapter, I leave open the possibility that agents can be blameworthy, and appropriately blamed, for actions or attitudes that are not wrong. See Macnamara (2013) for discussion of this kind of blame.

[2] In this very volume, Dana Nelkin points to one such difference involving the degree of blame that is appropriate in cases of self-blame versus other-directed blame.

understanding of the moral value of self-blame as well as the nature of blameworthiness itself.

My plan for this essay is as follows. In Section 2, I make some preliminary remarks about how to go about developing an ethics of self-blame. In Section 3, I present what I call the "Don't Suffer in Silence" norm of self-blame. According to this norm, agents who blame themselves should not do so privately. Rather, they should express their self-blame to those they've wronged. In Section 4, I address three questions about Don't Suffer in Silence in order to clarify its normative scope and how it relates to other norms governing the appropriateness of self-blame. Finally, in Section 5, I conclude by outlining how discussions of self-blame can inform our understanding of blameworthiness.

2   Preliminaries

What does it mean to blame oneself? Like other-directed blame, self-blame has proven to be the topic of controversy. Several accounts of the nature of self-blame have been put forward in this volume alone. Some have argued that self-blame is best understood as the experience of guilt (Carlsson, this volume; Portmore, this volume), while others argue it should be understood in terms of goal-frustrated anger (Shoemaker, this volume). Still others argue that self-blame is not necessarily connected to a particular emotion and take self-blame to be a kind of protest against oneself (Pereboom, this volume) or negative self-evaluation (McKenna, this volume; Thomason, this volume). I will remain (relatively) silent on these matters. In this chapter, I'll focus on the *ethics* of self-blame, as opposed to its *nature*.

To construct an ethics of self-blame, we must determine the set of conditions under which expressions of self-blame are appropriate.[3] When it comes to other-directed blame, these conditions are divided into three categories: those that apply to the target of blame, those that apply to the blamer, and those that apply to the act of blame (Coates & Tognazzini, 2013). Conditions governing the target of blame typically address whether this agent is the object of fitting, appropriate, or deserved blame, that is,

[3] I focus on the appropriateness of *expressions* of self-blame because, as Nelkin notes, expressions of blame are within our control and can thus be governed by norms of obligation and permissibility (this volume). However, as Nelkin also notes, there is a degree of control we can exercise over our attitudes themselves, either in cultivating or discouraging them, so the ethics of self-blame may well govern both expressions of self-blame as well as self-blaming attitudes.

whether the agent is blameworthy. Many of the essays in this volume do an excellent job of exploring the relationship between self-blame, fittingness, and desert, so I will focus on the second and, to a lesser extent, third categories of blaming norms in this chapter.

In the context of other-directed blame, blamers must meet a range of norms in order for their blame to be appropriate, the most discussed of which are standing conditions. Having the standing to blame others depends on the blamer's relationship to the wrongdoer and their wrong. For example, if the blamer performed a relevantly similar action to that of the wrongdoer, and never apologised or rectified their wrong in any way, then the blamer would lack standing because their blame would be hypocritical. And, if the wrongdoer engaged in, or helped the wrongdoer commit, the very wrong that they blame the wrongdoer for performing, then the blamer would lack standing because they are complicit. Additionally, if the wrongdoer's actions are simply none of the blamer's business, then the blamer would lack standing because their blame would constitute meddling.[4]

It's hard to see how the above standing conditions could apply to expressions of self-blame. It's not clear that an individual could be complicit in their own wrongdoing, or that their wrongdoings were none of their business. And what it would mean for a wrongdoer to blame themselves hypocritically is presumably very different than what it means for an agent to blame another individual hypocritically.[5] But just because typical standing conditions cannot easily apply to self-blame does not mean that there are no blamer-specific norms that govern how we blame ourselves.[6] A wrongdoer can still express self-blame inappropriately even if they are in fact blameworthy and are the fitting, appropriate, or deserving target of (self-)blame. But in these cases, what renders the expression of self-blame inappropriate has little to do with the relationship between the blamer and themselves or their wrong. Rather, it has to do with *to whom* and *how* they express their self-blame. When we blame ourselves, we typically express our self-blame to others. But there are better and worse audiences for our expressions of self-blame. In the next section, I present the (self-)blamer-specific norm

---

[4] The standing conditions discussed in this paragraph are not uncontroversial. For critical discussions of these norms, see Bell (2013) and King (2019).

[5] See Shoemaker's essay in this volume for a discussion of self-blame and hypocrisy.

[6] This also does not mean that there are no standing conditions on self-blame. In "Hypercrisy and Standing to Self-Blame," I argue that standing to self-blame depends not on how the blamer relates to herself, but rather on how the blamer relates to those she has blamed for relevantly similar wrongs (2021b).

"Don't Suffer in Silence" and explore what kinds of audiences are appropriate for expressions of self-blame.

3   Don't Suffer in Silence

In this section, I will argue that when we blame ourselves, we ought not do so privately. Rather, our self-blame should have an audience. Furthermore, we should direct our expressions of self-blame to the victims of our wrong-doings. These claims can be captured in the following norm:

> **Don't Suffer in Silence:** If A blames themselves for wronging B, then, *ceteris paribus*, A should express their self-blame to B.[7]

To defend this norm, I will centre my discussion around a paradigmatic form of expressing self-blame: expressing guilt.[8] This is because most theorists accept that expressions of guilt are expressions of self-blame, even if they do not take self-blame to be identical to the experience of guilt. For example, though Michael McKenna argues that guilt does not constitute self-blame, he takes the two to be importantly connected because guilt and the other blaming reactive attitudes "provide the medium within which we normally express our blame" (McKenna, this volume). In fact, McKenna goes on to argue that because our blaming practices developed around expressions of guilt, resentment, and indignation, we ought to theorise about blame by attending to the expression of these reactive attitudes (McKenna, this volume). I will heed McKenna's advice and focus on expressions of guilt when defending Don't Suffer in Silence.

When we feel guilty for committing a wrong, we do not usually keep it to ourselves. Rather, we tend to express our guilt to those we have wronged, typically via confession (Baumeister, et al., 1994). In fact, while some philosophers tend to conceive of guilt as a purely self-regarding emotion (e.g., Macnamara, 2015b, footnote 1), many psychologists take guilt to be a fundamentally social emotion. Guilt has been characterised as

---

[7] Note that this norm does not govern self-blame for victimless wrongs. While there may be reasons to express self-blame for victimless wrongs, they will likely diverge from the reasons to follow Don't Suffer in Silence.

[8] However, this is not to say that expressions of guilt are the only way to express self-blame or that a successful ethics of self-blame will only apply to expressions of guilt. After all, not everyone agrees that we express self-blame when we express guilt. David Shoemaker, for example, argues that guilt is not self-blame, but is rather a *response* to being blamed. On Shoemaker's account, a paradigmatic expression of self-blame is talking angrily to oneself (this volume). While my defence of Don't Suffer in Silence focuses on expressions of guilt, I take the norm to also apply to other expressions of self-blame, including expressions of angry self-talk.

"an interpersonal phenomenon that is functionally and causally linked to communal relationships between people" (Baumeister, et al., 1994, p. 243). And Brian Parkinson recently argued that "...the self-accountability appraisals associated with guilt may be associated with taking on the interpersonal role of a culpable transgressor and communicating your blameworthiness to the victim" (2019, p. 226). Of course, it does not follow that guilt *should* be expressed simply because guilty people tend to do so. Perhaps the guilt-ridden would do well to keep these feelings to themselves. To understand the moral importance of expressing guilt, it will be helpful to understand how expressions of guilt typically function.

Expressions of guilt do important interpersonal work. In confessing our guilt to those we have wronged, we begin the process of repairing our relationships with them. And confession is not the only means by which we express guilt. As many others have noted in this volume, guilt is characterised by a variety of reparative behavioural tendencies. When we feel guilty, we typically feel motivated to apologise, make amends, and minimise or eliminate the negative consequences of our actions (Lazarus, 1991; Baumeister, et al., 1994; Greenspan, 1995; Parkinson, 1996, 2019; Nichols, 2007; Tangney, et al., 2007). And, just as we express anger when we engage in the threatening behaviours that are characteristic of that emotion, we express guilt when we engage in the distinctive confessional and reparative behaviours that are associated with it. By focusing on these characteristic ways of expressing guilt, I will now build a case for Don't Suffer in Silence.

Victim-Based Reasons to Express Self-Blame

When we engage in the confessional and reparative behaviours that are characteristic of guilt, it benefits those who we have wronged. Expressions of guilt can ease victims' suffering, restore something important that they have lost (or was taken from them), and re-affirm their standing in the moral community. In fact, many have argued that wrongdoers and blameworthy agents *owe* this kind of care and concern to their victims (Radzik, 2009; Wallace, 2019; Tierney, 2021a). Because it's morally valuable to express guilt to victims in this way, it follows that we should, all else being equal, express self-blame to the victims of our wrongs – they are the appropriate audience of such expressions. Something of moral importance would be lost if a guilt-ridden agent refused to express their guilt and insisted on engaging entirely in private self-blame. Victims would be left without restitution, apology, or even acknowledgment of the harm they have suffered.

Notice that private self-blame which violates the above norm can be morally deficient even if the guilt-ridden agent experiences a fitting (or deserved) amount of guilt in virtue of being blameworthy. Imagine that Rose promised to visit her friend Sophia, who is in the hospital recovering from a difficult surgery, but breaks this promise in order to paint her bedroom. Rose does not tell Sophia that she is not going to visit her, and Sophia is hurt when she realises her friend will not be coming. The next day, Rose reflects on her behaviour and comes to understand that what she did was wrong and feels quite guilty about not visiting Sophia. However, Rose does not express her guilt to Sophia or anyone else and she keeps her self-blame entirely private. Even if Rose feels adequately guilty for what she has done, there is still something criticisable about her self-blame. Though an *expression* of self-blame could serve a reparative function, merely blaming oneself cannot. While Rose's private self-blame may be fitting and/or deserved in light of her blameworthiness, this in and of itself does nothing for the person she wronged.

There are also instances of self-blame that violate Don't Suffer in Silence even if they are not entirely private. Imagine that Rose eventually expresses her self-blame, not to Sophia but to their mutual friend Edna. A few weeks after the incident, Rose confesses to Edna what she's done and communicates to Edna that she is blameworthy for, and feels guilty about, her behaviour. While there is nothing morally objectionable about Rose expressing self-blame to Edna, and indeed expressing self-blame in certain public contexts can serve a morally important function, Rose should still express self-blame to Sophia. Without expressing self-blame to the person whom she hurt, Rose fails to engage in the reparative behaviours that would benefit Sophia. Importantly, the reparative function of self-blame would not be served even if Sophia came to know that Rose blamed herself for what she did. Imagine that Edna reports to Sophia that Rose feels guilty for what she's done. While Sophia might take some solace in knowing that she and Rose are in agreement about one feature of what transpired between them, namely that Rose is blameworthy, there is something upsetting about this development as well. Sophia would surely wonder why Rose failed to communicate her blameworthiness *to her*. Learning that the individual who wronged you blames themselves is not the same thing as receiving an apology or even acknowledgment of wrongdoing. And the relationship between the victim and wrongdoer will likely remain damaged even if both know that the wrongdoer is blameworthy *and* that they blame themselves. Thus, when we blame ourselves for how we have treated someone, we have good reason to express our self-blame to them. In so doing, we can begin the reparative process that benefits our victims.

Wrongdoer-Based Reasons to Express Self-Blame

Expressing self-blame via the reparative behaviours that are distinctive of guilt not only benefits victims, it serves an important ameliorative function for wrongdoers as well.[9] Philosophers and psychologists largely agree that guilt has a negative affect – to feel guilt is to suffer to at least some extent. But feelings of guilt can be resolved when one engages in the reparative behaviours that are distinctive of the emotion. That is, expressing guilt can reduce the experience of guilt. This has been noted in the empirical literature (Quiles & Bybee, 1997) and demonstrated in studies with both adults and children (de Hooge, 2012; Donohue & Tully, 2019).[10]

Arguing that expressing self-blame can benefit wrongdoers by ameliorating their feelings of guilt is not to say that experiencing guilt is in and of itself bad or to be avoided. It's surely appropriate to blame oneself when one is blameworthy and it may very well be that feeling guilty when one is blameworthy is non-instrumentally good, as some in this volume have argued (Carlsson, this volume; Portmore, this volume). However, *privately* blaming oneself is maladaptive: experiencing but not expressing guilt fails to serve guilt's interpersonal function. And this can have very negative effects on the guilty party. Not only do agents who privately blame themselves continue to feel guilty for their transgressions, they also tend to feel *guiltier* for what they've done (Silfver, 2007; Tilghman-Osborne & Cole, 2012; Riek et al., 2014). This makes it more likely that those who privately self-blame experience more guilt than they deserve to feel because they experience guilt longer and to greater degrees than those who express their self-blame. And while it may be non-instrumentally good to experience *deserved* guilt, it's non-instrumentally bad to experience *undeserved* guilt. Furthermore, maladaptive and excessive guilt is associated with higher rates of depression and anxiety and lower rates of social functioning (Jones & Kugler, 1993; Quiles & Bybee, 1997; Luby et al., 2018).

In a recent interview with Conan O'Brian, Terry Gross (2019) noted something interesting about self-punishment:

> You know, with self-punishment, I sometimes think there's a sense of … if you punish yourself and if you're penitent in some way, that it will avoid a harsher externally given punishment. Like, I know I did wrong. I've punished myself, so you don't have to do anything. I've taken care of it. It's almost like … [p]reemptive punishment. But it could be … so damaging.

---

9 Expressing self-blame can also benefit wrongdoers by improving others' treatment of them. For example, expressing guilt can stop victims from engaging in punishing and punitive behaviour towards wrongdoers (O'Connor, 2016; Rosenstock and O'Connor, 2018).

10 Interestingly, de Hooge (2012) found that transgressors' guilt feelings decrease even if *others* repair the transgressors' wrongs.

While Gross doesn't articulate the ways in which pre-emptive self-punishment is damaging, given the context, I suspect she had in mind the destructive effects of private self-blame described above. If you punish or blame yourself, perhaps in order to avoid greater punishment or blame from others, this can ironically cause you to suffer much more in the long run. This is a result of both the elevated guilt one suffers over the particular wrongdoing as well as the more general suffering caused by the negative impacts on one's mental health that maladaptive and excessive guilt can cause.

Even if one's private self-blame does not calcify into depression or anxiety, I take it that many readers are familiar with the distinctive unpleasantness of private self-blame. Take Rose as an example. Imagine that Rose decides not to apologise or acknowledge her callous behaviour to Sophia because she is afraid of how Sophia would react. Perhaps she worries that Sophia's resentment will make her feel worse than she already feels and she wishes to avoid such suffering. So, she keeps her guilt to herself. But without expressing her guilt to Sophia, there is no way to alleviate her guilty feelings. Whenever she thinks about what she's done, she feels fresh pains of guilt. And while she may try to avoid these unpleasant feelings by attempting not to think about them, this is an all but impossible feat. Guilt, like other emotions, is not easily ignored. Even if Rose were to succeed in ignoring her guilt for a time, it would reignite as soon as she is reminded of her blameworthy behaviour. Eventually, Rose may very well suffer significantly more by virtue of experiencing excessive and maladaptive guilt than she would have had she expressed her guilt to Sophia and been the target of her resentment.

While it may be conceptually possible to privately blame oneself, it is not advisable. Expressions of self-blame can serve reparative and ameliorative functions, which are morally important for both victims and wrongdoers. Such expressions can have a restorative effect on the victim as well as their relationship with the wrongdoer, and these expressions can also help wrongdoers avoid the undeserved suffering and negative mental health effects that are associated with private self-blame.

4   Caveats and Clarifications

In this section, I will address three questions regarding Don't Suffer in Silence in order to clarify its normative scope and how it relates to other norms governing the appropriateness of self-blame.

Should We Always Express Self-Blame?

Simply put: no. Don't Suffer in Silence states that agents who blame themselves should, *ceteris paribus*, express their self-blame to those they have wronged. But other things are not always equal and so it will not always be appropriate to express self-blame. Like other norms that govern expressions of blame, there will be circumstances in which the morally best thing to do will be to violate Don't Suffer in Silence. It will be interesting to explore at least a few of the conditions under which Don't Suffer in Silence ought to be disregarded.

One of the most important reasons to express self-blame is because such expressions typically serve a reparative function. But there will be situations in which expressing self-blame cannot serve this function. The most straightforward situation in which this occurs is when the victim's relationship with the wrongdoer has already been repaired via some previous expression of self-blame. I will modify the Rose and Sophia case to illustrate this point. Imagine that Rose, upon realising that she was wrong to skip her visit with Sophia to paint her bedroom, blames herself and calls Sophia to express her self-blame. She apologises for letting her friend down and promises to visit the next day, which she does. Over the coming weeks, Rose works to repair her relationship with Sophia and eventually Sophia forgives Rose. But years later, Rose continues to blame herself for how she treated Sophia – she still feels guilty for what she did. In this situation, it's not clear that Rose should express her self-blame to Sophia. The expression of self-blame won't succeed in having a reparative effect, because there is nothing left to repair. In fact, it's imaginable that Sophia could be annoyed or even distressed by Rose's expression of self-blame all these years later. Perhaps it serves only to remind Sophia of a difficult time in her life, one in which she was in the hospital and mistreated by a friend. In this case, it could very well be inappropriate for Rose to express her self-blame to Sophia because doing so would not serve a reparative function and could even cause harm.[11]

---

[11] Another kind of case that is often said to have this structure is one in which the victim does not know that the wrongdoer has wronged them. For example, it's sometimes argued that individuals in monogamous relationships should not confess to cheating on their partners because doing so will only cause their partners to suffer. However, I am not confident that Don't Suffer in Silence should be violated in such cases. Even if a victim is unaware that they have been lied to or betrayed, they have still been wronged (according to most normative views) and this wrong should be repaired. And it's hard to see how a broken promise or betrayal could be repaired without first being confessed to. After all, the victim should have some agency in determining how the wrong is addressed, which cannot happen if they are kept in the dark about the wrong that occurred. Confessing to someone that you have wronged them will no doubt cause them to

However, it's possible that Rose's expression of self-blame, while it would not benefit Sophia, could benefit Rose. Recall that there are wrongdoer-based reasons to express self-blame in addition to victim-based reasons. Expressing guilt can help wrongdoers avoid the undeserved suffering and negative mental health effects that are associated with excessive and mal-adaptive guilt. One could argue that Rose is no longer blameworthy for her treatment of Sophia.[12] And perhaps if Rose expressed her self-blame to Sophia, she would cease feeling guilty for something that she ought not feel guilty for anymore. In this case, it may be permissible for Rose to express self-blame to Sophia. It could even be permissible to do so if it negatively affects Sophia. While it can be painful to be reminded of a difficult time in one's life, it could be worthwhile if it alleviates another individual's undeserved suffering.

However, just as expressions of self-blame do not always serve a repara-tive function, they can also fail to ameliorate feelings of guilt. Indeed, in the case of Rose, one might wonder why she continues to feel guilty for her treatment of Sophia even after she successfully repaired their relation-ship. It's possible that if Rose were to once again express her self-blame to Sophia this would not ease her suffering at all. Perhaps the guilt that Rose feels is both excessive and recalcitrant. If this is the case, then it's not clear that Rose should express her self-blame to Sophia. Rather, she should take other measures to ameliorate her suffering. It's possible that her feelings of excessive and recalcitrant guilt are linked to underlying mental health issues that could be addressed with therapeutic and/or medical treatment.

The above are cases in which the reparative or ameliorative functions of expressing self-blame cannot be served and thus warrant the violation of Don't Suffer in Silence. But there are also situations in which these functions *ought not* be served, and would also require the violation of the norm. A case in which the power dynamic between the wrongdoer and victim is wildly out of alignment can have this structure. Imagine that

---

suffer, but the badness of this suffering may well be outweighed by the goodness of the reparative process that the confession initiates. Of course, there are bound to be exceptions. For instance, some individuals make clear to their partners that they would not want to know if they are cheated on. Confessing to such a partner would not give them agency in the reparative process, but would rather further violate their trust. In this kind of case, expressing self-blame would likely fail to serve the reparative function, and the best thing to do may be to violate Don't Suffer in Silence. Notice, however, that failing to confess would mean that the relationship would go unrepaired and the wrongdoer could experience heightened and maladaptive guilt. This is cer-tainly a bad state of affairs, but may well be better than the alternative. Thanks to an anonymous reviewer for encouraging me to discuss this kind of case.

[12] Whether and why Rose continues to be blameworthy for her treatment of Sophia is an interesting question and one I will return to in the conclusion of the chapter.

the relationship between Rose and Sophia is quite fraught – Sophia has bullied and manipulated Rose for years and demanded a level of care from Rose that she herself does not reciprocate. On the day that Rose decided to paint her bedroom instead of visiting Sophia in the hospital, she had simply had enough of this treatment and decided to take a stand. Rose could still be blameworthy and fittingly guilty for her behaviour in such a case. Sophia, despite her flaws, was in a time of need and there are other ways to take a stand against a bully than to abandon them when they need you most. Nevertheless, if Rose were to express her self-blame to Sophia, perhaps by apologising, this would simply re-establish their toxic relationship. While some relationships are improved through the reparative processes initiated by expressed self-blame, some simply go back to how they were. And in the case of Rose and Sophia, it's not difficult to imagine that an apology from Rose will only feed into the unbalanced power dynamic between the two. However, if Rose refused to express her self-blame to Sophia without even an acknowledgment of her blameworthiness, then their toxic relationship could come to an end. In this case, it may be best if Rose violates Don't Suffer in Silence and keeps her self-blame private, ending her relationship with Sophia. This could be so even if it means that Rose would always feel a bit guilty for how she treated Sophia and Sophia would never receive an apology or acknowledgment for how she was treated. Such a scenario is certainly unfortunate, but the scenario that would arise if Rose expressed self-blame could well be worse.

Just as there are cases in which the reparative function of blame ought not be served, there will also be situations in which blame's ameliorative function should be avoided. A case where the power dynamic between the wrongdoer and victim is heavily asymmetrical can also illustrate this point. Imagine again that the relationship between Rose and Sophia is very dysfunctional, this time because Sophia is terrified of losing Rose as a friend and wants to ensure that Rose never feels discomfort in their relationship. Because of this, Sophia is quick to accept any of Rose's attempts at amends as sufficient to repair their relationship, no matter how meagre or half-hearted. Thus, if Rose were to express the slightest degree of self-blame to Sophia for failing to visit her in the hospital, Sophia would quickly forgive Rose and assure her that she should not feel bad about what she did. And while this would likely ameliorate Rose's guilt, it's not clear that this is a good thing. Those who take blameworthy agents to deserve to feel a particular amount of guilt will likely agree. One could argue that Rose experiences less guilt than she deserves because her expression of self-blame alleviates her guilt too quickly. But one need not be committed to the view that blameworthy agents deserve to feel guilty to think that there is something objectionable about this scenario. Feelings of guilt can lead us to improve our behaviour over time and become better, more respectful agents (Ketelaar & Au, 2003). But if Rose experiences an abbreviated bout of guilt only because her expression of self-blame is met with forgiveness and grace by Sophia, then it's unlikely that Rose will be able to grasp the badness of her actions or be motivated to change her behaviour in the future, which is an unfortunate outcome. In this case, it might be best for Rose to delay expressing her self-blame to Sophia and spend some time blaming herself privately. While this will lead to more suffering on Rose's behalf, it will also allow her to come to see the seriousness of her wrong and truly commit to being a better friend.

This is far from an exhaustive discussion of the situations in which it could be appropriate to violate Don't Suffer in Silence. But the cases discussed above help to illuminate the moral value of expressing self-blame and provide a sense for when all else is not equal when it comes to these expressions. The moral value of expressing self-blame rests on the reparative and ameliorative functions such expressions can serve. But this value can be outweighed, as in cases where reparation and/or amelioration ought not occur, or undercut, as in cases where expressions of self-blame cannot perform their paradigmatic functions.

Is There a Wrong Way to Express Self-Blame?

The answer is surely yes. While I have focused on expressions of self-blame via the reparative behaviours that are characteristic of guilt, there are many ways to express self-blame, and some are worse than others. And though Don't Suffer in Silence, because it is a blamer-specific norm, cannot capture the dimensions along which expressions of self-blame can be better or worse, other conditions can. Just as there are norms that govern acts of other-directed blame, there are also norms that govern acts of self-blame. For example, it's often argued that blame ought to be proportional to the wrong in question, and this surely applies to self-blame as well. In addition to considerations of proportionality, philosophers also evaluate the vices and virtues expressed when we blame others. Gary Watson (2013) argues that blame should not evince the vice of judgmentalism, while Miranda Fricker cautions against blame that reflects a "controlling and censorious attitude towards others" (2016, p. 169). Similarly, there are likely virtues and vices that are distinctive of self-blame which we can evaluate.

For example, simply telling the person you have wronged that you blame yourself is not a particularly good way of expressing self-blame. Philosophers and psychologists have long noted that emotions, including guilt, are effective forms of communication because they convey both sincerity and seriousness (Frank, 1988; McGeer, 2013). After all, expressions of guilt, especially via reparative behaviours, are costly to the wrongdoer and hard to fake. But this is not so for an affectless statement like "I take myself to be blameworthy for how I have treated you." One could easily lie about taking oneself to be blameworthy and such a statement comes with little cost to the wrongdoer. Thus, non-affective statements regarding one's self-blame may very well be dismissed. And if these claims are not believed, then it's hard to see how they could fulfil the reparative function that makes expressions of self-blame morally valuable in the first place. So, one could argue that non-affective expressions of self-blame exhibit the vice of coldness, which renders them inappropriate.[13]

A wrongdoer can also express self-blame poorly even if they express guilt over what they have done. Engaging in the reparative behaviours that are characteristic of guilt is one way to communicate that one feels guilty, but one could also communicate one's guilt by articulating, in great detail, the degree to which one is suffering. But expressing guilt solely by describing the quality and degree of one's suffering would not be a very good way of expressing self-blame. This is not because expressing guilt this way would fail to convince a bystander that one blames oneself – such expressions might very well be successful in this regard. Rather, these expressions of self-blame are criticisable because they do little to serve the reparative function that makes expressing self-blame valuable. Being told by the person who wronged you that they feel very bad for what they have done is a lot like a third-party report on the wrongdoer's guilt. While it might give a victim some comfort to know that the person who wronged them blames themselves for their behaviour, this alone cannot repair the relationship. Victims should be given moral attention and care in light of being wronged, but expressions of self-blame that focus only on the negative affect of feeling guilt cannot do this. Such expressions focus attention

---

[13] This is not to say that the only appropriate way to express self-blame is by expressing an emotion like guilt. It's possible that an agent could blame herself without experiencing guilt, or any other relevant emotion, but express her self-blame by providing her victim with significant restitution or reparations. Because these behaviours are costly to the wrongdoer and hard to fake, they may well be accepted as sincere by the victim. Thus, though affectless, such expressions of self-blame would not exhibit the vice of coldness and could serve to repair the relationship between wrongdoer and victim. Thanks to Carrie Figdor for discussion on this point.

on the wrongdoer, not the victim, and self-blame should not be solely self-regarding. Thus, one could argue that suffering-forward expressions of self-blame exhibit the vice of self-centeredness.

There are likely many other virtues and vices that are exhibited by expressions of self-blame, and there are surely many other objectionable ways to blame oneself. I take this to be an interesting and promising direction for future research, but one that I will not explore further here.

What if the Victim Is Unreachable?

According to Don't Suffer in Silence, we should, other things being equal, express our self-blame to those we have wronged. But what if the victims of our wrongdoings are dead or otherwise inaccessible to us? Don't Suffer in Silence does not have much normative force in such cases, since it makes little sense to argue that an agent should communicate with someone they cannot reach. These are clearly cases where other things are not equal. Still, it's worth considering whether, and how, we should express self-blame when our victims are unreachable.

On first pass, one might argue that while there may be an ameliorative benefit to expressing self-blame in cases where the victim is unreachable, there is no reparative value. After all, expressions of self-blame clearly cannot benefit the victim in such cases. However, I think this would be too quick. Though I have largely focused on expressions of self-blame to victims in this essay, it will be worth briefly considering another audience for our self-blame: the public. Just as we can confess our wrongdoings to our victims, we can also confess them to other members of the moral community. And, public self-blame can serve a reparative function and mend the wrongdoer's relationship with these individuals. When we harm someone, though we only harm them, we also alter our relationship with the moral community at large (Scanlon, 2008). Others come to see us as disrespectful and untrustworthy and alter their relationships with us in light of this fact. Public expressions of self-blame, even if they cannot be expressed to one's victims, could serve to repair one's relationships with the moral community.

But what would expressions of public self-blame look like? When we express self-blame to our victims, we typically do things like apologise, make amends, and remedy the negative consequences of our actions. But it would be ill-fitting and even impossible to engage in these kinds of reparative behaviours with those we have not wronged. Still, there are a variety of behaviours we can utilise to communicate to others that we feel guilty for what we have done. In fact, there is interesting empirical work on how agents express guilt when they cannot repair their relationships with their victims. Rob Nelissen and Marcel Zeelenberg (2009) found that guilt evoked self-punishing behaviours, but only if there was no way to compensate for the guilt-inducing transgression. The researchers labelled this the Dobby Effect, a reference to the house-elf in the *Harry Potter* series who was forced to punish himself if he violated his masters' orders. While this kind of behaviour may seem maladaptive and morally suspect,[14] Nelissen and Zeelenberg suggest that it could have an important function: "Self-punishment may signal appreciation of and future compliance with violated standards … The Dobby Effect then, is a public sign of reconciliation that occurs if actual reconciliation (by compensating the victim) is impossible" (2009, p. 121).

So, one could argue that wrongdoers should express self-blame to the public even if they cannot express self-blame to their victims. While distinct norms would no doubt govern expressions of public self-blame, it's interesting to note that the reasons to engage in this practice are very similar to the reasons to express self-blame to victims: both forms of self-blame can serve a reparative function. Indeed, reparative factors have played an important role in evaluating a number of the dimensions along which expressions of self-blame can be better and worse. Given the important role reparative concerns play in the ethics of self-blame, perhaps they play an important role in blameworthiness itself as well. I'll explore this possibility in the concluding section of this essay.

5 Conclusion: Insights into Blameworthiness

Until now, I've focused on the ethics of self-blame and remained silent on matters of blameworthiness. But the two are intimately connected, and developments in the ethics of blame can shed light on the nature of blameworthiness (and vice versa). For example, when determining *to whom* and *how* agents should express self-blame, questions regarding reparations play a central role. Given the importance of reparative factors in the ethics of self-blame, they may also be relevant to blameworthiness. And, perhaps by developing an account of blameworthiness that makes room for

---

[14] One might raise Terry Gross's worries about pre-emptive self-punishment, for example. But pre-emptive self-punishment is very different from public self-punishment. When we engage in pre-emptive self-punishment, we do so in order to avoid engaging in the reparative process with our victims. But public self-punishment, when done well, is a way of engaging in the reparative process with the public, despite being unable to do so with our victims.

reparations, we can begin to solve difficult problems that other accounts of blameworthiness have faced.

Take the puzzle of blameworthiness over time, which Andreas Carlsson considers in his contribution to this volume. On the one hand, if an agent is blameworthy simply because they performed some wrong action, then this fact will always be true of them, and one could conclude that they are blameworthy forever. But this seems counterintuitive – surely blameworthiness should diminish over time. But if blameworthiness doesn't depend solely on wrongdoing, what other feature is at play that allows blameworthiness to diminish? Given our discussion above, one potential answer is: reparations. If an agent is blameworthy for wronging someone, they will remain blameworthy for their wrong until they try to make reparations. This account can easily explain how blameworthiness can diminish over time – agents cease to be blameworthy when they repair their wrongs and the relationships they have damaged.[15]

This view has the interesting implication that two agents can perform qualitatively identical wrong actions but be blameworthy, and the fitting targets of blame, for drastically different periods of time. But this strikes me as quite sensible. If two friends each break a promise to me, but one apologises while the other never acknowledges the wrong, I find it perfectly appropriate to cease blaming the first friend while continuing to blame the second. This view also has the implication that some agents will be blameworthy forever. Recall the case of Rose and Sophia in which it was better, all things considered, for Rose to never express self-blame to Sophia because in doing so she could end their toxic relationship. In this case, Rose would continue to be blameworthy for how she treated Sophia for all time, since she never attempted to repair her wrong. While this is surely unfortunate, I also take it to be a defensible implication of the view. After all, Rose never acknowledged or addressed

---

[15] Carlsson provides his own elegant solution to this puzzle. First, he defends the Blameworthiness as Deserved Guilt (DG) view, according to which blameworthy agents deserve to suffer a particular amount of guilt. On this view, once an agent experiences the requisite amount of guilt, they will no longer deserve to feel guilty, and will thus no longer be blameworthy. There is a way of rendering the view sketched above as consistent with Carlsson's view. For example, one could argue that reparations play a role in determining how much guilt an agent deserves to experience. According to this account, an agent would remain blameworthy, and thus deserving of guilt, until they try to repair their wrong. But there is also a way of rendering the two views distinct. One could argue that being blameworthy involves both deserving to feel guilty *and* owing reparations to one's victims (where reparations don't determine deserved guilt). On this view, an agent who doesn't attempt to make reparations would continue to be blameworthy *even if* they suffered the requisite amount of guilt. It's beyond the scope of this chapter to explore these views more fully, though doing so could prove to be an interesting future project.

her wrongdoing to Sophia. It would be appropriate for Sophia to harbour resentment towards Rose just as it would be appropriate for Rose to feel guilty for what she had done.

The above is far from a full articulation of an account of blameworthiness, and much more would need to be said to make it theoretically palatable. This is merely an illustration of how insights from the ethics of self-blame can alter our understanding of blameworthiness. By coming to understand the important role reparations play in the ethics of self-blame, we can begin to develop accounts of blameworthiness that make room for reparations as well.

6 Acknowledgments

I am grateful to Jahsie Ault, Luara Ferricioli, Carrie Figdor, David Glick, and an anonymous reviewer for providing comments on earlier drafts of this chapter. I would also like to thank the audience at my University of Sydney seminar presentation for their very helpful questions and feedback.

CHAPTER 7

How Should We Feel about Recalcitrant Emotions?

Krista K. Thomason

In everyday moral experience, we judge ourselves for our emotional responses. We feel guilty when we are irritated with our children. We are horrified by a sudden malicious pleasure. To awkwardly paraphrase Joan Jett, we hate ourselves for loving people we shouldn't. Often the emotions that we criticize are recalcitrant emotions: they are emotions that we do not endorse or that conflict with our considered judgments. Fear of things that are not in fact dangerous is often taken to be the paradigm case of a recalcitrant emotion – I sincerely believe that the spider on the bathroom floor is not dangerous and yet I fear it anyway.[1] Most of the philosophical literature on recalcitrant emotions focuses on (a) whether and how they are possible or (b) whether and how they are irrational (see, for e.g., Greenspan, 1988; Mele, 1989; D'Arms and Jacobson, 2003; Räikkä, 2005; Brady, 2009; Benbaji, 2013; Döring, 2015; & Helm, 2015). My interest here is in the ways we blame ourselves for recalcitrant emotions. On the surface, this self-criticism seems familiar and straightforward. If I have an emotion that I think I shouldn't have, it seems natural for me to judge myself for it. I aim to show that it is harder than it looks to explain self-blame for recalcitrant emotions. I will argue recalcitrance alone does not give us a reason to feel any particular way about our emotions and it is not sufficient grounds for self-blame.

To make my case, I will first survey three possible ways of understanding self-blame for recalcitrant emotions: we blame ourselves because they are irrational, we morally blame ourselves, and we blame ourselves for lacking self-control. I explain the disadvantages of each of these possibilities. I then conclude by arguing that in order to determine how we should feel about our recalcitrant emotions we must first do what I will call emotional self-interpretation. We have to work out the relationship between the particular emotion and our sense of self in order to know how we should respond.

---

[1] Greenspan (1988), D'Arms and Jacobson (2003), Brady (2007, 2009), Tappolet (2012), Benbaji (2013), Döring (2015), and Helm (2015) all use fear as an example of a recalcitrant emotion.

Before I begin, let me make some preliminary remarks. I will not stake out a position about what emotions are or are not – whether they are judgments, perceptions, or construals. I am interested in the phenomenology of self-blame, and when we blame ourselves for our recalcitrant emotions, it's not clear that we're using any of these distinctions to make sense of what we're doing. Additionally, I will not stake out a position about the precise nature of self-blame. I will not assume that there is one specific attitude or emotion that counts as self-blame. Although guilt is often taken to be the primary emotion of self-blame, anger, frustration, horror, shame, embarrassment, and disappointment also seem to be ways of experiencing self-blame. Here I will just say that I blame myself for an emotion when I *negatively evaluate* myself for feeling it. "Negatively evaluate" can mean that I make a negative judgment about myself for feeling a certain emotion or that I feel a second self-critical emotion (sometimes called a meta-emotion) about the first emotion.[2] Since I am adopting this wide definition, I use terms like "self-blame" and "self-criticism" interchangeably. Finally, I leave aside the question of whether other people have standing to blame us for recalcitrant emotions. Although the arguments I make here could potentially be used to explore that question, I will assume that self-blame and other-blame require separate accounts.

1   Are We Blaming Ourselves for Irrationality?

Although there is some debate in the literature about the precise definition, the best rough description of a recalcitrant emotion is that it conflicts with an agent's considered (or better) judgment or belief. An emotion is recalcitrant because it is "at odds with a decisive better judgment of the subject" (Mele, 1989, p. 279), because it "conflicts with an evaluative judgment" (Benbaji, 2013, p. 577; Brady, 2009, p. 413), because "the world is not as the emotion presents it" (Helm, 2015, p. 420), because it "persists despite the agent's conflicting judgment or belief" (Döring, 2015, p. 381), or because it "exists despite the agent's making a judgment that is in tension with it" (D'Arms & Jacobson, 2003, p. 129). Since we usually claim that we feel recalcitrant emotions for no reason and since we are often critical of ourselves for these emotions, it's easy to draw the conclusion that we must be blaming ourselves for being irrational.[3] Although

---

[2] For an explanation and defense of meta-emotions, see Jäger and Bartsch (2006).
[3] Greenspan (1988), Mele (1989), D'Arms and Jacobson (2003), Brady (2009), Benbaji (2013), and Helm (2015) argue that recalcitrant emotions are irrational.

this move appears straightforward, explaining exactly how this irrationality works turns out to be harder than it looks.[4] Conclusions that we
draw about the irrationality of recalcitrant emotions partly depend on
what we think emotions are,[5] but to get a sense of why explaining the
irrationality is difficult, let us consider Greenspan's famous case of Fido
the harmless dog.

Greenspan describes the case this way: "Ever since an attack by a rabid
dog, we suppose, an agent has felt fear in the presence of all dogs, including Fido, though Fido is well known to him" (1988, pp. 17–18). As the story
goes, the agent has recalcitrant fear: he judges that Fido is not dangerous
and yet he is nevertheless afraid. Philosophers who use this case sometimes
ignore Greenspan's opening phrase, namely that the agent was some time
ago *attacked by a rabid dog*. Those who have never been charged by an
angry dog might not quite grasp the power of this opening moment. Being
attacked by any dog is terrifying enough; being attacked by a rabid dog
ups the ante. Our agent could have been killed by this rabid dog. Luckily,
he survived, but then had to go on to receive (no doubt painful) rabies
treatment because the rabies might also have killed him. Given his experience, every dog he sees might reasonably dredge up a painful and terrifying
memory. Described this way, what is it exactly that makes this person's fear
irrational?

The main reason that his fear seems irrational is because Fido is not in
fact dangerous. The case in favor of irrationality for recalcitrant emotions
relies heavily on the notion of emotions having "fit" or "formal objects."[6]
Fear tracks, arises from judgments of, construes, or perceives the dangerous. Fido is not dangerous; therefore, fear is tracking, perceiving, or
construing something that isn't there. This is why we say that we have "no
reason" to feel whatever emotion is identified as recalcitrant. The trouble with the Fido case is that the agent's fear is tracking the dangerous

---

[4] For discussions of the problems with identifying irrational emotions, see Davidson (1985) and
Döring (2015).
[5] Solomon (2007) and Nussbaum (2001) provide examples of broadly judgmentalist accounts,
which are thought to have special problems explaining recalcitrant emotions. For explanations
as to why, see Greenspan (1988), Helm (2001), D'Arms and Jacobson (2003), Brady (2009), and
Benbaji (2013). Brady (2007), Döring (2015), and Tappolet (2012) offer explanations of recalcitrant emotions using perceptual analogies. For criticisms of this strategy, see Helm (2001,
2015). As Benbaji summarizes it, "Cognitivists ... cannot avoid ascribing a contradiction to the
agent, while non-cognitivists cannot explain why the recalcitrant emotion is irrational at all"
(2013, p. 580).
[6] For discussions of fit, correctness conditions, and formal objects, see D'Arms and Jacobson
(2000), Teroni (2007), and Deonna and Teroni (2012a). For arguments against emotional fit, see
Yang (2016).

under some description of "the dangerous." Maybe Fido poses no immediate danger, but this account of "the dangerous" is too narrow. The agent's bad experience provides him some reason to be uneasy about all dogs, including Fido. We can argue that the agent's fear in the Fido case is tracking or perceiving "the dangerous," but in a non-obvious way. There is nothing irrational about being afraid of the type of animal that at one point threatened your life.

Additionally, fear that looks irrational might be tracking something that is outside the scope of an emotion's typical fit or formal object. Return to the example of the non-venomous spider in the bathroom. What if my fear of the spider is not because it is dangerous, but because it is creepy-crawly? We are not only afraid of things because they are dangerous; we are also afraid of the disgusting, the eerie, the creepy, or the uncanny.[7] I see the spider in my bathroom, watching its little hairy legs creep across the floor. I imagine if I get too close it might suddenly scurry madly across my foot or up my leg. Notice that my fear of the creepy-crawly is not mitigated if you tell me that the spider isn't venomous – creepy-crawlies don't have to be venomous to be scary. People sometimes have a difficult time explaining why they are afraid of things that other people aren't afraid of, and so they respond to persistent questioning with "I don't know why I'm scared, I just am."[8] Our reasons aren't always easy to articulate, especially when we are afraid of things that don't seem obviously fearsome.[9] Fears that looks to be irrational might not be once we realize that they are attuned to atypical objects.[10]

Setting aside these issues, let's suppose we have a genuine case of recalcitrance with my fear of the spider on the bathroom floor. Let's stipulate that there is no context we can give for the fear and that I have no other reason to be afraid. If I blame myself, we now need to understand why or how I am blaming myself for experiencing an irrational emotion. What

---

[7] Windsor (2019) argues for a claim like this about the uncanny, although he maintains that we find the uncanny threatening in some way.

[8] In my view, this point wrongly gets cashed out as "unconscious" judgments or beliefs (Greenspan, 1988, p. 19; Räikkä, 2005, p. 477; Benbaji, 2013, p. 579). We can feel and think things that we cannot readily put into words, but those things aren't unconscious.

[9] Objectless emotions illustrate this: we can be sad or happy without being able to explain exactly why. Oddly, objectless emotions don't seem to strike people as particularly irrational. See Lamb (1987) and Price (2006) for helpful discussions. For questions about the articulacy requirement for reasons, see Ebels-Duggan (2019).

[10] These explanations help explain why agents might not warn others about the things they fear (Greenspan, 1988, p. 19). Fears that involve past history are likely attached the memories of the agent; he is reliving his own terrifying experience. There's no need to warn others of the creepy-crawly because it's not dangerous.

rational requirement is my emotion violating? Philosophers are divided on this question: some have provided possible answers while others deny that there is any such requirement.[11] Although I can't fully argue for this conclusion here, I agree with the latter camp that there is no rational requirement to avoid emotional recalcitrance.

Consider how difficult it is to identify the rational requirement that we supposedly violate when we feel recalcitrant emotions. Let's examine one plausible candidate: an emotion is irrational when its correctness conditions fail to hold. Fear, in this account, is irrational when its object is not really dangerous. The rational requirement we violate here would be something like: we (rationally) should only be afraid of things that are really dangerous.[12] As I've just pointed out, however, fear does not always track the dangerous and what counts as "dangerous" will vary with the personal history of the agent. Additionally, the claim that recalcitrant fear violates a rational requirement of correctness presupposes the idea that there is some identifiable standard that we can use to determine which objects are "really" dangerous. As Todd writes, "Even if … fear [is properly directed] at the 'dangerous,' this tells us nothing in itself about what features of the world will or ought to be construed as … a danger" (2014, p. 98). For example, a bear attack can cause serious physical harm, but it is also statistically unlikely, even among hikers.[13] Suppose I am hiking and I want my emotions to meet the rational requirement: should I be afraid of a bear attack or not? Should my fear track the statistically likely or the physically damaging? There seems to be no non-arbitrary way to answer this question.[14] Additionally, there seem to be cases where it is rational to not fear things that are actually dangerous. Driving poses a great deal of danger to human beings, but given how prevalent it is in our daily lives, we are likely to think that someone who actually fears driving – someone who tries to avoid driving and warns others against it – is irrational. We also know that our emotional responses to the same object vary for reasons that

---

[11] Brady argues that recalcitrant emotions violate both practical and epistemic norms of rationality (2009, p. 427). Helm argues when our judgments and emotions conflict, we experience rational pressure to resolve the conflict, in part because emotions are motivating (2015, p. 431). Tappolet argues that we face a rational requirement to make our emotional systems more reliable (2012, p. 221). Döring denies that recalcitrant emotions violate any rational requirement (2015).

[12] D'Arms argues in favor of this sort of view (2005). For arguments against this position, see Todd (2014).

[13] From the U.S. National Park Service website: "Since 1979, Yellowstone has hosted over 118 million visits. During this time, 44 people were injured by grizzly bears in the park. For all park visitors combined, the chances of being injured by a grizzly bear are approximately 1 in 2.7 million visits." See www.nps.gov/yell/learn/nature/injuries.htm.

[14] Todd raises similar issues with regard to emotions and the objectivity of values (2014).

have nothing to do with rationality.[15] As Döring puts it, "The evaluative properties that the different emotions attribute to their targets thus are relative to the individual: what is dangerous to me need not be dangerous to you" (2015, p. 394). We feel different emotions about the same object because we value it or judge it differently. You love roller coasters because you are thrilled by their speed, and I hate them for exactly that reason. We both appeal to the same facts in explaining our emotions: the speed of the roller coaster. If we know this variation occurs, there is no way to determine which of us feels the right emotion unless we assume there is only one correct way to value or judge roller coasters.

One way to address this problem might be to adopt the claim that recalcitrant emotions are irrational when they conflict with an agent's "better" judgment. Determining what counts as an agent's better judgment will be complicated if we accept the idea that emotions and judgments can both track values or features of the world.[16] Because of this, we can't assume that when there is a conflict the emotion will be wrong and the judgment will be right. There are times when our emotions are telling us the "right" information and our considered judgments are not.[17] For example, feelings of unease and discomfort have led people to get out of situations that were in fact unsafe even though they had no concrete evidence that something bad was about to happen. An emotion that conflicts with our judgments might turn out to be more accurately tracking values or features in the world than our judgments.

There is no doubt something intuitive about the idea that when we blame ourselves for recalcitrant emotions we're blaming ourselves for irrationality. As D'Arms and Jacobson point out, people "often say things like 'I can't help being afraid' or 'fear isn't rational'; that is, they do not claim their fear to be responsive to evidence" (2003, p. 130). Intuitive appeals aside, we seem unable to articulate what rational requirement recalcitrant emotions violate or why we blame ourselves for failing to meet it.

2 Are We Morally Blaming Ourselves?

If the irrationality of recalcitrant emotions doesn't seem to capture our practices of self-blame, there is a second option. Perhaps when we blame ourselves for recalcitrant emotions, we are simply blaming ourselves for moral failings. For example, Tom has long been envious of the success

---

[15] Helm refers to this as the "subject-relativity of evaluative properties" (2015, p. 429).
[16] For lengthy discussions of these sorts of claims, see Greenspan (1992), Helm (2001), Roberts (2003), D'Arms and Jacobson (2003), Teroni (2007), and Deonna and Teroni (2012a).
[17] Helm (2001, 2015) and Arpaly (2000) have examples like this.

of Betty, his colleague. Tom learns that Betty has just received the fifth rejection on a paper she is trying to publish and "he finds that he is pleased by the news" (Mele, 1989, p. 283). Tom believes his feelings of pleasure are unwarranted, but "unwarranted" can be interpreted in two different ways.[18] Tom might believe that he has no reason to feel pleasure at this news – that this news is not the proper object of pleasure.[19] But Tom might also think that his pleasure is morally unwarranted. He might believe that he is feeling some sort of malice or *Schadenfreude*, and that feeling plea- sure at another person's pain is morally wrong. His feelings are "unwar- ranted" in the sense that they are morally unjustifiable.

Although examples like these are common, it is unclear whether morally unjustifiable emotions are recalcitrant.[20] We typically think of recalcitrant emotions as somehow mistaken: my fear of the spider is incorrect because it wrongly presents the spider as dangerous. Tom's malicious glee at Betty's failure does not incorrectly characterize her failure.[21] Since Tom is already envious of Betty's success, her successes will pain him and her failures will please him – this is how envy works. The fact that Tom's envy is petty, immature, or vicious does not entail that his malicious glee toward Betty's failure is mistaken. We can say that Tom feels malicious glee against his better judgment, but what "better judgment" means here is different than what it means in the spider case. In Tom's case, "better judgment" means morally better or more virtuous whereas in the spider case "better judg- ment" means correct or accurate judgment.

There is another way we might understand self-blame that might pre- serve the recalcitrance. We can see how it works by appealing to Smith's rational relations view (2004, 2005, 2018). In Smith's view, we can blame ourselves for what we feel because our emotions reflect our values, moral judgments, or characters.[22] Our values and judgments are not always obvi- ous or transparent to us, so our emotional responses can sometimes be more morally telling than what we claim. When we morally blame our- selves for our recalcitrant emotions, it's because they reveal moral defects that either we would rather not acknowledge or that we do not realize are

---

[18] I take this wording from Stocker (1987, p. 60) and Mele (1989, p. 280). Mele does not explain exactly which interpretation of "unwarranted" he means in the example.

[19] I'm relying here on the distinction between fit and appropriateness. See D'Arms & Jacobson (2000, pp. 77–82).

[20] D'Arms and Jacobson (2000) have made a similar argument about the assumption that morally bad emotions are irrational.

[21] Roberts resists this conclusion in regards to envy. He argues that envy wrongly presents its target as a competitor (1991).

[22] For problems with Smith's account of attributability, see Shoemaker (2011).

there. I say I trust my partner, but my jealousy shows I do not. My anger over the small slight signals that I am petty or impatient even if I don't see myself that way. My fear of the spider is showing that in spite of how I see myself, I am actually cowardly. In cases like these, our emotions conflict with what we claim to value or judge, so they share this feature with typical recalcitrant emotions. Instead of blaming myself because it is irrational to fear the spider, I blame myself because I ought to be brave and my fear of the harmless spider is revealing that I am not.

This description still doesn't quite preserve recalcitrance. It turns out that our emotions are reflecting our values – just not the ones we claim to have. The emotions conflict with our declared values, but they reflect latent or concealed values. Unlike the typical case of recalcitrance, the emotions are not groundless or without reason. I fear the spider in the bathroom because deep down I am a coward. Cowards are afraid of things like harmless spiders, so my fear is not mistaken in this respect. It is working as it should, given that I am a coward. When I judge that I shouldn't fear the spider in this case, what I am actually saying is I shouldn't be a coward. Blaming myself for that fear is really no different than Tom blaming himself for his malicious glee. The only difference is that while Tom recognizes and acknowledges his envy toward Betty, I claim not be a coward even though I am. The object of my blame is not my emotion itself, but rather the hidden moral defect my emotion reveals.

The trouble with moral blame for recalcitrant emotions is that if we preserve true recalcitrance, the conditions for moral blame seem not to be met. If an emotion is truly detached from what we value or judge, then we cannot be answerable for it in the right way. As Shoemaker argues, "Your demand to me to justify an attitude reflecting a groundless emotional commitment will be without a point as a demand, for I am simply devoid of the resources necessary to engage with your communicative attempt" (2011, p. 611). If my fear of the spider is not a reflection of latent cowardice or the result of a concealed judgment that the spider really is dangerous, my fear is not really a part of my "rational network" (Smith, 2005, p. 255). Without this connection, it is unclear how I could be answerable for my feelings in the way that seems to be required for moral self-blame.[23] To see the problem, compare fear that is sufficiently detached from values or judgments to an irritable mood. Surely there are times when an irritable mood arises for reasons (stress at work or strained family relations), but

---

[23] For arguments about when self-blame is deserved or appropriate, see Clarke (2016) and Carlsson (2017).

sometimes moods arise for no reason. We blame ourselves when we act like jerks because we are in a bad mood, but we typically don't morally blame ourselves for just being in a bad mood. In part, we don't blame ourselves because a mood is just a mood. It's precisely not a reflection of a larger problem, a bad judgment, or a character flaw.

If moods float free from our rational network, surely emotions can as well. We have plenty of examples of what we might call intrusive emotions: unwelcome or surprising emotions that from our perspective seem to come from nowhere. Baier gives the example of someone who suddenly feels suicidal while standing in front of the sea (1990, p. 17). Shoemaker talks about a parent continuing to love a child even though the child is a serial killer (2011, p. 610). Philosophers who work on emotions have spent years trying to show that they are not arational forces that overtake us. In doing so, we have tended to forget that emotions are not always susceptible to reason. We can surely point to examples where people have talked themselves out of a feeling, have habituated themselves out of damaging emotions, or have over time come to care about something that originally meant nothing to them. But these strategies don't always work; human experience is littered with examples of people trying to unsuccessfully exert this kind of pressure on their emotions. All the right judgments can be in place yet the emotion comes anyway or it does not come when we expect it to. Our emotions can surprise and confound us.

If there are times when our emotions really are unconnected from our judgments, moral self-blame would seem like an odd reaction. Emotions that are detached from our evaluative judgments don't reveal anything morally dubious. It seems that we would no more blame ourselves for them than we would blame ourselves for our moods. If my emotions are surprising to me, I might be confused or bewildered by them. Confusion and bewilderment, however, do not seem to amount to moral self-blame.

3   Are We Blaming Ourselves for Lack of Self-Control?

Another way to understand self-blame for recalcitrant emotions is that we blame ourselves for insufficient self-control.[24] When we experience emotions that seem unwarranted or baseless, we often say things like "Get a hold of yourself" or "Pull yourself together." Blaming ourselves for a lack of self-control might explain our frequent feelings of frustration toward

---

[24] See Korsgaard (1996) for an example. For arguments that raise questions about this claim, see Adams (1985) and Smith (2008).

recalcitrant emotions. We're often frustrated at things we can't control – I can't get the lawnmower to start, so I kick it because I can't do anything else. As Smith puts it, "We expect grown-up people to exercise some control over the behavioral manifestations of their attitudes" (2008, p. 118).[25] Being in control of our emotions is a mark of maturity or adulthood. Children emote at the drop of a hat, but grown-ups aren't supposed to.

Some philosophers have pointed out that self-blame for lack of self-control appears similar to self-blame for akratic actions (e.g., Mele, 1989; Benbaji, 2013). I ought to be able to stop myself from eating that extra slice of pizza, but alas the pizza wins. If this is so, then perhaps this form of self-blame is rational criticism after all. What makes akratic action irrational and to what extent it is a rational requirement that we not act akratically is a storied debate that I cannot delve into (for a small sample, see Davidson, 1985, 2006a, 2006b; Mele, 1989; Arpaly, 2000; Jones, 2003; Kolodny, 2005; Kalis, 2018). What I can do is point out the questions that others have raised about the connections (or lack thereof) between akratic actions, self-control, and rationality. As I will suggest, these same questions can be raised about recalcitrant emotions, self-control, and rationality.

Is there a rational requirement to control our emotions? We should be wary here. Part of the reason that exercising self-control over our emotions seems like a rational requirement might have to do with the long-held belief that emotions are essentially irrational. Even though philosophers have long argued against this view, that doesn't mean it has translated into everyday practice. As Calhoun puts it, there is "a lingering sense that emotions are not trustworthy" (2004, p. 191).[26] Despite philosophers' efforts, it is common for people to think that emotions cloud judgment rather than enhance it or coexist happily with it. It is common for people to think that "emotional" is just a synonym for "irrational." Self-blame for being unable to control our emotions may in many cases be a shadow of the problematic conceptions of emotions as unruly forces that lead us astray.

If we do think that exercising control over our emotions is a rational requirement, we are still faced with the task of explaining how. Once again, the connection is not as straightforward as it seems. To see the difficulties, consider first the case of akratic actions. For instance, Mele argues that not every exercise of self-control is in the service of one's better judgment (1989,

---

[25] Smith cashes out this criticism in terms of moral blame.
[26] For examples of feminist critiques about the irrationality of emotions, see Jaggar (1989) and Calhoun (2004). For arguments about the intersection between emotional criticism and race, see Spelman (1989) and Cherry (2018).

pp. 54–55). Suppose I forgo the extra pizza because I am some strange sort of Pythagorean and I have a belief that one should refrain from destroying too many triangle-shaped objects. It's hard to say that my self-control is working in favor of my better judgment. Additionally, Arpaly argues that there are times when acting against one's better judgment is more rational than acting in concert with it (2000, pp. 491–493). Suppose I am extremely regimented in my food intake: I never indulge even on my birthday or other celebrations. My food inflexibility actually makes me rather joyless to be around. In this case, my temptation to indulge in the extra pizza might be a kind of nascent awakening that my rigid attitudes about food are preventing me from enjoying my life. If I were to lack self-control and act akratically in this case, it would be the more rational thing to do.

These same problems arise in the case of recalcitrant emotions. I may exercise self-control over my fear of the spider because I wrongly believe that if the spider senses my fear it will summon especially fearsome battle spiders to come to its aid. Alternatively, I might control my feelings of fear because I aspire to a warrior ethic that holds any and all emotions to be a sign of weakness. Somewhat silly fictional cases aside, we can point to examples where an emotion that appeared to be recalcitrant was actually attuned to something real and serious that the agent overlooked in her reasoning (for examples of cases like this, see Jaggar, 1989; Arpaly, 2000; & Jones, 2003). Likewise, it isn't always the case that failing to control our emotions is rational. A sudden outpouring of love, a genuine flood of tears, or an outburst of anger from someone pushed too far may all be akratic and yet rational at the same time.

Perhaps self-blame for a lack of self-control is instead a species of moral self-blame. If we think that mature people are able to keep their emotions in check, maybe a lack of emotional composure could be understood as moral failing. Similar to the problem of rationality and akrasia, it is notoriously difficult to explain how self-control is morally good in general (see Kalis, 2018; Brownstein, 2018 for detailed discussions). One problem is that there is no single answer about what self-control amounts to. As Brownstein points out, people can exercise their capacity for self-control when they develop bad habits, harm other people, and harm themselves (2018, pp. 588–590). By contrast, some philosophers have argued that self-control has a built-in normative dimension because of its relationship to moral agency (see, e.g., Kalis, 2018; Korsgaard, 2009). In views like these, self-control provides the pre-conditions for acting morally because it is what allows us to act on reasons (Kalis, 2018, p. 76; Korsgaard, 2009, pp. 69–72). Even if we grant that self-control has a built-in normative dimension, it may not follow from this conclusion that we should exercise control over our emotions. The kind of self-control needed for moral agency need not dictate control over emotions unless we think that emotions are threatening to moral agency. The impetus to control our emotions is often driven by the underlying assumption that they are arational disruptive forces. Once we abandon this idea, it is harder to claim that we should, all things considered, control our emotions as best we can. Additionally, our emotional experiences can reflect morally valuable responses and commitments, and not feeling strong enough emotions can be a mark of moral insensitivity. In some circumstances losing one's emotional composure can be more morally praiseworthy than keeping it.

4   Self-Blame and Self-Interpretation

So far I have argued that self-blame for irrationality, moral self-blame, and self-blame for lack of self-control do not fully capture our practices of self-criticism for recalcitrant emotions. One possible result of my arguments is that our practices of self-blame are simply misguided. Maybe we are simply wrong to blame ourselves for our recalcitrant emotions. Perhaps we would be better off developing a more accepting attitude toward emotions that conflict with our judgments, especially if we are willing to grant that there are times when our emotions are right and our judgments are wrong.

Although this conclusion is appealing, it too quickly dismisses our practices of self-criticism of our emotions. Emotional self-blame is ubiquitous, and even though common practices can be misguided, we should at least try to explain it before rejecting it. Rather than dismissing the practice of self-blame altogether, I will defend the claim that emotional recalcitrance all by itself is not sufficient for self-blame. Instead, emotional recalcitrance indicates the presence of a conflict within what Döring has called "agential identity" (2015, pp. 399–400). Döring appeals to agential identity as a way to explain the appearance of rational conflict in recalcitrant emotions. On this view, an agent has reason to resolve a conflict between her emotion and judgment if it forces her to deny an important part of herself, but not because she is rationally required to resolve it (2015, p. 400). The reason a hiker, to use Döring's example, should conquer her fear of heights is because the hiker would have to deny part of her identity by giving up hiking (2015, p. 400). I suggest that Döring's arguments can be extended to self-blame for recalcitrant emotions. That is, the mere presence of an emotion that conflicts with my judgment doesn't give me a reason to blame myself nor does it give me a reason to resolve the conflict. Expanding on Döring's arguments,

I argue that in order to determine how we should feel or what we should do about our recalcitrant emotions, we first have to do the work of what I call emotional self-interpretation.[27] Emotional self-interpretation involves working out the relationship between our emotions and our sense of who we are.

To help illustrate, start with a case of emotional self-interpretation that is straightforward. I hate roller coasters. I've ridden them a few times and every time I've been afraid. My fear comes as no surprise to me, given that I don't think of myself as a thrill-seeker. In this case, my sense of myself and my emotions point in the same direction. Moreover, my emotions and my sense of myself developed together. I tried roller coasters, I hated them, and I started to realize that these sorts of experiences weren't for me. Initially, I thought my fear might have been due to inexperience with roller coasters, so I didn't take it as definitive. Over time, I realized my fear was more telling than I first believed, especially when I found myself afraid in other thrill-seeking scenarios. My emotions helped me learn that I am not a thrill-seeker, and now that I think of myself this way, they are reflections of that trait. What I have described here is the "ongoing emotional-reflective process" where our emotional responses and our sense of ourselves develop and change together (Solomon, 2007, p. 265).

By contrast, recalcitrant emotions pose a self-interpretative problem for us. When we experience a recalcitrant emotion, we are faced with parts of ourselves that point in different directions. Return to my fear of the spider. On the one hand, I have my belief that the spider cannot hurt me and my desire not to be a coward. On the other hand, I have my emotional reaction to the spider. These two conflicting pieces of information force me to start asking questions about myself. Am I a person who is afraid of spiders even when they are not dangerous? If I am, does this make me a coward or not? Is my fear just a reaction or are my judgments about the harmlessness of spiders actually false bravado? Notice that the mere fact that my emotion conflicts with my judgment tells me nothing other than that there is a conflict. We know that emotional reactions can sometimes be more revealing than our stated judgments. I can't decide that my fear is the false thing without doing the work of self-interpretation.

Suppose it turns out that I am afraid of spiders even though I know they aren't harmful. What should I do? The implication of the arguments I made earlier is that there is no generalizable answer to this question. What

---

[27] I'm borrowing this term from Taylor (1985). Solomon argues that our emotions are part of having and creating a "sense of self" (2007, p. 222). Smith also uses this terminology; she claims that spontaneous attitudes present us with an "interpretative difficulty" (2005, p. 255). I have elsewhere discussed self-interpretation and shame (Thomason, 2018, pp. 169–172).

I do about my fear or how I feel about it will depend on my emotional self-interpretation. If I conclude that independent adults should take care of bugs in their houses and I aspire to this, then I should do something about my fear. I could try to conquer it by reading articles about the positive role that spiders play in the ecosystem or anthropomorphizing spiders so that they no longer seem scary. Notice, however, that doing something about my fear might just require me to figure out a way to manage it without getting rid of it. For example, I might have to coach myself through the process of catching the spider and putting it outside or squishing it with a long-handled broom. Alternatively, I might conclude through the process of self-interpretation that I am an arachnophobe. Plenty of people simply live with an intense fear of spiders. If they manage their lives in relatively healthy ways, there's no reason to think that they should work extensively to get over their fears. If they find that their arachnophobia interferes significantly with their lives or prevents them from being who they want to be, they may then have a reason to conquer their fears or blame themselves. When our emotions conflict with our judgments, it is the process of emotional self-interpretation that will determine what we do next.

One of the possible results of emotional self-interpretation is that we should remain emotionally ambivalent. We often assume that emotional ambivalence is a bad state to be in because on the whole it's best not to be conflicted or confused. Yet, as Coates has argued, there are reasons to resist this view. Coates gives the example of Agamemnon in Aeschylus's tragedy *Oresteia* (2017, p. 436). Agamemnon is faced with an impossible choice: he must either sacrifice his daughter or abandon the Greek expedition to Troy. As Coates argues, one of Agamemnon's major flaws is that he makes up his mind too quickly when he decides to kill his daughter (2017, pp. 438–439). It would have been better for Agamemnon to remain conflicted over his decision because the absence of conflict signals a failure to appreciate the seriousness of his crime. Coates's arguments are focused on ambivalent agency, but we can extend these arguments to ambivalent emotions. Imagine someone who becomes estranged from her family after years of conflict. Although she feels relieved, she also feels guilty for withdrawing. In this case, her ambivalent feelings may indicate that she recognizes that she too played some role in the conflict that ended the relationship or that ending family relationships is a difficult decision that ought not be taken lightly. Even if her guilt conflicts with her considered judgments, getting over those feelings might be a sign that she has too quickly absolved herself of responsibility or that she fails to realize the gravity of her decision. Emotional ambivalence can be part of the process of emotional self-interpretation, but it can also be the outcome of the process. It might be better in some situations for us to remain emotionally conflicted.

Emotional self-interpretation can also explain cases when our emotions turn out to be *just* reactions. The result of self-interpretation might turn out to show that there is no relationship between the emotion and my sense of self. In the same way that I might find something funny that isn't characteristic of my sense of humor, I will have feelings that I can't always control or explain. For instance, in spite of the fact that I have been teaching for years, I still get anxious on the first day of classes. Sometimes these feelings are brief, and I can shake them off without much trouble. Sometimes they are more persistent, and it might take me time to get over them. But there is nothing deeper to them; there is no special story to tell about why I have them. I have accepted that they are "just feelings." Of course, the only way I could come to this conclusion is to self-interpret. I have tried to figure out if I'm worried about something going wrong or if I feel unprepared. Over time I've come to realize that there is no reason why I am nervous. Does this mean I should try to conquer these feelings? I think the answer is no. In accepting that they are "just feelings," I no longer feel the need to try to influence them with rational pressure. They are not hindering my life, and I know they will go away eventually. This is one way to deal with the conflict that recalcitrant emotions present: we can just accept that they come upon us passively and have no deeper ties to our rational network or sense of self.[28] In cases where our emotions are just reactions, there is often no need to exert rational pressure in order to change them. They come unbidden, and they will eventually just go away.

Of course, there are cases when our recalcitrant emotions are more than just feelings. Just because I don't endorse or embrace a particular emotion doesn't mean that it says nothing about me. Our stated judgments and beliefs can be wishful thinking or self-deception, and what we care about or what we value isn't always obvious to us. Our emotions can mean many different things. Sometimes they are clues that something is wrong. Sometimes they are the result of old habits we're trying to get over. Sometimes they are affirmations that we're on the right track. Sometimes they are just feelings. But they don't always come affixed with a clear label. We have to do the work of self-interpretation to determine what they do and don't say, which is why recalcitrance alone provides no reason to feel one way or another about our emotions.

---

[28] This is a strategy one finds especially in Buddhist philosophy. For an example, see McRae (2012).

PART III

Self-Blame and Moral Responsibility

CHAPTER 8

Guilt and Self-Blame within a Conversational Theory of Moral Responsibility[1]

Michael McKenna

What is self-blame, and what role should it play in a theory of moral responsibility? Moreover, what of the emotional response of guilt? In what follows, I will examine the role of both self-blame and guilt within the context of a conversational theory of moral responsibility.[2] Some philosophers have recently placed guilt and self-blame at the heart of moral responsibility's nature. They have also made the deservingness of both the most fundamental normative consideration in justifying the harms of blaming (e.g., Nelkin, 2013a, 2019; Carlsson, 2017; Duggan, 2018; and maybe Clarke, 2016). Doing so appears to threaten conversational (McKenna, 2012) and other communicative theories of moral responsibility (e.g., Watson, 1987; Hieronymi, 2004; Macnamara, 2015a). This is because the central and exemplar cases of blame according to these communicative theories involve others overtly and directly blaming the one who is blameworthy, and so communicating in some way to the culpable party. But if one blames oneself, and if one feels guilt for her culpable wrongdoing, nothing needs to be communicated. And if guilt and self-blame are most fundamental, providing the grounds for the other responsibility-related phenomena, then considerations about the communicative or conversational features of our moral responsibility practices seem to be of secondary importance.

[1] I am grateful to Andreas Carlsson for inviting me to participate in the conference *Self-Blame and Moral Responsibility* held at the Department of Philosophy, University of Oslo, in September of 2019. I wrote this paper for that occasion. I also presented it to the Philosophy Department at Bowling Green State University in December 2019, and to the Michigan Mind and Moral Psychology Conference sponsored by the Philosophy Department at the University of Michigan, Ann Arbor. I am grateful to members of these audiences for their many insightful remarks. For especially helpful comments from those in attendance at one of these talks, or in personal correspondence, I would like to thank Andreas Carlsson, Randy Clarke, Justin D'Arms, Christel Fricke, Chris Howard, Dan Jacobson, Coleen Macnamara, Wade Monroe, Dana Nelkin, Derk Pereboom, Doug Portmore, Piers Rawling, David Shoemaker, Victor Tadros, Mark Timmons, Brandon Warmke, and Michael Webber.
[2] I limit my discussion to the accountability sense of moral responsibility, wherein if one is blameworthy, others are justified in holding a person to account (see Watson, 1996; McKenna, 2012; Shoemaker, 2015).

One option for defending the conversational theory against such worries is to treat guilt and self-blame as derivative of, or as parasitic upon, the more central interpersonal cases of blaming others and of attendant reactive emotions like resentment and indignation (McKenna, 2012). Self-blame is then to be understood as a form of self-conversation – analogous to the way one talks to oneself when engaged in silent soliloquy. Guilt would then be the affective vehicle for this intrapersonal practice. But this will not work. It will not account for the central role of both self-blame and guilt, nor will it account for the normative basis for either. Regardless, guilt and self-blame cannot play the fundamental grounding role in a theory of moral responsibility that others have recently identified for them – at least not to the exclusion of interpersonal forms of blame. As a result, conversational and other communicative theories are not in jeopardy.

In what follows, I will argue for three interrelated points. First, the aims and norms of our blaming practices show that guilt and self-blame can be usefully understood in terms of responses to the blame of others. A conversational theory is well-suited to account for this. Second, self-blame and guilt are distinct things. While it is natural to think that to experience guilt just is to blame oneself, this is not so. Although the two are tightly connected, the relationship is nevertheless contingent; one can blame oneself without experiencing guilt, and one can experience guilt without blaming oneself. Finally, I will explore the normative basis for self-blame and guilt as it is frequently understood when theorizing about moral responsibility. Most appeal to basic desert. However, some philosophers have instead recently appealed to fittingness as an alternative, arguing that this allows them to dispense with considerations of desert. In response, I will argue that desert in these contexts is best construed as a species of fittingness so that self-blame and guilt are both fitting and deserved.

1   Self-Blame and Guilt: My Proposal

Communicative and other conversational theories of moral responsibility take instances of directed blame to be paradigmatic or exemplar cases of holding morally responsible. *Directed blame*, as I understand it (2013), overtly expresses in publically accessible form a blamer's inner blaming attitudes and directs them *toward another* who is the blamed person. These are the central cases that need to be accounted for in developing a theory of moral responsibility, at least as communication-based theorists see it. In these cases it is natural to understand blame as communicating some content to another who is the target of blame and who can come to grasp the meaning in what is communicated. By contrast, when one blames oneself, she does not need to be the recipient of a meaning that is communicated in blaming.

The same remarks about other-directed blame also apply to other-directed reactive emotions that many philosophers following P. F. Strawson (1962) take to be essential to blaming – in particular resentment and indignation, which we can think of as distinctive forms of anger. These stand in contrast with the self-directed reactive attitude of guilt. Plausibly, these other-directed emotions are the central ones figuring in a communication-based theory. Indeed, communicative theories of responsibility were originally inspired by Gary Watson's insightful remark that these reactive attitudes are "incipiently forms of communication" (1987, p. 264). Hence, just as self-blame is not treated as paradigmatic of the central cases of holding responsible that need explaining in a communicative theory, so too is guilt not treated as paradigmatic. The focus is understandably on the other-directed emotions.

Given these reasons to favor the other-directed forms of blaming and the other-directed emotions, in earlier work (McKenna, 2012) I mistakenly treated self-blame and guilt on the model of other-directed blame. That is, I built an account of them out of and treated them as parasitic on my proposed communicative and conversational account of other-directed blame. Let me explain.

In the view I defend, other-directed blame and the overt and directed manifestation of attendant emotions of moral anger express a meaning as if they are responses in a conversation to another who initiated it (McKenna, 2012). A morally responsible agent whose action is a candidate for blame displays through her conduct a significance or meaning – I call it *agent meaning* as an analog to the Gricean notion of *speaker meaning*. Agent meaning is a function of quality of will. When one holds another agent responsible, one responds to that agent in light of an interpretation of the agent meaning expressed in that agent's conduct. By responding with an other-directed morally reactive attitude as an expression of blame, one who directly blames conveys a meaning revealed in the altered interpersonal practices within which pertinent action tendencies of these emotions are expressed. That form of reactivity, I have argued, is like a move in a conversation wherein one replies to another who initiated that conversation. Building on this analogy with speaker meaning and the structure of conversational exchange, I explained the nature and norms of blaming and other forms of holding responsible.

Self-blame and guilt, I argued (McKenna, 2012, pp. 72–74), should be accounted for in similar ways. We can understand self-blame on analogy with talking with oneself. And we can treat guilt as a reactive response to one's presumed culpability, as if one is directing moral anger toward oneself in the same manner that we direct our moral anger at another when we directly blame her. But on its face this proposal is implausible. It's phenomenologically inaccurate to think that in paradigmatic cases of self-blame, when we hold ourselves to account, we conceive of our culpable conduct as something that we need to take up with our own selves. Of course, this might happen, and sometimes does, such as in moments of uncertainty and struggle, or when we engage in self-remonstration for some shortcoming or failure. One thinks to oneself, "My God! You fool! You ass! How could you have done that? And after all she has done to support you." But often, without any need to address ourselves, as it were, we seamlessly register and hold ourselves to account. When we do, at least for those of us who are neuro-typical, we experience an episode of guilt.

As for guilt, it is inaccurate to conceive of guilt as a form of self-directed anger, as I had in earlier work (McKenna, 2012, p. 66; see also Greenspan, 1995, p. 130; and Shoemaker, 2015, p. 111). Admittedly, like anger, guilt involves a pained response, but it is a pained response to registering one's own blameworthiness or culpability rather than as a response to a threat or harm (Morris, 1976b, p. 104; Clarke, 2016, p. 124). Also, guilt's action tendency, unlike anger, is not to retaliate, strike back, seek revenge, or even just confront. It is, rather, to self-correct. One seeks reconciliation or reparation with those whom one has wronged (e.g., see Baumeister et al., 1994; Prinz & Nichols, 2010).

To do better, reflect on the target phenomena a communicative or conversational theory of moral responsibility is meant to explain: A practice of holding one another to account via our praising and blaming responses for our morally significant conduct. Such a practice, as P. F. Strawson (1962) convincingly argued, was poorly justified by theorizing exclusively in terms of social utility as a grounds for forcing others to pay costs for wrongdoing, while rewarding others for morally exemplary conduct. What is needed, Strawson taught us, is an explanation of our responsibility practices wherein we presume that we are morally licensed to hold each other to account in ways that, as Strawson put it, *express* our nature rather than merely exploit it. This involves accommodating the sorts of reasons that actually matter to and motivate us. So it is that in holding each other to account, we are liable to and often assume we are justified in doing "blamey" things to one another *for* certain reasons, and with certain emotional proclivities. In these ways, communicative theories of responsibility are supposed to treat our practices of holding responsible, including the directed expression of our emotional responses, as having certain aims. These aims can be justified or unjustified, and so subject to critical assessment. Crucially, according to communication-based theorists, they can be illuminated by reflecting on their communicative features. This is the deep insight in Gary Watson's original suggestion that we think about the reactive attitudes in communicative terms. So, what roles do self-blame and guilt play in accounting for these aims involved in holding each other to account?

In light of these considerations, I propose that self-blame should be accounted for as the desired or preferred response at which we aim, expect, or demand by way of our other-regarding blame when we hold others to account. The same applies to guilt.

Consider self-blame first. To explain self-blame within the context of a communicative theory, then, we need not understand it as if an agent is addressing herself. Rather, it is the attitude or stance an agent ought to adopt as a fitting response to our blaming her were we to do so. This is consistent with self-blame in contexts in which, as a matter of fact, no one else blames the self-blamer. In conversation, we aim for our audiences' understanding and agreement, anticipating further responses should we be successful in our audience both *understanding* and *endorsing* what we mean to communicate. So too in blaming another, at least in many familiar cases, we seek our target's appreciating and endorsing what we convey in morally engaging with them. Thus, if self-blame involves any communicative properties, in exemplar or paradigmatic cases it should not be thought of as the self-blamer's conveying to herself that she is blameworthy. Instead it should be understood in terms of two features that work together. First, self-blame can be understood in terms of a proper received response from others who would be warranted in expressing their blame were they to do so. Second, self-blame provides reasons and motivation for further sorts of communicative – and, in my view, conversational – engagement with others in the form of apology, contrition, reconciliation, reparation, acceptance of punishment, penance, and so on.

Now consider guilt. If guilt is the expression of self-blame, we can treat it in a like manner. Hence, guilt should not be thought of as angrily blaming oneself, as if one is then motivated to confront or retaliate against oneself. It is, rather, the *preferred or desired* response at which other-regarding blaming emotions aim. My proposal here is inspired by and is close to Coleen Macnamara's (2015b).[3] According to her, moral anger in the form

---

[3] According to Macnamara (2015b), reactive attitudes have a nonintentional purposiveness in that their functional role is to seek uptake in their targets. The nonintentional aspect accommodates the fact that an agent can privately experience an emotion of, say, resentment with no intention of expressing it at all, much less conveying it to its target – the blamed person. Regardless, like a note written and never sent, the purposive character of these emotions is to play the role of sending a signal. Were it "sent," it would have a communicative content.

of resentment and indignation seeks an uptake of guilt from its targets. Perhaps Macnamara is correct about this, but I have reservations. I suspect that moral anger itself, and its functional role in a set of moral responsibility practices, is more permissively to be understood simply in terms of seeking *understanding* in the process of confrontation, and not necessarily endorsement (see also Shoemaker, 2015, pp. 103–112). After all, many of those we blame and at whom we direct our resentment and indignation are not compliant, welcoming recipients of our anger. Nor should we expect that. Sometimes our blaming anger is unjustified, and sometimes we are blaming assholes who will resist regardless of their culpability. Still, plausibly, these uncooperative targets can be engaged so long as they understand us when we confront them. Nevertheless, it is true that, as I put it above, the preferred or desired response, at least in paradigmatic cases, is that those at whom we direct our moral anger will register it and have uptake by way of guilt. In such cases, a blamed agent would express an *endorsement* of the moral demands attendant with others' resentment or indignation. Hence, in my proposal, guilt is the response a blameworthy agent ought to have were others to blame her via their moral anger. Its appropriateness is in part a function of it being a fitting response to the fitting blame of others *when one is in fact blameworthy*.

Thus far, I have considered the nature of self-blame and guilt rather than ask about their norms. Of course, implicit in the discussion so far is that there are normative standards in play. For instance, if self-blame is or can be a meaningful response to the blame of others, as with guilt, and if meaningfulness includes a communicative or conversational dimension, then one normative constraint will be a function of intelligibility. Just as in actual conversations, where some replies to a speaker will be intelligible and so felicitous, rather than unintelligible and so infelicitous, so too some forms of self-blame and some guilty responses can be evaluated as meaningful or intelligible responses to the blame of others and to the wrongdoing that is a basis for it. Others, not so much. Still, as I have argued elsewhere (McKenna, 2012, 2019) norms of meaningfulness or intelligibility are not sufficient to capture the sort of ethical or moral foundation required for *directed* blaming responses to the blameworthy, at least when what we are interested in is moral blameworthiness. This is because, like punishment, even if less so, blame involves exposing its targets to the liability of harms and other forms of unwelcome treatment, treatment we have moral reasons to avoid in the absence of an adequate justification. At this juncture, various philosophers have appealed to a range of different normative grounds, but most working in this area focus on desert. In what follows, I will too.

I will assume that when an agent is blameworthy for something, the salient justification of her self-blame and guilt is a matter of desert; she deserves to blame herself, and she deserves to feel guilty.

I will now develop this proposal.

2 Appropriateness, Fittingness, and Desert

In order to take up these normative issues regarding desert, I turn to conceptual spade work, along with a bit of linguistic legislation. What follows applies to blame and the negative reactive emotions in general, not just to self-blame and guilt. To begin, consider the following biconditional, paraphrasing R. Jay Wallace (1994, p. 91):

> R-HR: A person is morally responsible for an action just in case it is appropriate to hold her morally responsible for performing that action.

As Wallace and others intend it, when applied to blameworthiness and blame, this claim of *appropriateness* reports that there exists some normative warrant of one sort or another for blaming one who is blameworthy.[4] So understood, R-HR can then be further developed by accounting for that propriety by way of some specific normative consideration, such as desert, fairness, contractualist considerations, or on consequentialist grounds.[5]

However appropriateness is explained in a principle such as R-HR, the justification supplied for holding responsible and blaming is only intended to provide *pro tanto* reasons. Suppose, for example, that appropriateness should be explained in terms of desert. If so, it might be that a person deserves to be held responsible and blamed for something even though all things considered, no one ought to do so. (Maybe doing so would cause the world to explode.)

Fittingness offers one appealing way to specify the normativity at issue in principles such as R-HR, as David Shoemaker has recently and forcefully argued (2015, 2017).[6] Fittingness identifies a rational relation that fits

---

[4] For example, see R. J. Wallace (1994, p. 92), and Joel Feinberg (1970, p. 56 and 82), who clearly use appropriateness in this way. See also myself (McKenna, 2012, p. 39).
[5] For justifications for blaming in terms of desert, see Feinberg (1970), McKenna (2019), Nelkin (2013a), Pereboom (2001), and Scanlon (2006). For justifications in terms of fairness, see Wallace (1994). For contractualist justifications, see Lenman (2006) or Scanlon (1998). And for consequentialist justifications, see Smart (1963), Bok (1998), and Vargas (2013).
[6] Some writers use "aptness" or "appropriateness" as a synonym for "fittingness" (e.g., Howard, 2018). In that case, their use of these terms needs to be distinguished from the meaning deployed above in R-HR, since fittingness is clearly not intended merely to report that some other, more specific normative ground exists to justify holding an agent morally responsible. Fittingness is intended to *be* that more specific grounds.

a response to a particular object in such a way that the response accurately represents its object. Hence, desire is a fitting response to the desirable; humor a fitting response to the humorous; belief a fitting response to the credible; fear a fitting response to the fearsome; and so on. So too, on such a proposal, blame is a fitting response to the blameworthy, and an emotion such as guilt is a fitting response to the fact that one is guilty (plausibly, of wrongdoing).

Fittingness also assesses its object by reference to standards of evaluation internal to the domain for its kind. Thus, a morally offensive joke can be positively evaluated for being humorous insofar as it is fitting to be amused by it (because it really is funny), even if a moral assessment is distinctly negative (e.g., see D'Arms & Jacobson, 2000).

Here I will add one further feature of fittingness as I understand it, one that perhaps involves an idiosyncratic bit of linguistic legislation on my part. As I understand it, fittingness fits a response to its objects in a way that is case-specific. That is, it tailors its proper response to particular instances in a manner that defies appeal to general principles or algorithms. For instance, as I have noted elsewhere (McKenna, 2012, 2019), a conversational reply to an interlocutor can be fitting or unfitting. That evaluation can only be settled by the particular meaning of an interlocutor's conversational contribution within the context of the assumptions shared in *that* conversation. I grant that this case-specific feature of fittingness is not explicitly recognized among philosophers who make use of this term of art. As a result, I am prepared to treat it as a stipulation of the term as I intend to use it. Nevertheless, I believe that this further feature is often implicitly assumed in the way fittingness is used (e.g., see Feinberg, 1970).[7]

Desert offers yet another appealing way to develop the sense of appropriateness at issue in principles such as R-HR. Indeed, it is perhaps the most widely accepted way of doing so (e.g., Feinberg, 1970; Pereboom, 2001, 2014; Scanlon, 2008, 2013; McKenna, 2012, 2019; Clarke, 2013, 2016; Nelkin, 2013a; Carlsson, 2017). Here I will limit attention to what is often referred to as *basic desert* (e.g., Pereboom, 2001, 2014). Basic desert has both a negative and a positive component.

---

[7] This is also borne out by considering belief. If p is believable, then believing that p is fitting. But note just how case-specific that relation of fit is. The accurate representation involved in believing that p is manifested in the particular sentences a believer would be willing to assent to in virtue of her belief, and in the inferences a (rational) believer would take to be licensed by the content of p rather than some other equally credible proposition q. (I am indebted to conversations with Mark Timmons here.)

Consider first the negative component. If a person basically deserves blame, there exists no more basic normative consideration of, say, a contractualist or consequentialist sort that would justify a claim of desert. The negative part is simply the denial of there being any other normative basis supporting desert.

Desert's positive thesis identifies the "desert base" in virtue of which a response of blame is deserved. In the case of deserved blame, the desert base is limited just to facts pertaining to the agent and her conduct in virtue of which a blaming response is deserved. A familiar cocktail of factors for a desert base for blame is that an agent freely and knowingly performed a morally wrong action.[8] In such a case, one might say that she deserves a suitably tailored blaming response *just because* she freely and knowingly did morally wrong. Here the "just because" is meant to express the thought that the justification for blaming is settled exclusively in terms of the features of the agent's act that merit or make her worthy of being a recipient of blame. In this respect, desert should be construed as one of the basic features of justice; deserving welcome or unwelcome treatment should be settled exclusively in terms of the worth of a person's actual deeds – nothing more, nothing less.

Elsewhere (McKenna, 2012, 2019), I have argued that a further feature of deserved blame is that it is noninstrumentally good. Indeed, I argued that the harm that is plausibly understood to be a constitutive ingredient of (successful) blaming is itself noninstrumentally good. While some (e.g., Wallace, 1994; Scanlon, 1998, 2008; Nelkin, 2019) strongly reject this axiological thesis, others take it to be an important element of basic desert for blame. It is part of what it most fundamentally is (e.g., Bennett, 2002; Clarke, 2016; Carlsson, 2017; McKenna, 2019; Pereboom, 2019).

Some philosophers clearly treat fittingness and desert as distinct bases for blame, so that desert is one thing, fittingness another (e.g., Shoemaker, 2015; Nelkin, 2016, 2019; Carlsson, 2017). I disagree. Granted, there are relations of fit that are not relations of desert. It is fitting to believe a true proposition, but true propositions do not deserve to be believed. We do them no injustice in failing to do so (cf. Howard, 2018). But as I understand it – in opposition to the philosophers cited above – *desert is a species of fittingness* (e.g., Clarke, 2016; McKenna, 2019; see also Feinberg, 1970, p. 82). As others have noted (Howard, 2018), it is a vexing question to ask just what distinguishes desert as a species of fittingness from those relations of

---

[8] I just use this as a placeholder for a more refined proposal. This clearly will not work, as a person can be blameworthy for acting from culpable ignorance.

fit that are not relations of desert. Perhaps a simple proposal will suffice, even if it is relatively uninformative: desert involves that sort of fitting- ness that is implicated in considerations of justice. A more substantive thesis, which I propose here, is that, first, desert requires agential con- trol (see Howard, 2018), or as I would prefer to put it, free agency (see also Carlsson, 2017); second, desert supplies reasons that justify forms of treatment that are otherwise morally problematic.[9] For instance, assuming blaming a person exposes her to certain harms, it might be argued that one is morally required to refrain from harming a person in these ways, unless blame is deserved.

3   Blame and the Reactive Attitudes

Set aside for the moment these normative considerations regarding fitting- ness and desert. We will return to these in the next section. How should we understand the relation between blame and the negative reactive atti- tudes? Thus far I have discussed self-blame and the reactive attitude of guilt separately. Above I characterized guilt as the affective complement or expression of self-blame. Some will balk. Why treat them separately? Following P. F. Strawson (1962), many treat blame exclusively in terms of the negative reactive attitudes of resentment, indignation, and guilt. In views of this sort, blame is simply identified with the pertinent reac- tive attitudes (e.g., Wallace, 1994; Russell, 2004, 2017). For instance, as Andreas Carlsson has recently argued, to self-blame just is to feel guilty (this volume). According to these philosophers, one blames just in case one experiences an episode of a negative reactive attitude of resentment, indignation, or guilt. I assume that many who defend this claim think of it as a necessary truth.[10] Getting clear on these issues bears on the above normative considerations regarding desert and fittingness. If after all guilt and self-blame are distinct, then perhaps we would do better to assess one in terms of desert – blame – and another in terms of fittingness – the reac- tive attitudes of resentment, indignation, and guilt.

So, should we *identify* blame with the negative reactive attitudes, and so self-blame with guilt? If so, should we take this identification to express a necessary truth? In response to both questions: no. Consider first the claim of necessity. Even if it is true of human beings that one blames just

---

[9] I recognize that this seems not to be so for deserving positive forms of treatment. But I'll ignore this problem here because it makes my bald claim less credible.

[10] It is hard to find in print anyone who openly discusses these modal issues. So this is mostly con- jecture on my part.

in case one experiences an episode of a negative reactive attitude, this is not a necessary truth.[11] My argument is simple. Grant that directed blaming is of a piece with a set of responsibility practices that involve holding members of a moral community to account relative to standards set by the moral community. These practices involve making demands that members act with a reasonable degree of good will toward one another. Community members respond negatively when other members do not act with sufficient good will, and they do so by means that communicate moral demands, and indicate expectations for apology, restitution, and modifications to objectionable behavior. In holding to account by blaming, they signal altered sanction-like policies toward the culpable in terms of the sorts of relations the blamed person might expect from others. And so on. Now imagine emotionless beings who are still motivated to care about and comply with such a practice. This is intelligible. Or instead imagine beings with quite different emotional profiles where their emotions do not play the central role they do for us in our responsibility practices. This is also intelligible. If so, it is not a *necessary* truth that to blame one must experience an episode of a negative reactive attitude. Hence, it is not a necessary truth that to self-blame one must feel guilty.

Some will be unimpressed by the preceding argument, countering that our theory of moral responsibility *should* be anthropocentric. We don't care about Martian self-blame. We care about us. Fair enough. Indeed, I agree (McKenna, 2012, pp. 110–112). So what if it is a contingent truth that one blames just in case one experiences a negative reactive attitude? It is still true of us, isn't it? (Some might argue that it is a necessary truth *about us*.) But I do not think it is true, even as a contingent truth restricted to critters like us. There are plausible cases where it seems a person self-blames and yet does not feel guilty, and there are also plausible cases where a person feels guilty but does not self-blame.

Let's start with cases where a person can credibly be said to self-blame but yet does not feel guilty. Maria is severely depressed. Prior to her depressive episode she treated Martin horribly at a party and went home thinking nothing of it. As her illness set in, and after a friend reminded her of the event in a conversation, it dawned on her that she wronged Martin. As her affect is so flattened by her current state, she simply does not have any distinguishable pained response at all to her poor conduct. All the same,

---

[11] Obviously, "just in case" expresses logical necessity, which is weaker than identity. Nevertheless, it is entailed by identity, and I argue here that even if we grant logical equivalence, we should not treat it as a necessary truth.

she recognizes that she has wronged Martin. Indeed, she is self-aware enough to know that were she not depressed, she would feel terrible. Still, as it happens, she doesn't. Yet she accepts that she was blameworthy for doing so, and somehow despite her illness she resolves to take steps to hold herself to account for treating Martin so poorly. She recognizes Martin's recent cool treatment of her as his way of blaming her, and she accepts it as fitting. She calls Martin and apologizes, makes various mental notes to herself to correct her behavior in future interactions, and takes steps to signal to Martin in future interactions that she'll take more care with how she treats him in social settings. I say Maria blames herself, but she feels no guilt.

Here is one more case. Double M has dropped acid with a group of friends.[12] In hysterics, he makes a wise crack about a fellow traveler, Crispin, and it cuts deep. It's a terribly cruel joke, even though by all accounts from those around it's hysterical. Except to Crispin. Poor Crispin is visibly wounded. With tears of laughter running down his face, Double M apologizes to Crispin profusely, "I am so sorry man! I should never have said that. Really, I mean it." He does everything he can in his drug-addled state to hold himself to account for what he clearly registers as a blame-worthy remark on his part. Still, *he feels no guilt at all*. He can't. His ability to do so is finked by the acid. He even goes on to laugh about his current psychic state, reporting to his fellow trippers that he knows he should feel terrible, but he just can't. It's all too hilarious. Here too, I say Double M blames himself, but he feels no guilt.

Now consider cases where a person feels guilty and yet she does not blame herself. Here I offer two sorts of cases. The first involves recalcitrant emotions. The second involves a failure of commitment. The first sort is familiar enough. Fernando has just had sex with Manuel, and though he fully believes there is nothing wrong with doing so, he feels terribly guilty. All of this he realizes is the upshot of his Catholic upbringing, wherein homosexual sex is regarded as a sin. But Fernando rejects all of it. In no way does he hold himself to account. He takes no steps to correct his behavior; rather, he redoubles his efforts to enjoy his sexual life as a gay man. He has no commitment at all to apologize to anyone for what he has done, and he is strongly disposed to resist rather than embrace the blaming behavior from anyone who would be inclined to blame him for doing something that they would regard as immoral. Here, Fernando's

---

[12] For the uncool, "dropping acid" means ingesting LSD, a hallucinogenic drug that can induce extreme euphoria.

recalcitrant emotion of guilt does not rise to the level of self-blame, so long as we understand self-blame as a means of holding oneself to account for conduct taken to be blameworthy.

The second sort of case involves a failure of commitment in the face of appropriate guilt. Both Buster and Manny join in with a bigoted crew who harass and berate a local Jewish family whose financial success in their community is interpreted through the lens of stereotypical Jewish caricature. Their piling on contributes to the local community shunning the family. As a result, the family moves out of town so as to protect their children from derision and isolation. Later, both Buster and Manny confess to each other that they feel guilty about joining in with that crew. They confess to each other that they now see it almost exclusively in terms of a tribal inclination to fit in. Indeed, they both agree that they are blameworthy. However, Buster and Manny respond to their guilt differently. Buster holds himself to account. He resolves not to treat members of groups such as Jewish people poorly and to resist those from the prejudicial group he previously went along with. He decides to apologize in person to the father and mother of the Jewish family if ever he has a chance to see them, and he accepts that any blaming treatment from the family or others in his community is fully legitimate. He'll not resist, and he'll be contrite if and when confronted. As for Manny, none of this is true. He feels guilt, but he does not commit at all to holding himself to account in light of the ethical considerations in virtue of which he is blameworthy. In this respect, he is morally weak – a coward. He won't commit despite his bad feelings. Indeed, the following week a Native American family moves into town, and yet again Manny joins in with that nasty crew, just so he can fit in. In this case, I say Manny feels guilty, but unlike Buster he does not blame himself.

The preceding four cases show that guilt and self-blame are distinct. Neither is necessary nor sufficient for the other. Nevertheless, they *are* intimately connected, as are other-directed blame and expressions of moral anger in the form of resentment and indignation. How so? Episodes of these reactive attitudes are the affective complements of our blaming in exemplar or paradigmatic cases.[13] They provide the medium within which we normally express our blame, and they offer the characteristic motivational source of our preparedness to blame. Moreover, because we characteristically blame in this way, our conventions for expressing our blame toward others have been built up out of the practices wherein

---

[13] I develop this general approach to theorizing about blame in my 2013 work. See also Miranda Fricker (2016), who independently develops a similar strategy.

these emotions are given expression. For these reasons, I propose that we theorize about both blame and the negative reactive attitudes by attending to paradigmatic or exemplar cases representative of the phenomena we are most interested in assessing. Thus, in the many familiar cases that come to mind, one self-blames *by way of feeling guilty*. Her guilt provides the motivational engine to respond to the blame of others in ways that express the fact that she does hold herself to account, does appreciate the moral demands of others, is motivated to improve herself morally, to reconcile, and so on. Because of this tight, albeit contingent, connection between the central cases of self-blame and guilt, we can still make sense of the contention that both self-blame and guilt can be fitting and can be deserved. Or so I will now argue.

4   The Fittingness and Deservingness of Directed Blame and Moral Anger

Returning to the normative questions we briefly set aside, the results of the last section undercut the following elegant way to argue that deserved blame is a species of fittingness: grant that blame should be evaluated in terms of desert, as numerous philosophers contend. If we *identify* blame with pertinent reactive attitudes, it follows that these reactive attitudes are deserved when blame is. Now grant that the emotions should be evaluated in terms of fittingness, as numerous philosophers of the emotions believe. Again, assuming *identity*, it follows that blame is fitting when an episode of one of these reactive attitudes is. But now add a further assumption: some relations of fittingness are not relations of desert, like the relation of fit between belief and a credible proposition. It follows that desert is a species of fittingness. But, alas, as argued in the preceding section, we cannot identify blame with the negative reactive attitudes; indeed, we cannot even hope for an extensional equivalence. So this argument fails. Is there another way to show that deserved blame is fitting, and that fitting moral anger is deserved?

Consider paradigmatic cases of directed blame in which one blames another. As explained above, within the context of a conversational theory, directed blaming can be assessed for being intelligible or unintelligible as a means of addressing a blamed party. Just as in actual conversations, some replies to an interlocutor can miss their mark while others are especially apt, so too when blaming, one can blame another in a way that is infelicitous rather than felicitous. An example I have used elsewhere (McKenna, 2012) involves Daphne and Leslie. Daphne directly blames Leslie for what she took to be Leslie's hurtful racist remark about Hispanics, expressed in the presence of several Hispanics in a local coffee shop, all of whom seem to have taken offense. Assume that Leslie is blameworthy and that she deserves blame. Daphne directly confronts Leslie, angrily telling her that her comment is disgusting. She storms off, cutting short a date they had set together, and then she alters later plans for getting together with Leslie and a mutual Hispanic friend. This suite of behavior has a meaning and is intelligible as a reply to the salience of Leslie's morally objectionable conduct. It is, one might say, *fitting*. And its fit is captured on analogy with conversational felicity.[14]

By contrast with the case as described above, imagine instead that Daphne had done none of the above, thought nothing of leaving the coffee shop, kept the planned meeting with their mutual Hispanic friend, but instead angrily told Leslie her breath stinks and then stuck her tongue out at her. In this case, we need not say that Daphne does not blame Leslie. Rather, we might say she does so in a way that is unfitting. Note that if we understand Daphne's blame as expressed through her indignation, we can then also say of her expression of moral anger that it is fitting for its object when it involves a mode of replying meaningfully to Leslie's offense.

Note two things. First, there is a sense in which, if appropriate, Daphne's meaningful reply *accurately represents* Leslie's offense, just as is required of fittingness. How so? Its intelligibility turns on responding to what Leslie really did and to the meaning that it reveals in terms of the quality of her will. (Suppose Daphne misheard Leslie, and Leslie was not talking about hating Hispanics, but about hating her cousin's histrionics.) Second, its fit captures something that is case-specific, a feature of fittingness noted above. For instance, as an expression of Daphne's blame, she cancels plans to get together with a mutual Hispanic friend, and she also cuts short a date already in progress in a coffee shop where Daphne presumes others might have taken offense or been hurt. These details are rendered appropriate means of Daphne expressing her indignation only in light of the prior relationship and shared expectations.

Just now, I offered a way to show that in paradigmatic cases of directed blaming, deserved blame and the other-directed emotion of indignation, a species of moral anger, can be usefully illuminated in terms of fittingness. What of desert? Can desert be used to help illuminate (some cases of)

---

[14] Christopher Bennett (2002) develops an example that serves purposes similar to mine involving a group coworkers responding to one of their own who treats another as no more than a sexual conquest. The coworkers' affect-laden responses display a meaning or significance that can plausibly be thought of as fitting – and on Bennett's account, deserved.

fittingness? Of course, I stipulated that Leslie deserves Daphne's blame. But does she deserve to be the target of another's directed moral anger or some other unpleasant emotional response? Here is the key question: will desert supply an illuminating way to understand the appropriateness of expressing the pertinent emotions, *or is fittingness alone adequate to account for the appropriateness of the emotional response*? Here is first a quick explanation of why Leslie deserves to be the target of these emotions, followed by a slightly more cautious justification. The quick explanation goes like this: the conventional resources for blaming and the characteristic motivation that gives rise to blaming practices are built up out of our modes of manifesting our emotions. As Strawson (1962) observed, these are our actual blaming practices because *this is what we are like*. In this way, if blame is deserved, it is deserved as expressed by beings like us with the sort of affect we deploy to hold others to account. So, yes, *if* the blame is deserved, then the directed anger of others, as modes of expressing blame, is deserved.

A slightly more cautious reply goes like this: deserved blame in these contexts involves justifications for modes of treatment in response to morally objectionable conduct. The justification desert offers supplies reasons for why, in holding each other to account, certain forms of treatment that would otherwise be unjustified are in these contexts justified. Those forms of treatment are conventionally understood to be not only unwelcome, but potentially harmful, for instance causing setbacks to the welfare interests of the blamed (McKenna, 2012, 2019). At least this is so in typical cases. Indeed, as noted above, in some views, these harms are even understood to be noninstrumentally good. But the harms involved in blaming that are registered by the blamed are often harms *precisely because* they are understood by their targets as expression of others' moral anger. The sting that is part of the deserved blame – the harm that is deserved – is a harm *constituted* by being the recipient of others' anger. So in these paradigmatic cases, if the blame of others is deserved, so is their anger as the means whereby that directed blame is expressed.

5   An Analog to "The Punishment Should Fit the Crime"

A further feature of deserved blame gives reason to appeal to considerations of fit to better understand deservingness. When it comes to punishment, it is commonplace to note that the punishment should fit the crime. In the case of blame, there is no such pithy statement. Still, it is plausible to suppose that in like manner the blame should fit the culpable wrong. Given the conversational theory, an appealing feature of the fittingness of a blaming reply to blameworthy conduct is that its meaning can be tailored specifically as a felicitous reply. If this sort of fitting reply is what is deserved, we have an elegant way to evaluate just how it is that one sort of blaming response is the one that is deserved rather than some other (McKenna, 2019).

To illustrate, consider again the case of Daphne and Leslie. Above I suggested an infelicitous blaming response by Daphne, spouting out "Your breath stinks!" rather than the fitting response described. Imagine a different sort of infelicity. Suppose Leslie had also culpably slacked off on some work and left it for others, including Daphne, as they are cowork- ers as well as friends. Now suppose *as a response to Leslie's racist remark*, Daphne does none of what I described above. Instead she leaves work she could help Leslie complete for Leslie to do on her own. Suppose it is the sort of work they would cheerfully do together when on friendlier terms, but now she does not help. Imagine also she angrily says to Leslie, "You know, you are taxing everyone else in the office by blowing us off!" Suppose that Leslie is upset by Daphne's display of anger, and that she is just as wounded and unsettled by it as she would have been had Daphne's reply been as described above.

Here is the point. Leslie might deserve *this* blame from Daphne just as much as she deserves the blame wherein Daphne confronts her about her prejudicial remark. It might sting just as much, and it might be of equal value in terms of being noninstrumentally good that she is so addressed. Nevertheless, *it is not fitting as a reply to her racist remark*.[15] So, though she might deserve it, it is not what she deserves for the offense in question. As philosophers like Feinberg (1970) might put it, the desert base is not fitted for the one response but is fitted for the other. This helps to show that an analog to conversational fittingness, a kind of intelligibility of replying to a meaningful contribution, is a feature of deserved blame. Hence, we get the result that desert in this domain is a species of fittingness.

6 The Fittingness and Deservingness of Self-Blame and Guilt

Thus far, I have argued that in the exemplar or paradigmatic cases of blaming the blameworthy, both the directed blame and the directed neg- ative reactive attitudes that express blame can be fitting and deserved.

---

[15] Of course, it *is* a fitting reply to an entirely different matter for which, by hypothesis, she *also* deserves blame.

This is so even if we cannot *identify* blame with episodes of these emotions. However, my argument so far has focused only on the blame of others and on the moral anger involved in resentment and indignation. What of self-blame and guilt? Here I can be brief.

Randolph Clarke contends that we should understand guilt as a pained response to the thought that one is blameworthy (2016, pp. 122–123).[16] I agree. Or at least I agree with the basic proposal that in some way the pained response of guilt is to be understood in terms of an agent's assessment of her own conduct as blameworthy or culpable. We can treat self-blame in like fashion. It is an attitude one adopts toward oneself as a response to her own presumption of blameworthiness. So understood, it seems on its face that we have no need to appeal to any communicative or conversational resources to understand either. But we do. Grant that guilt is a pained response to registering one's own blameworthiness. Still, it is a response that, if properly grasped, involves an appreciation of the reasons others have for communicating their blame to that person.[17] It also can be understood as the sort of attitude others would prefer or desire that she have in light of her treatment of those whom she wronged. The same applies to her self-blame. In all of these ways, we can understand her guilt and her self-blame in terms of the sorts of actions that would involve fitting expressions. That is to say, as part of a set of practices of holding each other to account, both guilt and self-blame can be assessed for their suitability in responding meaningfully to others in a moral community, and most crucially those one has wronged.

To illustrate, imagine that Leslie receives Daphne's blame as Daphne prefers for Leslie to receive it. She comes to blame herself, and she feels guilty. Plausibly, that requires her blaming herself in a certain way and feeling guilty in a manner that renders certain sorts of conduct fitting expressions of her holding herself accountable. This in turn involves the way she is disposed to respond to others. Suppose instead, drawing upon the example of infelicitous other-regarding blame above, that in

---

[16] Others would offer a different diagnosis. Some, for instance, might characterize guilt in terms of one's having slighted another (Shoemaker, 2015, p. 107), or in terms of one having displayed ill will or indifference toward another (Hieronymi, 2004, p. 133).

[17] In personal correspondence, Derk Pereboom has asked whether this is sufficient to show that communication of blame by others is more fundamental. In reply, no. But it bears emphasizing here that my thesis need not rule out self-blame as one essential element in a proper account of our practices and norms of holding morally responsible. All that matters to preserve the relevance of any communicative theory is that other-regarding blame is *as* fundamental. It only needs a place, not an exhaustive place, in the basic or fundamental resources required to supply an adequate theory of holding (and being) morally responsible.

blaming herself and feeling guilty *for her hurtful racist remark*, Leslie does not apologize for that. She makes no effort to alter any of her modes of interacting with Hispanics, including her and Daphne's mutual Hispanic friend, and she persists in making racially derogatory remarks. Instead, Leslie self-corrects at work and carries more of the weight to help out Daphne and her coworkers with the more unpleasant tasks. She makes extra efforts to be kind in the workplace, and so on. All the while, what she feels terrible for is her racist remark, not her poor behavior at work. But to this hurtful remark, she signals in no way in her expressions of guilt that she takes a stance toward objectionable racist attitudes. Her holding herself to account involves nothing recognizable to other would-be blamers that would communicate that she has taken a stance against her own culpability. In this case, in some perverse way, Leslie might feel guilty for and blame herself for that remark, but it is not fitting, and it is not what she deserves. She deserves to feel a guilt that tends to and is a response to the nature of the wrong for which she is blameworthy. And she deserves to blame herself and hold herself to account in a way that is fitted for that wrong. The conversational theory of moral responsibility illuminates this in terms of intelligible – and so fitting – responses to the blame of others were others to blame. This applies to cases of self-blame and guilt wherein, as a matter of fact, no one else does blame the blameworthy person.

7 Assessing Carlsson's Guilt-Based Theory of Blameworthiness

In an impressive paper, Andreas Carlsson has recently argued that to be blameworthy is simply to deserve guilt (2017). Identifying guilt with self-blame, he writes, "[To] blame oneself – to feel guilty – necessarily involves suffering" (90). He also argues that other-regarding directed blame cannot credibly be what a blameworthy person most fundamentally deserves. Why? It is a contingent matter whether one who is blameworthy suffers due to the blame of others (99–100). After all, a culpable person might not care at all about the blame of others. It might not bother her in the least. Not so with the guilt involved in self-blame. It is necessarily painful. Hence, what a blameworthy person deserves most fundamentally is to feel guilt. He also denies that we should evaluate guilt in terms of fittingness, since responses can be fitting even when a person did not freely act to bring them about, but this cannot be used to justify aiming to bring about responses that are intrinsically painful. Desert requires freedom, and is itself distinct from fittingness. It supplies the needed normative warrant of guilt, and it helps justify why we ought to blame others and so seek a response of guilt from them (110–113). Finally, Carlsson rejects Clarke's (2016) minimal desert thesis that agents who are blameworthy deserve to feel guilty *because they are blameworthy* (Carlsson, 2017, p. 91). His objection to Clarke's proposal is that it presupposes a prior understanding of blameworthiness (91). Carlsson instead argues not just that blameworthiness necessarily involves deserved guilt, but that deserved guilt *grounds* blameworthiness. When a person is blameworthy, it is in virtue of deserving guilt.

Carlsson's proposal is intriguing and thoughtfully developed. Much is consistent with the conversational theory as developed here. For instance, if we restrict our attention to actual human beings and set aside thought experiments about possible beings without emotion, it is plausible that a person is blameworthy just in case she *deserves* to experience guilt as a response to her wrongdoing. Nothing as set out above is incompatible with this. Consider, for instance, Maria and Double M. Neither was in a position to experience guilt. But this does not mean they did not deserve it. They were simply not equipped to receive something they deserved. Of course, contra Carlsson's proposal, the cases of Maria and Double M show that in blaming oneself, one does not necessarily feel guilty. But Carlsson's contention that guilt is a central concept that can be used to elucidate blameworthiness is not impugned. Nor is it in tension with the thesis developed here that fitting and deserved guilt needs to be understood by reference to the communicative features that would make it salient as a meaningful way of responding to the blame of others.

Nevertheless, there are four points where in my estimation Carlsson overreaches. First, Carlsson is correct that fitting feelings of grief might be noninstrumentally good but not deserved, and he is correct that we should not aim to bring out that pained response of grief in others as something they deserve. But this is no reason to think that desert in the case of guilt is not a *species* of fittingness. In this proposal, some fitting responses for some evaluative domains have further features involved in their satisfaction conditions in virtue of which they are also deserved. I have proposed that they are features pertaining to justice that turn on an agent's acting freely and thereby proving *pro tanto* reasons for forms of treating her that would otherwise be morally problematic. This, I take it, is how Feinberg understood desert (1970, p. 82).

Second, Carlsson's reason for rejecting the contention that other-regarding blame can be used to ground blameworthiness is that it does not *necessarily* involve the suffering of the blamed. Rather, the relation between the potential harms in the blame of others and the person blamed is contingent and indirect (Carlsson, 2017, pp. 99–100). So, if a culpable person deserves to suffer for her wrongdoing, it cannot be that what she deserves is the blame of others. This is a point Carlsson shares with Dana Nelkin, (2013b, p. 124). This, however, is not a good reason to reject the thesis that we can ground blameworthiness in deserving the blame of others, especially in the form of directed moral anger. To begin, one might simply tweak the thesis in a plausible way and avoid the worries about contingency. We could say, for instance, that what a blameworthy person deserves most fundamentally is not simply others' blame, but to have a pained response to registering the moral anger expressed in others blaming her. Indeed, I suspect this is what most have in mind when they link a desert thesis about other-directed blame to the blameworthy. Of course, this is consistent with its *also* being true that a blameworthy person deserves to feel guilty.[18]

Also, Carlsson and Nelkin assume it is problematic to identify what a person deserves with something that is only contingently related to its being harmful or unpleasant for the person who deserves it. I disagree. Not everything a person deserves is something she is assured of getting. Sometimes efforts to give a person what she deserves fail, yet that is no reason to think she does not deserve it. To put the point differently: a person may deserve to be treated in a certain way partly on account of the intended consequence of the treatment. Suppose the intended consequence doesn't come about. It may still be true that she deserved, fundamentally, to be treated in that way. So, for example, the person who deserves to receive the trophy for winning the race might drop dead or turn into a turnip before receiving it. She did not get it, but she deserved to. So one key premise in Carlsson's argument for favoring guilt over the angry blame of others is false. The angry blame of others and the harm or suffering conventionally associated with it can be something a blameworthy person deserves. This is so even if she would not find it unpleasant or regard it as a setback to her interests.

Third, between the deserved angry blame of others, and deserved self-blame and guilt, which is more fundamental? Which provides the grounding considerations in an account of blameworthiness? I would say neither. They both have a grounding role to play if either does. This is borne out by the explanation I offered regarding the aims of the blame of others and of the uptake others would prefer of the blamed. Carlsson,

---

[18] I take it to be a virtue of Clarke's (2016) minimal desert thesis that his proposal is silent about these matters. That is, nothing in his formulation linking blameworthiness to deserved guilt rules out other things like the blame and moral anger of others also being deserved and also being fundamental to blameworthiness and moral responsibility.

I take, treats self-blame as the fundamental notion; the blame of others is a secondary matter. But in many cases, it is not just that a person deserves to experience the pain of guilt for her wrongdoing. What she deserves is to be confronted by those whom she has wronged and to come to experience guilt as a response. In this way, one of the things that makes it good that she experiences the pain of guilt is that it is an expression of her respect or concern for those who have reason to blame her, and it is so as an apt response to a phase in a moral conversation. For cases of this sort, we cannot leave out of the picture reference to the desert of other-regarding blame. This is just an application of a more general feature of the phenomena that needs to be explained. Accountability is about our relations with each other whereby we hold *each other* to account. Guilt's role, and its value as something that is deserved, is connected with our relations of mutual regard and the general demand, as Strawson put it, that we show a certain degree of good will toward one another. So, guilt has its place, but is it *more* fundamental to accountability than the role played by the blame of others? No.

Fourth and finally, Carlsson joins the impressive company of philosophers like David Shoemaker (2015, 2017), R. Jay Wallace (1994), and Gary Watson (1996) in arguing that blameworthiness is grounded in the appropriateness conditions for holding morally responsible. On such approaches, it is not that holding someone morally responsible is appropriate because that person is morally responsible. Rather, a person is morally responsible because it is appropriate to hold her morally responsible. Thus, on Carlsson innovative and distinctive version of this general strategy, he is committed to the following:

> Deserved Guilt (DG): A person is blameworthy for performing an action if and only if and in virtue of deserving guilt for performing that action.

Elsewhere (McKenna, 2012), I have offered reasons for resisting this general strategy. Applied specifically to DG, one simple reason why this approach will not work is that on careful inspection we cannot make sense of deserved guilt without reference to blameworthiness, as is suggested by views according to which guilt itself involves a pained response to the thought that one is blameworthy.[19] Note, moreover, that when there is controversy over whether an agent deserves guilt, what we most naturally

---

[19] My own view is that the opposing parties to this debate both have it wrong (2012). We can no more ground the appropriateness and more specifically the deservingness of blaming by reference to an independent notion of blameworthiness than we can work in the direction favored by Carlsson. But this is not the place to advance my arguments for this interdependence thesis.

attend to as a way of assessing the desert claim involves attending to features of the agent. Did she really act with poor regard for the interests of others? Did she act freely? Was she duped into acting as she did? Were there unfortunate circumstances in her history that made it hard for her to value things properly? In all of these cases, what we attend to are considerations that bear on her blameworthiness.

8   A Final Consideration

In this chapter, I have argued for the thesis that we should understand deserved blame as a species of fittingness. I did so by deploying features of the conversational theory to show that we can help understand what sorts of blaming and self-blaming responses are deserved in terms of conversational fittingness. So too for the negative reactive emotions characteristic of blaming, both the angry blame of resentment and indignation, as well as guilt. A critic might protest that we can assess both blaming practices and pertinent emotions via various norms. One might be a matter of fit, while another might be a matter of desert. Perhaps they co-occur in a certain domain and even have the very same objects, as would be the case if, contrary to my counterarguments, we identify blaming with the pertinent negative reactive attitudes. Still, fittingness and desert are distinct. One is not a species of the other.[20]

I reject this alternative proposal. For one reason, it does not allow us to illuminate what sorts of blaming responses are deserved by reference to considerations of fit. Treating desert as a species of fittingness does, as I argued above. Nevertheless, there is a more cautious objection, or rather qualification, to my proposal that I endorse. Fitting accounts of the emotions in general are well-supported. As guilt is such a pervasive emotion, it would be perverse to think that we could not illuminate a normative assessment of it in terms of fit along with the full suite of human emotions. This supplies a strong incentive to endorse a fittingness account of guilt. But both our blaming practices involved in our ordinary folk understanding, and our folk assessments of emotions like guilt, also seem subject to considerations of desert that plausibly turn upon assumptions about free agency or free will as a condition of desert, and so justice. This then supplies a strong incentive to endorse a desert-based account of norms bearing on both blame and guilt.

Granting the two preceding points, it is also quite plausible to think that if free will and moral responsibility skepticism are true, no one

---

[20] Justin D'Arms thoughtfully suggested this proposal.

basically deserves directed blame and the accompanying harms involved in expressions of anger and guilt. But it is equally *implausible* to think that the central emotions in play here would be unfitting if free will and moral responsibility skepticism are true. Suppose no one does have free will and that no one deserves the harms of blaming, punishing, and so on. Surely in some way guilt might still accurately represent to a guilty party that her treatment of another was objectionable – say as manifesting ill or insufficient good will toward another. This sort of fittingness as accurate representation would not itself, in the absence of appeal to desert, involve any further judgment that it is intrinsically or noninstrumentally good or just to experience the pain intrinsic to guilt.

So, my final proposal is this: if persons have free will and are morally responsible, then self-blame and guilt are both things that a moral agent might deserve. If not, guilt and other emotions are still subject to evaluation in terms of fit, even if they are not deserved. Since desert on my proposal supplies *pro tanto* reasons for forms of treatment that are otherwise morally problematic, while fittingness alone does not, the forms of treatment that fitting moral anger and guilt can help to justify in the absence of desert are far more limited.[21]

---

[21] This is a partial concession to David Shoemaker's (2015, pp. 222–223) contention that we should develop a theory of moral responsibility in terms of the fittingness of emotions and treat considerations of desert and blaming practices as a further ethical matter beyond the scope of a theory of responsibility. I do not agree. But my conclusion here is meant to accommodate an important insight that I believe he aims to capture.

CHAPTER 9

Deserved Guilt and Blameworthiness over Time

Andreas Brekke Carlsson

1 Introduction

The literature on moral responsibility is ripe with accounts of what it takes for an agent to *become* blameworthy. Typically, a responsibility theorist will say that the agent must act wrongly and display an objectionable quality of will. Moreover, she must have generated this action, attitude, or omission knowingly, voluntary, and under control. When this happens, she is worthy of blame. But for *how long*? Very little is written about what it takes for an agent's blameworthiness to cease or diminish.[1]

One reason for the lack of interest in this question might be that many philosophers share the assumption that blameworthiness is *forever*: once you're blameworthy for something, you're always blameworthy for that thing. But it is by no means obvious why this should be the case. Most philosophers working on moral responsibility also accept that an agent is blameworthy for something if and only if it is appropriate to blame her for that thing. This generic biconditional entails that if blaming S for x is no longer appropriate, *then S is no longer blameworthy for x*. Suppose that blame is equated with the reactive attitudes resentment, indignation, and guilt. The question of whether an agent remains blameworthy then boils down to the question of whether resentment, indignation, and guilt remain appropriate. Once we frame the question in this way, there seem to be reasons to doubt that blameworthiness is forever. The diminution of blame, towards oneself, as well as towards other people, is a familiar phenomenon. The intense and painful guilt we might feel in the hours, days, and weeks after we have done something wrong rarely persists. Similarly,

---

[1] Notable exceptions are Tognazzini (2010), Coleman and Sarch (2012), Khoury and Matheson (2018), and Clarke (forthcoming). Shoemaker (2021) provides an interesting and relevant discussion, although the paper is framed in terms of forgiveness rather than blameworthiness. Callard (2018) and Marušić (2020) provide interesting discussions of the rationality of anger over time, without linking this discussion to blameworthiness.

resentment or indignation can change and disappear in time. Of course, many of the reasons for why blame diminishes seem to have little to do with the agent's blameworthiness. It would be puzzling if the mere passage of time could render an agent less blameworthy for what he has done. A victim might decide to let go of blame because he needed to move on with his life. Such prudential reasons might outweigh other reasons the victim has for continuing to blame the wrongdoer. But it would not make the agent any less blameworthy.

However, there seem to be certain things a victim or a wrongdoer can feel or do that might change the wrongdoer's status as blameworthy. A wrongdoer might experience guilt, atone, apologize, and make reparations. A victim might forgive. Such actions and emotions seem to be reasons for why the victim should stop feeling resentment, or at least for resentment to diminish and for why the wrongdoer should stop feeling guilt for their action, or at least for guilt to diminish. Moreover, these reasons seem relevant to the agent's blameworthiness, and not merely to the overall justification of continued blame.

My aim in this chapter is to answer the question of how and why blameworthiness can cease or diminish. In order to investigate this question, we need to consider what it is to be blameworthy. I will begin by discussing several ways in which a theory which understands blameworthiness in terms of the fittingness of resentment and indignation might attempt to answer this question. I will argue that all of the most plausible candidates face serious difficulties (Sections 3–5). The problem is that it is very hard to develop a view of the representational content of blame that can account for the ways in which, intuitively, blameworthiness might diminish or disappear. The solution, I will argue, is to adopt a different account of blameworthiness, which does not rely merely on the fittingness of other-directed blame, but rather on the desert of self-directed blame. If we understand blameworthiness in terms of *deserved guilt*, we can give a plausible account of how blameworthiness can change over time. In Sections 6 and 7, I present this account. The thesis I will defend is this: whether an agent remains blameworthy will depend on whether she has experienced the guilt she deserved to feel for her action, attitude, or omission.

2   Blameworthiness and the Reactive Attitudes

The starting point for my discussion is the following, commonly accepted, generic biconditional:

Blameworthiness: An agent S is blameworthy for x if it is appropriate to blame S for x.[2]

However, sometimes we use the word "blameworthiness" in a different way. We talk of an agent being *guilty of a wrongdoing*, meaning simply that S did some wrongful action x at some point t and that they satisfied the control and knowledge conditions for being morally responsible for x at t. No matter what happens after, it remains the case that the agent did x under certain conditions. In this sense, it will remain true that they are guilty of the wrongdoing.[3] Note however that this conception of blameworthiness does not say anything about how we should treat or feel towards agents who are blameworthy in this sense. Consider an analogy.[4] An offender who serves his time is nevertheless still guilty of his crime. It will remain true that he has committed the crime, acting with the relevant capacities. However, it would no longer be appropriate to keep him in prison. After all, he has gotten what he deserved. Whereas punishment was appropriate when he was sentenced, it no longer is when he has served his time. Similarly, although a culpable wrongdoer will always remain guilty of his wrongdoing, it is by no means obvious whether it will always be appropriate to blame him for his wrongdoing. What gives the debate about moral blameworthiness its urgency is the question of whether our practices of feeling and expressing blame are appropriate at a particular time. Therefore, I will be concerned with blameworthiness in the sense that is identified by the appropriateness of blame, and not with blameworthiness in the sense of being guilty of a wrongdoing.[5]

The accounts of blameworthiness I will focus on in this chapter understand blame as an emotion.[6] Blame is typically understood either as resentment or indignation (Hieronymi, 2001; Graham, 2014; Menges, 2017b; Strabbing, 2019). Appropriateness is understood as fittingness. Emotions are commonly taken to represent their objects as having evaluative properties. Envy portrays one's rival as having something that one lacks, and casts this circumstance in a negative light. Regret represents one's action as a mistake. Emotions are fitting only when such representations are correct or accurate. As D'Arms and Jacobson (2000, p. 72) put it, in this respect, "the fittingness of an emotion is

---

[2] See, for example, Wallace (1994), Fischer and Ravizza (2000), McKenna (2012), Brink and Nelkin (2013), Pereboom (2014), Rosen (2015), Shoemaker (2015), and Menges (2017a).
[3] Khoury and Matheson (2018, p. 207) call this the trivial sense of blameworthiness, since it follows trivially from the fixity of the past.
[4] I borrow this analogy from Clarke (forthcoming) who argues that blameworthiness ought to be understood analogous to legal guilt rather than analogous to the appropriateness of punishment.
[5] Thanks to Michael McKenna for pressing me on this point.
[6] I will also focus on moral blameworthiness as accountability in this chapter. For discussions of other kinds of blameworthiness, see Watson (2004), Shoemaker (2015), and Carlsson (2019).

like the truth of a belief." This conception of fittingness is sometimes called alethic (Rosen, 2015).[7] Once we specify the relevant notions of blame and appropriateness, we get the following account of blame:

> **Blameworthiness as fitting resentment:** An agent S is blameworthy for x if it is fitting to resent S for x. (Hieronymi, 2001; Graham, 2014; Strabbing, 2019)[8]

According to **Blameworthiness as fitting resentment**, an agent is blameworthy to the extent that resentment is fitting. Whether blame is fitting will thus depend on what resentment represents. Different views give different accounts of the representational content of blame. Graham (2014), for example, takes resentment to be constituted only by a thought about the wrongdoer's insufficiently good will.[9] Strabbing (2019) adds to that a thought about the wrongdoer's capacity to have acted better than she did. Such differences will yield different accounts of the conditions of blameworthiness.

However, to answer the question of whether blameworthiness can change over time, we also need to know how these thoughts are indexed to time.[10] Does resentment represent the wrongdoer's quality of will or capacity to act better at the time of the wrongful action, or does it rather represent these attributes at the moment of blaming?

3   Resentment Indexed to the Past

Let us begin with the first option. Although few accounts have addressed this issue explicitly, it is possible to draw conclusions from how the representational content is formulated by different philosophers. Graham writes: "the content of a blame emotion felt toward a person for phi-ing is that, in phi-ing, that person *has* violated a moral requirement of respect" (Graham, 2014, p. 408, my italics). Similarly, Strabbing defines the two constitutive thoughts as follows: "(1) In doing A, S *expressed* insufficient good will (toward me), (2) S could have done better" (2019, p. 3136, my

---

[7] Note that this sense of fittingness is different from the ones typically employed in value theory. The alethic sense of fittingness is neither analysed in terms of reasons nor value, nor is it a *sui generis* normative concept. For discussion of different senses of fittingness, see Howard (2018) and Macnamara (2020).

[8] Shoemaker (2015) shares this framework but argues that we should rather understand blaming emotions in the accountability sense as what he calls agential anger.

[9] More specifically, he takes the blaming emotions to represent the wrongdoer as having violated "a moral requirement of respect."

[10] Coleman & Sarch (2012, p. 14) note that this may be a way that reactive attitude accounts of moral blameworthiness might attempt to deal with the issue of blameworthiness over time.

italics). Both of these formulations define the representations in the past tense. Resentment represents something in the past. This gives us:

> **Resentment indexed to the past:** Resentment represents the blameworthy agent as having acted wrongly, with ill will, sufficient control, and so on *at the time of wrongdoing.*

This emotion will be fitting if what the emotion represented is correct: an agent is blameworthy if and only if she acted wrongly with control, knowledge, insufficient quality of will, and so on at the time of action. As a matter of phenomenology, this way of indexing the representational content seems plausible. Blame is typically backward-looking, so it seems natural to take its representational content to be about the past: about the wrongness of the action and the agent's mental states, at the time of action, or prior to the action. When we blame other people, it is directed towards them as they are now, but what we blame them *for* is typically not about who they are now, but rather about what they did in the past.

An implication of this view is that blameworthiness is forever. On this view, resentment represents what happened in the past, and nothing that happens in the present can change the past. Resentment will always be fitting, no matter what happens afterwards, since the content of this representation will always be correct. Therefore, the agent will always be blameworthy. This is a problematic implication of the view. Guilt, atonement, reparation, and forgiveness seem able to lessen or extinguish one's blameworthiness. But if resentment is indexed to the past, those actions and emotions would not make resentment any less fitting.

The most principled reply on behalf of **Resentment indexed to the past** is to maintain that resentment is *always* fitting when its representational content is correct, so the wrongdoer would always be blameworthy. We should, however, distinguish between fitting blame *and an all things considered justification* of blame. Although resentment is always fitting, on this view, there are often reasons against feeling resentment, and these reasons can gain strength over time. These reasons will not bear on the blameworthiness of an agent. In this sense, they are reasons of the wrong kind. However, that doesn't make them any less important when considering whether to continue to blame. First, one may perhaps lack the standing to blame. Over time, for example in a long relationship, one might have come to commit many of the wrongs for which one initially blamed the other. This provides reasons against blaming. Second, continued resentment over long stretches of time will often be damaging to our relationships and detrimental to our own well-being. This fact gives us both moral and prudential reasons to let go of blame.[11] Third, and perhaps most importantly, the *significance* of the wrongdoing in one's life will change over time. The reason why we resent someone who wronged us depends on many factors: a comment might be hurtful because of one's vulnerability at a certain point in life, or because of the role the wrongdoer played in our life at that moment. These things might change and this may change one's reasons to feel resentment, although resentment will nevertheless continue to be fitting. Given the prevalence of strong, albeit wrong, kinds of reason not to feel resentment for wrongs that happened long ago, the proponent of **Resentment indexed to the past** could provide a debunking explanation for why one might think that blameworthiness can diminish or disappear over time: blameworthiness is forever, but our (wrong kinds of) reasons for continued blame are not.

I don't think this reply is successful. Although many of our reasons to stop blaming do not have any bearing on whether an agent remains blameworthy, there are many reasons which do. Consider self-blame. As Douglas Portmore has argued, the fact that an agent already has blamed herself by feeling guilty seems to matter to whether it is appropriate for her to continue blaming herself (Portmore, 2019b, p. 15). Unlike the reasons for ceasing to blame discussed above, the fact that you already have blamed yourself does seem to affect your blameworthiness. We can illustrate this with a comparative case. Consider two agents who both acted wrongly. Suppose that their wrongdoings are similar in all relevant respects. Their actions were equally wrong, committed with the same quality of will, knowledge, and control. One of the wrongdoers experienced guilt for what he did: he was pained by the recognition of his wrongdoing. The other wrongdoer did not experience guilt. Although both were equally blameworthy at the time of action, it seems, at the very least, that the former wrongdoer is *less* blameworthy than the latter at some later point in time. Yet, according to **Resentment indexed to the past**, it follows that they are equally blameworthy, since by stipulation, they were similar in all relevant aspects at the time of action. Similar cases could be constructed where one but not the other wrongdoer not only experiences guilt, but also apologizes, atones, and is forgiven. Intuitively, these kinds of actions will make the wrongdoer less blameworthy than he otherwise would have been, but **Resentment indexed to the past** has no way of explaining why this should be the case.

---

[11] For an interesting discussion of letting go of resentment, see Milam and Brunning (2018).

4   Resentment Indexed to the Present

To avoid these problems, a natural solution would be to think that resentment is not indexed to the past, but rather to some objectionable quality that the agent displays at the present. Call this view **Resentment indexed to the present**. Recently, Khoury and Matheson (2018) have defended this kind of view. The main point of their paper is to show that blameworthiness can diminish over time, depending on the wrongdoer's psychological connectedness to her past self. Even though a wrongdoer is psychologically continuous with her past self (through overlapping chains of strong psychological connectedness), it does not follow that she now shares any of the objectionable psychological features of her past self. It is possible to be psychologically continuous with one's past self, but at the same time be psychologically disconnected to it. If that is the case, the agent is no longer blameworthy. They illustrate their claim with the example of Leon, who drinks from the well of immortality. At the age of 30 Leon commits a terrible crime. However, at the age of 530 Leon "is a perfect time-slice psychological twin of your favourite moral saint. At 530 Leon shares no distinctive psychological features with Leon 30 but remain psychologically and biologically continuous with him" (Khoury & Matheson, 2018, p. 214). Khoury and Matheson argue that at 530, Leon is not blameworthy for the atrocity he committed when he was 30, because he no longer shares any of the psychological features that were essential to his performing the atrocity.

They rely on the following version of **Blameworthiness as fitting resentment:** "we claim that the intentional content of blame involves the attribution of a flaw to the subject. That is, blaming involves thinking or representing the subject to have a flaw. And a necessary condition of the subject being a worthy target of blame is the truth of this thought or accuracy of this representation" (Khoury & Matheson, 2018, p. 222). It is clear from the context that they take resentment to represent the wrongdoer as having a flaw at the moment of blaming. They use this account to explain how someone whose psychology changes radically can cease to be blameworthy: if the agent no longer displays the flaw, the representational content is no longer correct. This means that resentment is no longer fitting, and thus, that the agent is no longer blameworthy. This view can better account for the comparative case presented above. This is not because guilt or apologies as such lessen the agent's blameworthiness, but rather because guilt and apologies can serve as *evidence* for the fact that the flaw is gone.

I think this account suffers from two problems. First, the intuition that guilt or apologies may lessen an agent's blameworthiness is not, it seems to me, best explained by the fact that these emotions and actions are evidence for a changed personality. To illustrate, suppose my flaw that made me blameworthy in the first place just disappears by accident. In that case, it seems to me that I would still be blameworthy. Or suppose I take a pill to remove the flaw, not in order to become a better person, but – knowing Khoury and Matheson's theory – in order to avoid fitting blame in the future. In this case, my decision to take the blame is obviously indicative of some kind of flaw. But the pill works and now I don't have the flaw anymore. Given that resentment in this theory is indexed to the present, it follows that I'm no longer blameworthy. This seems to be the wrong result.

Second, it also seems that the theory can sometimes make it too hard to avoid blame. Suppose you acted wrongly because of some flaw. Afterwards you feel guilt, sincerely try to reform, and ask for forgiveness. However, the flaw remains. It does not seem obvious that you are still blameworthy (at least to the same extent) for that very action.

5   A Mixed Account

Both of the accounts of resentment considered so far assume that resentment has a simple representational content. But perhaps resentment is more complex? According to Pamela Hieronymi (2001) resentment is constituted by several judgments. Hieronymi's account is particularly relevant for our purposes because it is developed with the aim of explaining how forgiveness could be "articulate." Forgiveness, she argues, requires an overcoming of resentment, but not every kind of overcoming would count as forgiveness. The fact that resentment can be painful, counterproductive, or damaging to one's relationships constitutes perfectly good reasons to let go of resentment. But letting go of blame for these reasons is not forgiveness. Hieronymi wants to develop an account of forgiveness on which it can, to use the terminology I have been employing in this chapter, be *fitting* to stop resenting. The challenge is to explain how it could be fitting to overcome blame without excusing the wrongdoer. To be blameworthy is to be an appropriate target of blame. David Shoemaker puts the challenge well: "how might one appropriately withdraw blaming emotions fitting for someone's culpable moral transgression without also withdrawing the judgment making them fitting, namely that that person culpably committed a moral transgression" (Shoemaker, 2021, p. 33). Hieronymi's solution is to develop an account of blame on which resentment is constituted by several different judgments. In order for me to resent a wrongdoer, she argues, I must make the following three judgments: (1) the action was wrong; (2) the wrongdoer was blameworthy for the action; and

(3) I, as the one wronged, ought not to be wronged (2001, p. 530). These judgments are necessary but not sufficient for resentment. Importantly, Hieronymi also adds a fourth judgment: (4) the past wrong makes the false claim that it is acceptable that I am treated this way, and this claim, if left unaddressed, poses a threat to me. Resentment, in Hieronymi's view, is fundamentally a *protest* against the past action that persists as a threat (2001, p. 546). These judgments allow Hieronymi to provide a solution to the puzzle of forgiveness. When a wrongdoer sincerely apologizes and repudiates his wrong, the fourth judgment is no longer true: the past wrong no longer makes a threatening claim. This means that the resentment can fittingly disappear. Moreover, this can happen without excusing the wrongdoer, since the first three claims remain true.

Hieronymi's project in that paper is to develop an account of forgiveness and not to explain how blameworthiness might change over time. However, we might use some elements from her account of resentment in order to address this problem. Hieronymi is offering a *mixed* account of resentment, where some of the constitutive judgments of blame are indexed to the past, whereas one is indexed to the present. Judgments 1–3 will always remain fitting. The judgment that the wrongdoing constitutes a threatening claim, on the other hand, might change depending on the wrongdoer's repudiation of his action.

Some tweaking is necessary for this account to work as a theory of blameworthiness. The third judgment seems superfluous for our purposes. The second judgment will not work when employed in the **Blameworthiness as fitting resentment** framework. If a constitutive judgment of resentment is that the agent is blameworthy, the account will be circular and noninformative. So for the purposes of this chapter, let us substitute it with a judgment about the agent's quality of will. We then get the following mixed account:

> **Mixed account:** Resentment represents the wrongdoer as having (a) acted wrongly; (b) with a bad quality of will; and as making (c) a threatening claim.

This account would have several benefits compared to **Resentment indexed to the past**. Like Khoury and Matheson's account, it can explain how blameworthiness can change over time: once the threatening claim is sincerely repudiated, the threat is no longer present and resentment is no longer fitting, so the agent is no longer blameworthy. On this view, blame is fundamentally a protest against the threatening claim. Once this claim is taken back, there is nothing left to protest against. Similarly, it can account for the intuition that guilt expressed to the victim through atonement and apologies can influence an agent's blameworthiness. These actions can all be seen as ways of repudiating the threat. Moreover, this view avoids some of the problems I raised for **Resentment indexed to the present**. In the mixed account, it is not sufficient to change one's quality of will or to remove a flaw. It matters how one does it. If one's psychology changed dramatically, either by accident or in an intentional attempt to avoid blame in the future, without a repudiation of one's past wrongdoing the agent will still be blameworthy, since the threatening claim will remain unaddressed.

However, the mixed account faces problems of its own. First, even though expressed guilt is one way of repudiating the wrongful claim implicit in one's action, it seems possible to renounce one's action in ways that do not involve any painful emotions whatsoever. The wrongdoer might simply apologize to the victim while calmly explaining that he now understands that his action was wrong and promise never to do anything like that again. This seems sufficient to retract the threat. Of course, the victim might have more confidence in the wrongdoer's sincerity if he also expresses guilt, contrition, or remorse for his action. But this painful emotion only plays an epistemic role for the mixed account. This leaves the possibility of a fully blameworthy agent who ceases to be blameworthy without ever being pained by what he has done simply because his action no longer constitutes a threat. This strikes me as implausible.

Moreover, even in cases where the wrongful threat is repudiated through sincerely felt and expressed guilt and apologies, it is not clear that it is sufficient to render blame inappropriate. It seems that agents who have sincerely repudiated their past wrongs might nevertheless remain blameworthy. Consider two cases:

> **Cheating.** Tom is married to Mary. He cheats on her. The morning after, Tom experiences a pained acknowledgment of what he has done. He feels guilty and apologizes to Mary. Nevertheless, upon hearing Tom's expression of guilt, Mary blames Tom. She will continue to blame him for a long time.

> **Assault.** John assaults Jerry. Jerry is traumatized physically and mentally by the ordeal. After being apprehended by police, John comes to feel guilty for what he done; he painfully acknowledges what he has done. During the trial, he expresses his sincere guilt to Jerry and repudiates his action. Nevertheless, Jerry continues to blame John for assaulting him.

As Hannah Tierney (2021a) points out, blaming wrongdoers who already experience and express their guilt is in many cases perfectly appropriate. This, Tierney, argues, seems to create a problem for Hieronymi's view.

In the cases above, it is not clear in which sense Tom's and John's actions persist as threats. If resentment is fundamentally a protest against an unaddressed threat, how could it be fitting to blame wrongdoers for wrongs which no longer count as threats on Hieronymi's account (Tierney, 2021a, pp. 191–192)? At this point one may appeal to the other constitutive judgments of resentment mentioned by Hieronymi. Although the judgment about the threatening claim is no longer true, it is still the case that Tom's and John's actions are wrong, that they acted with insufficiently good will, and that their victims ought not to have been treated as they were. However, the mixed view would need to choose between two options. If the truth of the threatening claim is *necessary* to render the agent blameworthy, it seems that Tom and John are no longer blameworthy. If, on the other hand, the truth of these other thoughts involved in resentment is *sufficient* to render the agent blameworthy, even without the threatening claim, the view collapses into **Resentment indexed to the past**. Tom and John will be blameworthy forever. But it seems plausible that if they keep on experiencing guilt and amend their wrongdoings, they will at some point stop being blameworthy. At the very least, they will be less blameworthy than they once were.

David Shoemaker (2021) develops a view that is in some ways similar to the mixed account sketched above. According to him, what he takes to be the paradigmatic blaming emotion – agential anger – represents actions or attitudes as *slights*. The anger is directed towards the wrongdoer's failure to take the victim sufficiently seriously and to properly acknowledge him. The action tendency of agential anger is to communicate the anger to the wrongdoer, thereby "delivering a request that the slighter empathically acknowledge what he did" (Shoemaker, 2021, p. 51). Shoemaker argues that the wrongdoer's lack of sufficient acknowledgment creates a normative disequilibrium between the victim and the wrongdoer. Whereas for Hieronymi blame is fundamentally a protest against a persisting threat, Shoemaker understands blame as an angry request for acknowledgment.

This account of the nature of blame also helps explain how blame can *cease* to be fitting.[12] When the wrongdoer has empathically acknowledged the victim, the normative equilibrium is restored. This happens, according to Shoemaker, when the wrongdoer feels *remorse*. Shoemaker understands remorse as a "painful emotional response to my recognition of having

---

[12] Shoemaker's methodological approach in this paper is to start out with an account of what makes anger go away. Just as with Hieronymi, Shoemaker develops an account of how blame can stop being fitting as a way of explaining the puzzle of forgiveness.

caused you irremediable loss of value, a response which constitutively involves my being moved to reflect on (over and over) what I did from your perspective" (Shoemaker, 2021, p. 37). For a wrongdoer to feel remorse he must take up the victim's perspective and be open to feeling some approximation of how the victim felt as a result of the wrongdoing. Shoemaker thus understands remorse as a painful empathic acknowledgment.

Hieronymi takes blame to represent an ongoing threat. This threat disappears when the wrongdoer repudiates his action. As a result, blame is no longer fitting. Shoemaker, on the other hand, takes blame to represent an ongoing slight: a failure of acknowledgment. In his account, the "offender's empathic acknowledgment is sufficient to make it the case that the slight *is no more*" (Shoemaker, 2021, p. 51). As a result, blame is no longer fitting. It remains true, of course, that there *was* a normative disequilibrium – a slight – so the victim can still view the wrongdoer as someone who merit*ed* anger. But because the victim has gotten what he requested from the wrongdoer – empathic acknowledgment – the victim no longer has a reason of fit to blame the wrongdoer. Hence, the wrongdoer is no longer blameworthy.

Shoemaker's account is an improvement on the mixed account. Whereas a repudiation need not involve any painful emotion, the empathic acknowledgment involved in remorse is painful. So Shoemaker's account is not vulnerable to the objection that a mere repudiation of one's action is insufficient to stop being blameworthy. It might seem, however, that Shoemaker is vulnerable to the counterexamples concerning serious wrongdoing discussed above. In **Cheating** and **Assault**, it would seem perfectly appropriate for Mary and Jerry to continue to blame Tom and John even if they had experienced and expressed remorse for their wrongdoing. Here, however, Shoemaker might object that the kind of remorse he has in mind involves *empathic acknowledgment*: the wrongdoers need to fully appreciate what it is like to be pained or damaged by the wrongdoing. For serious wrongdoing, it may take time to fully appreciate this.[13] Shoemaker might thus argue that the reason why Mary and Jerry still have reasons (of fit) to blame Tom and John is that these wrongdoers have not yet fully appreciated the pain they caused.

Nevertheless, I believe that Shoemaker's account suffers from serious problems. The crucial element in Shoemaker's story is the wrongdoer's emotional perceptual stance rather than the duration and intensity of his painful emotion. If I wronged you, I must take up your emotional perspective and come to imagine how it must have felt for you when I treated you badly.

---

[13] See Shoemaker's contribution to this volume, footnote 28.

I will then have experienced a simulacrum of your pain. Once that happens, Shoemaker argues, "it looks appropriate for you to abandon hard feelings in favor of forgiveness *just as soon* as you have witnessed (and believed) my own sincere emotional devastation in light of what I did. It is, after all, obvious that I *clearly and truly get what I did*, which looks to be enough to disarm your blaming appraisal of me" (Shoemaker, 2021, p. 41, my italics).

However, one might appropriately continue to blame a wrongdoer even after it becomes obvious that they clearly and truly get what they did. This seems clear in cases of serious wrongdoing. The fact that I have taken up your emotional perspective and that I am pained by the loss I caused you is one crucial step in a process towards blame becoming inappropriate, but it is not its end point. Once I have truly acknowledged the pain I caused you, it will be appropriate for me to apologize, try to make up for my wrongdoing, and ask for forgiveness. These practices make sense in light of the fact that the victim's blame continues to be appropriate. But in Shoemaker's account the blame would cease to be fitting as soon as the wrongdoer truly get what they did. Moreover, Shoemaker's account will also struggle to make sense of the appropriateness of *self-blame*. If it is no longer fitting to blame the wrongdoer, he is no longer blameworthy. If the wrongdoer is no longer blameworthy, it would also, presumably, no longer be fitting for him to blame himself. But the fact that a wrongdoer has truly acknowledged the pain he has caused his victim does not mean that it is appropriate for him to (immediately) stop blaming himself. That acknowledgment seems to be the *beginning* of a process of appropriate self-blame. Once this acknowledgment happens, the wrongdoer will typically begin to feel guilty, and it seems appropriate to do so, at least for some time.

6 Blameworthiness as Deserved Guilt[14]

I have argued that accounts of blameworthiness that understand blameworthiness in terms of fitting resentment or agential anger will face difficulties in explaining how blameworthiness may change over time. Intuitively, there are certain things that a wrongdoer can do or feel that will diminish her blameworthiness. She can experience guilt, apologize, or make amends. Versions of **Blameworthiness as fitting resentment** struggle to account for this, either because resentment is indexed to the past, or because it is indexed to the present. What matters to a wrongdoer's blameworthiness *now* is not merely her mental state at the time of the

---

[14] This section summarizes arguments presented more fully in Carlsson (2017, 2019).

action, nor her mental state at the present time, but also the *moral process* she has undergone since the wrongdoing in the past. Even accounts, like Hieronymi's and Shoemaker's, that aim to capture these features struggle to get the details right. Fitting resentment views seem ill suited to capture this drama of atonement.

In this section, I will present an alternative theory. Accounts of blameworthiness tend to start with other-directed blame: agents are blameworthy for x to the extent that it is appropriate that others blame them for x. I suggest that we instead build our theory of blameworthiness around blaming *oneself*. To blame oneself is to experience guilt (Wallace, 1994; Clarke, 2013).[15] Guilt is characterized by its action tendencies, its representational content, and its affect. The action tendency of guilt is to express the guilt and attempt to repair the relationship that has been damaged by the wrongdoing (Lazarus, 1991; Baumeister, et al., 1994; Haidt, 2003; Nichols, 2007). I do not want to attempt a full account of the representational content of guilt. This strikes me as an extremely difficult empirical question. Answering it requires introspection, and there is no guarantee that people will find the same thing when they look inside. I think the best we can do is to give a rough gloss. In an earlier paper, I suggested (following Graham, 2014) that the representational content of guilt might simply be that one acted with insufficiently good will (see Carlsson, 2017). It now seems to me that one can feel guilty for cases in which one does not have an insufficiently good will, for example, for unwitting omissions. It seems to me now that the most promising gloss on what guilt represents might be that *one has violated a legitimate normative expectation* (Wallace, 1994), or perhaps simply that one has engaged in either a *wrongdoing or in a personal betrayal* (D'Arms and Jacobson, this volume).

Importantly, guilt is also characterized by its painful affect. When one experiences guilt, one is pained by the thought that one has violated a legitimate expectation. The thought does not necessitate the unpleasant affect. It is possible to believe that one has violated a legitimate expectation without being pained by this thought. But in that case it would not be guilt. In this sense, guilt is *constituted* by its painful affect. This is important and sets guilt apart from other-directed blame. Unlike resentment

---

[15] More specifically, to blame oneself in the accountability sense is to experience guilt. I believe that to blame oneself in the attributability sense is to experience shame. See Carlsson (2019). For alternative accounts of self-blame, see McKenna's, Pereboom's, and Shoemaker's contributions to this volume.

and indignation, guilt is necessarily experienced by the wrongdoer: the suffering involved in guilt is a necessary part of what it is to blame oneself. This suffering comes in different degrees. It can vary from a mild discomfort to a prolonged state of agony (Clarke, 2013, p. 155). But if the emotional state does not involve suffering at all, it is not guilt.

An agent is blameworthy, I suggest, to the extent that it is appropriate for her to feel guilt for what she has done. What is the relevant notion of appropriateness? I want to argue that the relevant notion is *desert*. Just as we can ask whether pain involved in punishment, sanction, or harsh treatment is deserved, we can also ask whether the painfulness of guilt is deserved.

Desert differs from fittingness in several respects.[16] First, desert, in contrast to fittingness, is a distinctly moral notion, which entails non-instrumental goodness (McKenna, 2012).[17] Although some fitting emotional responses, such as grief or gratitude, may be non-instrumentally good, non-instrumental goodness is not entailed by fittingness. It can be fitting to feel envy or disgust or to be amused by a cruel joke, but it is not non-instrumentally good to be envious, disgusted, or amused by cruel jokes. Moreover, whether an agent deserves something harmful is a consideration of justice (Feinberg, 1970; Clarke, 2016). It can be fitting to feel regret or grief, but it is not just. Finally, desert is uncontroversially a robustly normative notion. The normative status of fittingness in the alethic sense, according to which the fittingness of an emotion just consists in the correctness of its representation, is less clear cut (Tappolet, 2012). In general, it is not obvious that we have reasons to have true representations.[18] It is even less obvious that the fact that an emotion would be an accurate representation of some evaluative property would be a reason to experience that emotion. It seems doubtful that we have any reason to feel schadenfreude, although schadenfreude might be fitting. By contrast, the fact that an agent is *deserving* of something provides pro tanto reasons to make it the case that the agent gets what he deserves. These features of desert help explain why it is prima facie permissible

---

[16] The sense of desert I'm concerned with here is what Feinberg (1970) calls "personal desert." It differs from the sense in which we sometimes say that an artwork deserves admiration or a problem deserves consideration. It seems that we can capture the latter sense of desert by using the word "merit." See Howard (2018) for some examples of how merit and personal desert differ.

[17] For an account of desert that neither entails non-instrumental goodness, nor provide pro tanto reasons to bring about what is deserved, see Nelkin (2019).

[18] Although there might be a standing reason against holding false beliefs. For discussion, see Sharadin (2016).

to impose deserved harms on people who deserve them. It is prima facie permissible to make a wrongdoer experience the guilt he deserves, for example, by blaming him. But it is not prima facie permissible to impose painful emotions such as grief, embarrassment, or regret. The reason is that these emotions can be fitting, but they are not deserved (Carlsson, 2017; Pereboom, 2017).

By substituting resentment with guilt, and fittingness with desert, we get the following account of blameworthiness:

> **Blameworthiness as deserved guilt (DG):** An agent S is blameworthy for x if and only if, and in virtue of the fact that S deserves to feel guilty for x (Carlsson, 2017).

An agent is blameworthy, I propose, because she deserves to feel guilt. Deserving guilt is both a necessary and sufficient condition on being blameworthy. DG provides an explanation of how blameworthiness relates both to emotions and to harm. Like **Blameworthiness as fitting resentment**, it understands blame as a matter of emotional reactions and not as an overt form of treatment.[19] This allows for the possibility of private blame. But unlike **Blameworthiness as fitting resentment**, it also makes sense of the thought that being blameworthy involves deserved harms or suffering. However, the suffering is of a special kind. When you feel guilt, you suffer in recognizing what you have done. I believe that this captures the kind of suffering that we take blameworthy agents to deserve. It is not suffering in general, but rather the specific pain of acknowledging that you have engaged in wrongdoing or violated a legitimate expectation. An agent may suffer as a result of being blamed, without recognizing his own fault, simply because he finds criticism unpleasant or because it affects his social standing. However, what he really deserves is the pain of guilt; the suffering involved in recognizing what he has done.

Guilt must thus be fitting in the alethic sense in order to be deserved. It is only when what guilt represents is correct that the agent will be deserving of the specific pain involved in guilt.[20] But although the fittingness of guilt is a necessary condition on blameworthiness, it is not sufficient. If an agent acted wrongly or violated a legitimate normative expectation, guilt will be fitting, but this does not mean that the pain of guilt is deserved.

---

[19] For accounts that understand blame as an overt treatment, see Wallace (1994) and McKenna (2012).

[20] See D'Arms and Jacobson (this volume) as well as Portmore (this volume) for more on this point.

If the agent had an excuse, it will be neither non-instrumentally good nor just that the agent is pained by the recognition that he acted wrongly.

Another strength of DG is that it can give a straightforward explanation of excuses and exemptions. A common way to explain excuses and exemptions is by appealing to the *harm* of blame. When these hostile emotions are expressed, they can be harmful. Because of this prospect of pain and hostile treatment, certain control conditions must be met for blame to be justified (Wallace, 1994; Nelkin, 2011; Rosen, 2015). The problem with this approach is that other-directed blame need not be expressed at all, and even when it is expressed it need not be harmful (Nelkin, 2013a). Self-blame, understood as guilt, by contrast, is necessarily painful. DG provides a forceful and straightforward explanation for why control is a necessary requirement on moral blameworthiness without identifying blame with any form of overt treatment. To be blameworthy is to deserve to feel guilt. To feel guilt is to suffer. But no one deserves to suffer for what they cannot control. So no one is blameworthy for what they cannot control. Similarly, when people act wrongly without having the capacity to recognize moral reasons, or under duress, or while being coerced, they are not blameworthy because they do not deserve to experience the pain of guilt. The benefits of this way of accounting for excuses and exemptions can be seen by comparing it to **Blameworthiness as fitting resentment**. For such accounts to explain the variety of excuses and exemptions, the conditions of blameworthiness would need to be a part of, or explained by, the representational content of resentment. The content of resentment could not simply be that the agent acted with an insufficient quality of will, nor could it be that she engaged in wrongdoing or violated a legitimate expectation, for it is possible for those representations to be true without the agent being blameworthy. A child might act with an insufficient quality of will and someone might be ignorant about the legitimate expectation he violated. A conjunction of such conditions would do better. However, to capture all of the commonly accepted conditions of blameworthiness, such as voluntariness, knowledge, and control in the representational content of resentment while at the same time maintaining psychological plausibility is very difficult. The content would become implausibly complex and run the danger of violating what Gideon Rosen (2015) has called the naivety constraint: the representational content of guilt must be framed in terms that everyone capable of guilt understands. DG avoids this problem by explaining exemptions and excuses not by the content of the blaming emotion, but rather by appealing to moral facts about when the pain of guilt is deserved.

DG also makes sense of a common observation about the nature of blame. Many philosophers have recently argued that the communicative aim of blame is to generate guilt or remorse in the wrongdoer. According to Miranda Fricker, "[I]n Communicative Blame the speech act is geared specifically to bring us to feel the proper pang of remorse, where remorse is understood as a cognitively charged moral emotion – a moral perception that delivers a pained understanding of the moral wrong we have done" (2016, p. 173). Macnamara argues, "Specifically, emotional uptake of the representational content of resentment or indignation by the wrongdoer amounts to guilt" (2015b, p. 559) (see also Mason, 2019). Other philosophers suggest that guilt is the retributive aim of blame. As Gideon Rosen notes, "The wrongdoer who responds to outward blame with a sincere and cheerful promise to do better next time but without a hint of guilt or remorse palpably frustrates a desire implicit in resentment" (2015, p. 83). Similarly, Susan Wolf argues that the point of angry blame is to get the target of blame "…to experience the painful feelings of guilt and remorse" (2011, p. 338).

If it is an essential part of the nature of blame that it aims at generating a painful emotional state in its recipient, this raises a question of how blame can be justified. DG provides a natural justification for this kind of blaming. When wrongdoers deserve to feel guilty, it will be prima facie permissible for others to induce guilt in the wrongdoer (see Clarke, 2013, pp. 158–159, as well as Pereboom, 2017; Carlsson, 2017). Moreover, the blameworthy wrongdoer cannot reasonably object to the fact that blame generates guilt in him, if feeling guilty is what he deserves.[21]

7   Deserved Guilt and Blameworthiness over Time

DG has the following implication: if an agent does not deserve to feel guilty, she is not blameworthy. This means that if an agent who did deserve to feel guilt for some reason no longer deserves to feel guilty, she is no longer blameworthy. How could one stop deserving guilt? One way would be simply by having experienced a certain amount of feeling guilty. To be blameworthy, I suggested, is to deserve to feel guilty. However, this claim must be modified. As Clarke (2013) has noted, the pain of guilt comes in different degrees and it can last for a longer or shorter time. A blameworthy agent deserves to feel guilty to the right degree and for the right

---

[21] However, he could object if blaming led to other kinds of harms, or to disproportionate guilt.

amount of time. Moreover, as Portmore (2019a) has argued, experiencing a certain amount of guilt for a particular wrongdoing will influence how much guilt one deserves to experience for that wrongdoing in the future. "After all, one deserves to suffer only so much self-reproach for any given wrongdoing" (2019a, p. 20). DG thus provides a clear explanation for how an agent's blameworthiness can change over time. A blameworthy agent deserves to feel a certain amount of guilt. When she has experienced the right amount of guilt, she has gotten what she deserves. It is no longer just and non-instrumentally good that she suffers the pain of guilt. Since being blameworthy on DG is to deserve feeling guilt, this means that the agent is no longer blameworthy. Moreover, the fact that she already has experienced some but not all of the guilt she deserves makes her less blameworthy than she otherwise would have been.

DG is well equipped to solve the problems I raised for **Blameworthiness as fitting resentment.** First, in contrast to **Resentment indexed to the past**, it can explain why experienced guilt matters to one's degree of blameworthiness. Recall the two agents whose wrongdoings were similar in all relevant respects. One of them experiences guilt afterwards, the other does not. DG can explain why the former seems to be less blameworthy than the latter. He has gotten more of what he deserved.

Second, in contrast to **Resentment indexed to the present**, DG can explain how one can cease to be blameworthy without the disappearance of a flaw being either sufficient or necessary: agents can remain blameworthy even though they no longer have the flaw. A person who simply loses a flaw by accident or takes a pill in order to remove the flaw so that they can avoid appropriate blame in the future will remain blameworthy because they still *deserve* to feel guilty. On the other hand, an agent may cease being blameworthy even though he still has the same flaw so long as he has experienced the right amount of guilt.

Third, in contrast to **The mixed account**, it can explain how agents can remain being blameworthy even though they have experienced guilt and repudiated their wrongdoing so that it does not persist as a threat. Tom and John are less blameworthy than they would have been without their guilt. But they are nevertheless still blameworthy since they still deserve to feel guilty. Their victims would thus have a pro tanto justification for continued blame. Similarly, in contrast to Shoemaker's account, it can also explain why both other-directed and self-directed blame can remain appropriate even after the wrongdoer has come to fully acknowledge the pain he caused his victim. Empathic acknowledgment does not settle the issue of whether the wrongdoer still deserves to feel guilty.

DG claims that an agent ceases to be blameworthy as soon as she has experienced the right amount of guilt. Is this plausible? DG is compatible with the claim that some agents who have committed grievous wrongs will always remain blameworthy. It might very well be the case that such agents will continue to deserve guilt for their entire life, and that no amount of experienced guilt will equal the guilt they deserve to experience. However, it seems that, at least for many kinds of wrongdoing, there are limits to the amount of guilt a wrongdoer deserves. When a wrongdoer has experienced the amount of guilt she deserves, she is no longer blameworthy.[22]

This raises three important questions for my account. First, does this mean that blame is never justified when the agent already experiences the guilt they deserve? Hannah Tierney (2021a) has emphasized that we often continue to blame wrongdoers who feel and express guilt to their victims. She argues that this raises a serious worry for my view. DG provides a pro tanto justification of blame because blameworthy agents deserve to feel guilty. When people already feel the right amount of guilt, this justification will no longer be applicable. Yet, Tierney argues, this kind of blame is often perfectly appropriate. She suggests that blame has two different characteristic functions. One is to make the wrongdoer feel the appropriate guilt. But another, equally important, function is to communicate to the wider community as well as to the wrongdoer that the victim possesses self-respect. In expressing blame, the victim, according to Tierney, communicates that she should not be treated this way, and that she deserves moral attention, care, or concern in light of the perpetrator's behaviour. I believe that Tierney is right that blame often serves this function. However, I also believe that DG can allow for

---

[22] According to Portmore (2019a, 2019b, 2019c, this volume), guilt is constituted by the thought that one deserves the unpleasantness of guilt. So, in Portmore's account, an agent is blameworthy only if guilt is fitting, and guilt is only fitting if the wrongdoer deserves the unpleasantness of guilt. It is an elegant package. Since both of our views take an agent's blameworthiness to depend on whether she deserves to feel guilty, Portmore could explain how blameworthiness can change over time in exactly the same way as I have outlined in Section 7. Why not embrace Portmore's account instead? A full comparison between Portmore's account and my own falls outside the scope of this paper, but I think that we have good reasons to doubt that guilt is in fact constituted by a thought about deserved unpleasantness. First, it seems highly unusual that the content of any emotion would be constituted by a representation concerning its own justification. It seems more natural that we often have *independent* thoughts about whether our emotional reactions are justified. Second, it is crucial to Portmore's account that guilt is constituted by a thought about deserved, rather than fitting, unpleasantness. But it in order to distinguish fittingness from desert, Portmore needs to appeal to notions such as non-instrumental goodness. If we accept the naivety constraint, the representational content must be framed in terms everybody capable of experiencing the emotions understands. I don't believe that this is the case when guilt is constituted by desert and desert is understood in terms of non-instrumental goodness and justice.

this. Blame can be justified in many ways. If an agent has already suffered the guilt he deserves, he is no longer blameworthy. This provides a pro tanto reason not to generate any more guilt in him. However, the importance of communicating self-respect to the wrongdoer and to the wider community provides a pro tanto reason to continue blaming. These considerations need to be weighed against each other. Moreover, I don't think that expressing the claim that the victim deserves moral attention, care, or concern in light of the wrongdoer's behaviour requires that the wrongdoer is blameworthy. It is, for example, contested as to whether people are blameworthy for their unwitting omissions. Suppose I forgot my brother's birthday. It may be the case that I don't deserve to feel guilty for this. Nevertheless, it seems quite clear to me that my brother ought not to be treated this way, and that he deserves moral attention, care, and so on in light of my omission. This aspect of blame will often be justified even when the agent is not blameworthy.

Another worry is that the explanation I have given is simply too focused on the wrongdoer's emotions. As I emphasized when criticizing versions of **Blameworthiness as fitting resentment**, it also matters what the wrongdoer *does* after his wrongdoing. Feeling guilty can lessen a wrongdoer's blameworthiness, but so, intuitively, can apologizing, compensating, and various sorts of making amends. It would be problematic if these sorts of actions matter to a wrongdoer's level of blameworthiness only to the extent that they served as evidence of her feelings of guilt. But DG does not have this implication. According to DG, an agent is blameworthy to the extent she deserves to feel guilt. Experiencing guilt is *one* reason why one might deserve less guilt, but it is not the only one. Intuitively, the fact that one has apologized, atoned, or made amends will also matter to how much guilt one deserves to feel. What a blameworthy agent deserves is typically understood as a direct result of the wrongness of her action, her mental states at the time of action, her opportunity to avoid what she did, and the difficulty of avoiding doing what she did. These features relate to the time of her action. However, when we investigate what an agent deserves *now*, it also seems relevant to ask what she has done in the interval between the wrongful action and the present. Plausibly, when one acts wrongfully, with knowledge and control, one will not only deserve to feel guilty, but also incur certain duties towards one's victim. These can come in various forms, but at the very least it seems that such wrongdoers often will have a duty to apologize, compensate, and make amends. It seems plausible that an agent will continue to deserve to feel guilty for his wrongful action until such duties are fulfilled.

A similar story might be told about forgiveness. Certain views on forgiveness, which I find attractive, argue that in committing a blameworthy wrongdoing a wrongdoer incurs a debt to the victim from which the victim might release the wrongdoer by forgiving him (Nelkin, 2013b). One might worry that if my account were correct, forgiveness would play no role in releasing the victim from this debt. But this does not follow from my account. At least for certain grievous wrongs, it may be that agents will continue to deserve guilt, not only until they have experienced a certain amount of guilt, and fulfilled the duties incurred by their wrongdoing, but also until they are released by their debts to their victims by being forgiven.

The final worry concerns fittingness. I have argued that we should understand blameworthiness in terms of deserved guilt. Whether a wrongdoer will continue to deserve to feel guilty can change. But, as mentioned in Section 6, for guilt to be deserved, it must be fitting in the alethic sense: it must be a correct representation. I also argued that guilt's representational content is indexed to the past. It represents the agent has *having* violated a legitimate normative expectation or *having* engaged in either wrongdoing or personal betrayal. Since it is indexed to the past this representation will be true forever. This means that guilt might be fitting although the agent no longer deserves to feel guilty, and thus, no longer is blameworthy. This, however, is not a problem for my view. As noted in Section 6, the fittingness of guilt is necessary but not sufficient for blameworthiness The possibility of fitting but non-deserved guilt might perhaps have been problematic if fittingness were analysed in terms of reason or value, or if it were understood as a generic notion of appropriateness. But this is not the sense of fittingness that I have been discussing in this chapter. On the alethic sense of fittingness, fittingness is simply a matter of correct representations. And the representation that I engaged in wrongdoing or violated a legitimate normative expectation is compatible with the fact that I no longer *deserve* to feel the pain of guilt for the wrongdoing, as well as with the fact that I'm no longer blameworthy for it.

8   Conclusion

In this chapter, I have argued that accounts that understand blameworthiness in terms of fitting resentment will struggle to make sense of how blameworthiness can change over time. It matters to an agent's blameworthiness whether she has experienced guilt, apologized, and made amends, but these views have difficulties in explaining why this is the case. The solution to the problem, I argued, is to adopt a different account of blameworthiness. An agent is blameworthy to the extent that she deserves to feel guilty. When she no longer deserves to feel guilty, she is no longer blameworthy.[23]

---

[23] Thanks to the participants of the workshop on self-blame at the University of Oslo in September 2019, including Randy Clarke, Justin D'Arms, Christel Fricke, Dan Jacobson, Coleen Macnamara, Michelle Mason, Michael McKenna, Dana Nelkin, Derk Pereboom, Doug Portmore, Piers Rawling, and Krista Thomason. Special thanks to Randy Clarke and Justin D'Arms for very helpful discussions of my chapter. For excellent written comments on my chapter, I'm very grateful to Leonhard Menges and Daniel Telech, as well as to an anonymous reviewer for Cambridge University Press.

CHAPTER 10

Blame, Deserved Guilt, and Harms to Standing

Gunnar Björnsson

Having unjustifiably and inexcusably wronged another person and blaming ourselves for it, we characteristically feel guilt. We feel bad in a way prompting us to accept the justified anger and judgment of the victim and to set things right: to apologize, mitigate the harm, and mend the relationship. Moreover, trying to set things right strikes us as the only unproblematic way to alleviate the pain – unless the suffering is disproportional to the seriousness of what we have done, and needs to be turned down a notch. When proportional, the feeling of guilt is, we sense, *deserved*. Mirroring all this is the characteristic angry blame directed at us from the victims or those reacting on their behalf, implicitly or explicitly calling on us to engage in self-blame. When one is guilty, this too seems deserved; when innocent, undeserved.

Reflecting on these phenomena, it is tempting to think that

> BLAME AND DESERVED GUILT: Blaming someone for something presupposes or involves the sense that they deserve to feel guilty about it.[1]

Moreover, our sense that guilt is deserved seems independent of any thought that it would have good consequences. Guilt, we feel, is deserved merely in virtue of what we have done.[2]

Relatedly, it is tempting to think that *being blameworthy* involves or implies deserving blame, that one deserves blame only to the extent that one deserves self-blame, that self-blame is guilt, and that blaming oneself more involves feeling more guilt. From these assumptions, it follows that

> BLAMEWORTHINESS AND DESERVED GUILT: One is blameworthy for something only if one deserves to feel guilty about it.[3] One is worthy of more blame only if one deserves to feel more guilt.

---

[1] For the latter, stronger idea, see Portmore's (this volume) suggestion that blame involves its seeming to the blamer that the target "deserves to suffer the unpleasantness of guilt, regret, or remorse."

[2] In the terminology of Pereboom (2001, 2014), the desert thus seems to be "basic."

[3] See, for example, Clarke (2016) about moral blameworthiness. Duggan (2018) defends the closely related thesis that one is morally responsible "in a liability sense for a transgression" only if one deserves to feel guilt.

More strongly, one might think that deservedness of guilt, or guiltworthiness, constitutes the explanatory core of blameworthiness.[4] First, an influential Strawsonian tradition understands other-blame as resentment or indignation (see, e.g., Wallace, 1994; Wolf, 2011, inspired by Strawson, 1962), and it is natural to see such reactive attitudes as aiming exactly at the target's pained recognition of what they have done (see, among many others, Darwall, 2006, ch. 4; Macnamara, 2015b; Rosen, 2015; Shoemaker, 2015, ch. 3; and Fricker, 2016). Given this, other-blame seems to presuppose exactly what feeling guilt does: that the target deserves to feel guilt. Second, one might think that it is the implication of deserved guilt that best explains the common idea that blame is a *sanction* that one can deserve more or less of, that degrees of blameworthiness are a matter of the *severity* of the deserved sanction, and that one can therefore only be to blame for things over which one had a high degree of control. This idea might seem to fit badly with an understanding of blameworthiness in terms of other-blame, as the severity of the sanctions imposed by indignation seems highly contingent on the blamed agent's dependence on the blamer's good will and the circumstances in which the indignation is expressed. By contrast, feeling guilt seems to be a form of suffering and so bad for one, and feeling more guilt is worse.[5]

These connections between blame, blameworthiness, and guilt are natural and have considerable explanatory potential. But as I will argue, they are fundamentally mistaken. Trying to account for a wider range of cases, we can see that blame does not presuppose that the target deserves to feel guilt and does not essentially aim at the target's suffering in recognition of what they have done, even when taking the form of resentment or indignation. And the blameworthy do not necessarily *deserve* to be blamed, and even when they do, they do not necessarily deserve to suffer.

On the constructive side, I will offer a new explanation of why, in *typical* cases of moral blameworthiness, the agent deserves blame, and in particular the pained recognition of guilt. The explanation will lean on (i) a general account of moral and non-moral blame and blameworthiness and (ii) a version of the popular idea that moral blame in particular targets agents' objectionable quality of will.

---

[4] Carlsson (2017, 2019) defends this thought for "accountability blame," which involves reactive attitudes like resentment, indignation, and guilt, but not for what he calls attributability blame.

[5] See Carlsson (2017, 2019). I reject the claim that the control condition of blameworthiness is explained by the sanctioning involved in blame because (i) non-moral blameworthiness can require at least as much control as moral blameworthiness without involving suffering and (ii) the control requirement seems well explained from the assumption that moral blame is grounded in demands that agents care about moral values. (Some of this will be clearer later on; also see Björnsson & Persson, 2012; Björnsson, 2017a.)

1   Non-Moral Self-Blame without Guilt or Desert

Though most who accept BLAME AND DESERVED GUILT or BLAMEWORTHINESS AND DESERVED GUILT have had moral blame in mind, our focus will first be on cases of non-moral self-blame. The reason for this is twofold. First, such cases show how some of the aspects that are also central to moral blame bring neither the suffering of paradigmatic feelings of guilt, nor any sense that suffering is deserved. Second, they illustrate the structure that moral and non-moral blame have in common, a structure that will be central to understanding what is special about moral blame and why paradigmatic cases of moral self-blame do involve something that is properly called suffering and is well understood as deserved.

For an example of the relevant sort of non-moral self-blame, contrast three cases where I form a false belief. Suppose first that I form it based on evidence that would mislead anyone. Later learning that the belief is false, I judge that it was in this way epistemically bad, but I don't blame myself for it: that I formed this false belief was merely a matter of bad epistemic luck. Suppose next that I form the belief based on evidence that would mislead nearly everyone, but not those with truly exemplary epistemic habits. Learning that it is false, I also learn that the evidence I relied upon had an esoteric statistical property revealing it as unreliable. With my formation of a false belief serving as a concrete lesson, I update my epistemic strategies accordingly, refining my doxastic heuristics. But I don't blame myself for the failure; though I hold myself to high epistemic standards, they don't require knowing about and keeping track of esoteric statistics that I haven't come upon before. Suppose, finally, that I form the belief based on someone else's authority, failing to check who they were and what their evidence was because the belief pleasingly seemed to support a hypothesis I hoped to be true. Upon discovering the falsehood of the belief and realizing why I had formed it, I not only see the episode as a lesson for future belief formation, but blame myself for having formed a false belief because of a substandard responsiveness to the evidence.

My self-blame here is not merely causal self-blame or some weak form of agent regret: In all three cases, my agency was involved in the regrettable formation of the false belief, but only the third occasioned self-blame. Nor is the self-blame merely a matter of pinning the belief on a failure to respond to available reasons, as my belief in the second case was due to my failure to take into account a statistical property of the available evidence. It is crucial that I fell short of standards that I hold myself to and take to have applied to me at the time. This is why the epistemically bad formation of a bad belief highlights something (perhaps mildly) alarming about me. And it is why self-blame of this sort characteristically involves an emotional reaction that not only has the bad action or outcome as its object, but also *targets* oneself, and is naturally expressed in a self-directed reprimand.[6]

To substantiate these claims, I will say more below about the nature of self-blame and blame generally. But pending further detail, we can recognize the difference between my reactions in the three cases. We can also recognize that the third case will characteristically involve a negatively valenced emotional response to the badness of the belief, my gullibility, and the involvement of my gullibility in the belief formation, likely in the form of irritation or anger directed at myself. This response is naturally understood as self-blame, and seems fitting in light of what I have done. Still, it does not seem to constitute even mild *suffering* of the sort characteristic of guilt, such that it is prima facie non-instrumentally *bad* for me to be in it.[7] It also does not seem to constitute a *sanction*, or a state that I *deserve* to be in. And it does not seem to presuppose or involve the sense that I deserve to suffer. Because of all this, it doesn't much resemble paradigmatic cases of moral guilt.

Take these points in turn, starting with the claim that the negatively valenced state of self-blame doesn't constitute suffering or make me prima facie non-instrumentally worse off. Admittedly, realizing that some substandard aspect of oneself has resulted in a bad outcome might be deeply painful, especially when the aspect is resistant to change or central to one's self-conception. But it doesn't have to be that way, and most often isn't. Noticing and being momentarily alarmed by my gullibly acquired misbelief, I commit to be more alert to the quality of certain kinds of evidence, and then move on. While my life might have been made marginally worse by my gullibility and my misbelief, it was not made prima facie non-instrumentally worse by fleetingly being in the negatively valenced state of self-blame. Perhaps the state disrupted other activities, and perhaps dramatically so. Indeed, it might be part of the function of this sort of state to

---

6 My self-blame thus goes beyond mere *criticism*, understood as attempts to get the agent to understand the reasons not to do what they did, why it was the wrong thing to do, and to change behavior (Jeppsson, 2016). It also goes beyond negative evaluative and emotional responses to *attributability*, that is, to bad aspects of agency that do not necessarily violate standards that the agent is held to (see, e.g., Watson, 1996; Arpaly & Schroeder, 2014; Shoemaker, 2015), and more characteristically involves self-directed anger or irritation rather than shame, and so isn't mere "attributability blame" in the sense of Carlsson (2019). But as I will stress, it also lacks the connection to sanctions and harsh treatment standardly associated with *accountability* blame.

7 I say prima facie non-instrumentally bad. One might think that some suffering is overall non-instrumentally good for someone because it is deserved, but that it is deserved exactly because it is prima facie non-instrumentally bad for them.

disrupt other ongoing activities by calling on me to immediately notice the role my gullibility played in the formation of a false belief and to commit to be less gullible. But suppose that any negative disruptive consequences were insignificant enough to be compensated for by my decreased gullibility. Then I wouldn't have traded anything of value to not be in that state.

One might perhaps think that negatively valenced phenomenal states are necessarily prima facie bad for one. But that's a mistake. What gives phenomenal states their negative valence is not that they are themselves bad, but that they present something as bad: in this case the false belief, my gullibility, and the role of my gullibility in forming the belief. Moreover, such states do not plausibly constitute even mild suffering as long as one is *at peace* with them; as long as one does not occurrently desire not to be in them. Consider sorrow as an example.[8] While sorrow is negatively valenced and can constitute suffering, sorrow with which one has found peace does not. Likewise for regret, disappointment, frustration, and even pain. While the moments of regret, disappointment, and frustration involved in practicing a skill might constitute suffering, they typically do not, and the same goes for the pains of physical exercise and sports massage.[9]

Because being in a negatively valenced state of self-blame doesn't itself constitute a cost to me, it is also not well understood as a sanction. One might naturally think that it is: It is the response to violated expectations, like legal sanctions, and arguably has as its psychological function to bring me to satisfy a certain standard, analogously to how legal sanctions (on some understandings) have as their function to promote abidance by imposing costs on transgressions. But unlike legal sanctions (so understood), it isn't that the state is bad for me that prompts me to be less gullible, to avoid being in that state. Rather, the state is one of being alerted to how the bad gullibility yielded a bad belief, and of being alarmed by this. Compare Christine Korsgaard's claim that "Pain is not the condition that is a reason to change your condition. ... It is your perception that you have a reason to change your condition" (Korsgaard, 1996, p. 148). Setting aside Korsgaard's claim about pain specifically, I similarly say that my negatively valenced feeling of self-blame is my vivid sense that forming the belief was bad, that being gullible in that way is unacceptable, and that my

---

[8] Duggan (2018) interestingly understands guilt as sorrow over what one has done, a kind of sorrow deserved by those "morally responsible in a liability sense for a transgression."

[9] For axiological purposes, one might want to understand pain as an occurrent experiential state that one occurrently prefers not to be in for its own sake. Given that notion, pain might perhaps always be prima facie non-instrumentally bad for one, but then some states that are naturally described as painful fail to be pains.

gullibility was instrumentally bad in virtue of its role in the formation of the belief. The role of the state is to alert me to reasons to improve, not to *be* such a reason (compare Bok, 1998, pp. 167–170).

Being in this state of self-blame is also not something I *deserve*. It might be natural to mistake it for such a state: It is a negatively valenced phenomenal state, and one that seems fitting in light of my gullible belief formation. But that's too quick. As I have just argued, the state isn't bad for me, and it seems that in order for me to deserve something, it has to be bad for me in some sense, not good or neutral. For example, suppose that I recklessly break something of yours. Then I might incur obligations to let you know and to do my best to mend the thing and our relationship, and it is natural to think that I deserve the hardships involved. But if I am eager to let you know what I have done to get on with the mending, and doing so is a relief rather than a burden, it is odd to say that I deserve letting you know (see Nelkin, 2013, p. 121, 2016, p. 177; Macnamara, 2020).

Moreover, even if my negatively valenced state of self-blame were bad and so could in principle be deserved, it wouldn't actually be deserved, even on the plausible assumption that it is in some intuitive sense fitting. Here are two ways of seeing this: First, if the state had been deserved in the way that feeling guilt is deserved in central cases of moral blameworthiness, it would be prima facie wrong or bad to decrease its intensity and duration. But it isn't: If I could diminish the state to a mere flicker through meditation, without undermining the lessons learned from the occasion, the diminishing of the state would not be a consideration against meditating. Second, for being in the state to be deserved in the relevant sense, it would have to be good *as a matter of justice*, because of what makes me blameworthy (see Macnamara, 2015b; Clarke, 2016). Now, being pained by my gullible misbelief might perhaps be seen as good in virtue of being an integral part of my caring about truth and knowledge, or an integral part of caring about living up to the standard I violated, analogous to how the pain of grief might be seen as good in virtue of being an integral part of caring about what has been lost.[10] And perhaps painful disappointment or self-scorn might seem "deserved" in the sense that it would correctly reflect that I fell short of standards I hold myself to. But it is hard to see how the degree to which I feel bad about my gullible misbelief is a matter of justice.[11]

[10] See McKenna (2019); though see Nelkin (2019) for criticism.
[11] Compare Macnamara (2020) about attempts to establish claims like BLAMEWORTHINESS AND DESERVED GUILT on the basis of claims about goodness or fittingness.

Neither my self-blame nor my sense that I am to blame for my gullible misbelief seems to come with the sense that I deserve to be pained by the recognition of what I have done. Nor does my self-blame seem to presuppose that I deserve this. As I have argued, the negatively valenced feeling involved is not itself prima facie non-instrumentally bad, and there is no sign that it aims or involves any disposition to impose suffering. While self-directed anger might be involved in this sort of self-blame – one might "feel like kicking oneself" – that anger craves no suffering in response, only that one start taking the standard with sufficient seriousness.[12]

Finally, and for all the above reasons, it should be clear that the sort of self-blame at work in many non-moral cases doesn't constitute guilt. I might be annoyed that I formed the belief and might give myself an angry reprimand before moving on. But the negatively valenced state I'm in lacks characteristic elements of guilt: The state isn't prima facie non-instrumentally bad for me, isn't plausibly or intuitively understood as deserved, and involves no sense that I deserve to suffer or that there is anything that has to be set right, apart from the sense that my way of responding to evidence won't do.

Admittedly, some of what I have said about my self-blame might be intelligibly resisted. For suppose that the operative epistemic standards are moral standards, perhaps grounded in the fact that substandard belief formation might harm others or constitute a kind of morally objectionable disrespect of reason or truth. Then it might seem less implausible that I deserve to feel bad about my gullible belief formation. (In Section 4, we return to how the nature of the standards involved matters for desert.) All I need here, though, is the idea that some clear cases of non-moral self-blame differ in relevant regards from paradigmatic moral self-blame. Thus, consider my case of epistemic self-blame on the assumption that while I violated standards that I justifiably hold myself to, satisfying these standards or holding myself to them is not morally required. Or consider the self-blame of Judy, a formidable juggler. Instead of forming a false belief like me, she miscalculates a throw and loses the rhythm necessary to complete an advanced sequence involving a chainsaw and two torches. Like my gullible belief formation, her sequence was botched because her skill-relevant responsiveness to the situation fell below the exacting standard that

---

[12] Portmore (this volume) points to psychological experiments confirming the presence of desert-related characteristics in central cases of moral blame, self-blame, and guilt. He further takes these experiments to suggest that the desert element is present also in non-moral blame, based on data indicating strong similarities between guilt and regret of self-inflicted harm (Zeelenberg & Breugelmans, 2008). As far as I can tell, however, the similarities in question do not involve what is essential to the relevant sense of desert.

she justifiably holds herself to. And like me, she blames herself for the resulting failure, annoyed, before giving the sequence another try and succeeding. What I said about my self-blame goes equally for hers: Though her response was substandard, botching the sequence bad, and her state of self-blame fitting, her fleeting negatively valenced state of self-blame didn't make her situation prima facie worse, isn't plausibly seen as a sanction, isn't plausibly something that she deserved in the way guilt seems deserved in paradigmatic cases of moral blameworthiness, and doesn't involve or presuppose the sense that she deserves to suffer.

In light of all this, it seems clear that BLAME AND DESERVED GUILT is mistaken if understood without restriction, as concerned with blame generally. Likewise, BLAMEWORTHINESS AND DESERVED GUILT is mistaken if understood as concerned with blameworthiness generally. For it seems clear that I am to blame for my gullible belief-formation and Judy is to blame for her botched sequence, and that we are thus in some sense correct in blaming ourselves for these things and so blameworthy for them (in senses of "correct" and "blameworthy" that I'll return to in Section 3).

2   Moral Blameworthiness without Deserved Suffering

Though reflection on non-moral blame and blameworthiness undermines unrestricted forms of BLAME AND DESERVED GUILT and BLAMEWORTHINESS AND DESERVED GUILT, most who have been tempted by claims like these have had restricted kinds of blame and blameworthiness in mind. For some, it has been *moral* blame and *moral* blameworthiness. For others, it has been blame that involves *holding someone accountable* and a corresponding relation of *accountability*, that is, the relation in virtue of which one is liable to be held accountable for something.[13] Eventually, I will argue that even restricted in these ways, the two capitalized claims fail. But pending that argument, the fact that they have to be restricted raises questions:

1. What is it about *moral* or *accountability* blameworthiness specifically that makes blame *deserved*?
2. Why is it that *guilt* specifically is deserved in cases of accountability or moral blameworthiness?

---

[13] Carlsson (2017) and Duggan (2018) defend the implication from accountability (or "liability" in Duggan's terminology) to deserved guilt. For the classic piece on the distinction between accountability and neighboring relations between an agent and a possible object of blame, see Watson (1996). Also see n. 6.

The answer to the first question will be based on an assumption about the standards violated by the morally blameworthy. I understand these as interpersonally valid demands to give people's perspectives and interest and other moral values a certain *weight* in deliberation and action, or to accord them a certain de facto "standing". In violating such standards, one has accorded some value too low a standing compared to one's own perspective or interests. One thus incurs obligations to restore its relative standing, by subordinating one's own perspective or interests to it, and becomes liable to be subordinated by others.

The answer to the second question is that paradigmatic cases of moral blame involve the sense that subordination is required, and specifically a kind of subordination that involves staying with the pained recognition of one's fault.

These answers vindicate the intuitions supporting the capitalized claims. But they also leave open the possibility that one might be morally blameworthy without deserving pain specifically, as well as the possibility of moral blame that works more like non-moral blame. Before spelling out the relevant account of blame and blameworthiness generally and the specifics of moral blame and blameworthiness, consider for illustration:

> *Jiro*: Because his writing has been unusually engaging, Jiro has knowingly ignored a promise to go visit his friend Joan, who is going through a crisis. When he sees that Joan is calling, presumably to hear what is going on, Jiro immediately regrets his priorities. Clearly, it was his insufficient concern for Joan and his exaggerated focus on writing that left Joan hanging at a difficult time. As Jiro has done similar things before, to others, and has become increasingly dissatisfied with this tendency, this realization prompts an immediate value conversion. As a result, he sincerely apologizes to Joan and sets out to make his way there as quickly as possible to make things right. Throughout, he feels a number of emotions. First, regret and horror at what he had done and concern for Joan, before the value conversion prompts empathy-driven somber determination to do right by Joan, initially accompanied by relief that he had cast off his mistaken values.

On natural ways of filling in this scenario, it seems that (1) Jiro is morally to blame for not visiting Joan prior to the phone call. (2) Jiro deserves blame for what he has done. (3) There is nothing that he deserved to feel or do in virtue of what he had done that he didn't feel or do. But (4) neither the explicit details of the story nor what needs to be filled in implies any *suffering* on Jiro's part. It is true that in attending to the fact that he had harmed Joan and made his own life prima facie non-instrumentally worse, he reacted with horror and regret. As noted, though, we shouldn't think that being in negatively valenced phenomenal states, including moments of regret or horror, is itself necessarily prima facie non-instrumentally bad for one. And because of Jiro's immediate value conversion, he found himself at peace with the fact that his old values and actions were unacceptable and that he would have to make up for what he had done.

Like our cases of non-moral blame, the case of Jiro suggests that blame and blameworthiness do not presuppose or imply that the target deserves to suffer. Some who have considered cases where the guilty party changes values and does their best to set things right but without suffering the pains of guilt have drawn the opposite conclusion. But they might have imagined the agent, not as Jiro, but as a "wrongdoer who responds to outward blame with a sincere and cheerful promise to do better next time but without a hint of guilt or remorse" (see Rosen, 2015, pp. 82–83). Considering such a character, it is natural to think that he "palpably frustrates a desire implicit in resentment" (Rosen, 2015, p. 83) or in any case that he doesn't get what he deserves. But cheerfulness isn't the only alternative to suffering. When we empathically hear someone out who has been harmed, or engage in hard and serious conversation, or humbly consider our faults, or do all these things intermixed, we are not cheerful, and our phenomenal states might be negatively valenced. But we also do not necessarily suffer, or find ourselves in states that are prima facie noninstrumentally bad for us. Jiro doesn't, and still his emotional response seems perfectly adequate to his blameworthiness.

In what follows, I will outline an account of blame and blameworthiness generally and an account of what makes *moral* instances of these special. These accounts, I will argue, can explain why the suffering of guilt is deserved in typical cases of moral blameworthiness but not in cases of non-moral blameworthiness, and not in cases like Jiro's.

3   Blame and Blameworthiness

Blame, whether moral or non-moral, has both a *target* and an *object*: *someone* is blamed *for something*. To account for blame, we thus need to understand how it relates to both target and object, what it presupposes about their relation, and what sort of a response it is to these matters.[14]

---

[14] The account here draws on accounts of blameworthiness and blame developed in Björnsson (2017a, 2020a, n.d.). For reasons of space, I cannot here motivate my preference of this account over its main competitors, but many of these have been designed primarily to handle cases of moral blame, and go wrong or stay silent about cases of non-moral blame that target failures of skill rather than failures of will and do not involve reactive attitudes, relationship modification, protests, or holding the object of blame against the target of blame.

At a natural level of description, the targets are uniform: agents with relevant capacities.[15] However, objects of blame vary immensely in salient ways, even restricting attention to moral blame. We readily blame people for attitudes, decisions, intentional actions and omissions, and acts and failures of noticing or remembering something important, along with various outcomes of all these things. As we look at other domains, it seems again that a wide variety of responses or failures to respond to aspects of the circumstances matter, as well as a variety of outcomes of such failures: failure to notice or appreciate an opening in a game of chess, to adequately balance force and direction of the foot hitting the soccer ball, or to balance colors or proportions for a painting, resulting in an avoidable loss, a failed pass, and forgettable art. One thing that objects of blame have in common, though, is that they are understood as bad within the relevant domain, as something to be avoided. Another commonality is that they are due to a substandard responsiveness to aspects of the circumstances: a responsiveness that falls short of the blamer's demands or normative expectations on the agent.

Our concern with this complex of conditions, I have argued, is primarily due to our concern with *outcomes in domains or skill*. A *skill*, in the relevant sense, is an *ability* to respond to circumstances so as to promote certain *values*. Specifically, it is a way of responding to circumstances that has been *improved* in response to successful or failed *promotion* of those values, an improvement that has been possible because the degree of promotion is systematically affected by how one responds to circumstances. Thus, acquiring knowledge or forming true, justified, or excellent beliefs are skills aimed at promoting epistemic values, as are abilities to notice, seek, and weigh evidence. Juggling is a skill aiming at excellent juggling, as are its component abilities, including various abilities to throw, catch, and track projectiles. Caring about what is morally important or valuable is also a skill, aimed at promoting the objects of caring, as are various aspects of caring well so as to better promote these objects, including dispositions to notice and be motivated by opportunities for promotion.

Blaming requires three interrelated abilities to identify certain kinds of conditions and responding to these so as to build and uphold certain levels of skill.

First, the ability to identify the value of relevant outcomes, required for learning what outcomes to promote or prevent.

---

[15] Blame can target both individual agents and groups of agents (see Björnsson, 2020b); focus here will be on the former.

Second, the ability to identify cases where good or bad outcomes are due to the responsiveness of agents so that the responsiveness can be evaluated as instrumentally good or bad and reinforced or adjusted accordingly. This involves distinguishing when modes of responsiveness explain outcomes in line with a systematic tendency to do so (in "normal" ways) and when they "just happen" to have these outcomes.

Finally, since we often rely on certain levels of skill, the ability to identify and react to instances falling below such levels so as to promote correction. Differently put: the ability to *demand* or *normatively expect* a certain skill level, in weak senses of "demand" and "normatively expect," or to *hold the agent to* a certain standard of skill.

When I say that we have *abilities* to do these things, I mean that we have mechanisms the function of which is to make it the case that we do these things, in the sense that these mechanisms continue to play the role they do in our psychology because they have done this.[16]

The mechanisms in virtue of which we have and exercise these abilities operate prior to intentional guidance, and without the involvement of reflective understanding of what exactly the values or demands are or what makes the explanatory connections relevantly normal. In a nonfactive and metaphorical sense, we just *see* these things. Specifically, in jointly exercising these abilities we can come to see something as someone's "fault":

> FAULT: For Y to be X's fault is for Y to be bad and explained in a normal way by X's responsiveness falling short of applicable standards.

Seeing something as someone's fault, I claim, is the *core* component of blaming someone for something. Judy immediately saw that the botched sequence was her fault, and Jiro immediately saw that having left Joan waiting was his fault.

Given the functions of the three abilities involved, seeing something as someone's fault plausibly has a more specific function:

> FAULT FUNCTION: The specific general function of seeing Y as X's fault is to prompt satisfaction of the relevant standard of responsiveness. The normal way for this to happen is (i) for the "demand" mechanisms to direct negative attention to X's substandard responsiveness, (ii) for the mechanisms for feedback learning to direct negative attention to the role of that responsiveness in bringing about Y, and (iii) for the negative attention to these features to prompt improvement of the responsiveness.

---

[16] For the sort of account of etiological function that I have in mind, see Millikan (1984).

The performance of this function is most straightforward in the case of self-blame, which is our main focus here. But we can be alarmed when the substandard responsiveness of another agent has bad outcomes, taking their case as a lesson for ourselves, or conveying the lesson to them as well as to third parties.

We can now spell out a general account of blame:

> BLAME: To blame X for Y is for one to see Y as X's fault and for the mechanisms normally performing the function of this state to be operative.[17]

On this account, if one thinks that something was someone's fault without that thought prompting activity in the demand and learning mechanisms, one isn't blaming (other than in a dispositional sense). Still, the mechanisms can be operative without successfully performing their full function.

I have said that blame is guided by our sense that something is someone's fault. Our intuitive sense that blame is fitting or correct in some cases but not others primarily tracks the very same condition.[18] Of course, this sense of fittingness might be guided by unjustifiable values or demands. But idealizing these away, we can say that:

> BLAMEWORTHINESS: X is *to blame* for Y, X is *blameworthy* for Y, and blaming X for Y is *fitting* or *correct*, if, and only if, Y is bad relative to a justifiable value and explained in a normal way by X's responsiveness falling short of applicable justifiable standards.

The account sketched in this section makes sense of blame's complex structure. Blame has an object and a target because it involves both a negative evaluation of the object and normative expectations directed at the agent whose substandard responsiveness explains the object. It also makes sense of blame's pervasiveness, because it relies only on abilities and responses that are central to domains of skill. And it explains why blame is embedded in or accompanied by a wide variety of emotional reactions:

---

[17] The quasi-perceptual state of seeing A as F is distinct from the explicit personal-level judgment that A is F. Indeed, I might accept that something isn't my fault but nevertheless, at some level, see it as my fault and so, at that level, blame myself for it.

The account concerns the psychological activity of blaming. There is also blaming as a communicative act or a speech act, as when someone says that Y was X's fault. Here my focus will be primarily on the former.

[18] Given FAULT FUNCTION, this is also arguably what blaming someone *represents*, in the sort of naturalistic sense of "represent" developed by Ruth Millikan, beginning with her 1984 work. That the activity of blaming is fitting or correctly represents the world doesn't mean that it is all things considered wise or morally appropriate; it might have bad consequences, or the blamer could lack standing to blame (see D'Arms & Jacobson, 2000).

disappointment or horror in light of the object of blame, regret of one's involvement in bad outcomes, often overshadowed by arousal in the form of irritation and anger aimed at dealing with the problem, and sometimes shame, disgust, and disdain, as agential failures are implicated. As we will see in the next section, the account can also help us understand what is distinctive about central cases of moral blame.

4 Moral Blame, Deserved Guilt, and Harms to Standing

Equipped with accounts of blame and blameworthiness, let us return to our questions from Section 2: Why do the *morally* blameworthy characteristically deserve certain negative consequences, and why do they often deserve to *feel guilt*, or to be pained by the recognition of their blameworthiness? The answer, I believe, is complex. It involves the nature of the normative expectations that ground moral blame, the nature of the objects of blame, and the relation between these. Seeing its complexity lets us understand both why the pain of guilt often seems deserved, and why it sometimes does not.

Start with four aspects of the demands at work in the moral domain. First, these demands concern agents' *quality of will*: They are demands that agents care about various values enough, often compared to other values. Second, these demands are *categorical*: They are demands that agents care about certain values whether they want to or not. Contrast these with some non-moral demands, such as the juggler's demands on her juggling skills, which she might understand as contingent on her own preferences. Third, these demands are at least typically *interpersonal*: Others justifiably have normative expectations that agents live up to these demands. Correspondingly, violations of the demands that ground moral blame tend to be violations of demands that not only the agent but others can justifiably make on the agent. Fourth, these demands tend to be *requirements of acceptable cooperation*. The categorical interpersonal demands are thus backed up by potential threats of partial or full alienation. If others see one as falling short, they will often be fully cooperative only after one has displayed commitment to the relevant standards.[19]

These first four features of moral demands partially explain the suffering of the morally guilty. The demands inherent in moral blame are demands that one change what one cares about. Doing so involves *abandoning* some things that one cares about, at least to some degree, by downgrading their

---

[19] For an influential discussion, see Bennett (2002).

relative importance. Prior to a completed change, this will be understood as pro tanto bad and will tend to be subject to partial inner resistance. When one is morally blameworthy, accepting these demands will thus tend to hurt.[20] Add to this that one might have been seen by others as failing expectations, and that one's valuable relationships might be threatened, and the pain of abandoning some things one values might be accompanied by social fear. Moreover, the process of coming to accept self-blame often involves coming to see clearly, with engaged empathy, not only how others might see one, but how they have been harmed. In such cases, the empathic mirroring of their pain and the regret involved in seeing what one has brought about can further contribute to suffering.[21]

All this also points to important reasons why moral self-blame triggers attempts to mend relationships and show others that one is committed to the norms one has violated.[22] And it explains why we might have not only reasons but obligations to engage in the processes that bring the suffering. For the following principles seem plausible:

> OBLIGATION FROM HARM: If some undeserved harm (material, psychological, social…) happened because of X, X acquires a pro tanto obligation to help set things right.

> OBLIGATION FROM POSITION: If X is in a unique position to help alleviate some harm, X has a pro tanto obligation to do so.

Given these, if I am morally to blame for harming a relationship, I typically acquire a pro tanto obligation to help mend it: The harm was due to me, and I am uniquely placed to set things right. And setting things right will mean accepting the demands of moral blame, and so enduring the suffering involved.

Still, what has been said thus far leaves unexplained the sense that the suffering characteristically involved in feeling guilty would be *deserved*. That sense, we have said, involves the idea that it is good as a matter of justice, in light of what makes the agent blameworthy, that the agent is subjected to it. But neither of the two principles above tracks whether the harm was due to the agent's substandard caring, or was the agent's moral fault: They would yield analogous obligations when someone harms a relationship because of a non-culpable confusion.

---

[20] Compare Bennett's (2002) suggestion that guilt is self-alienation.
[21] See Shoemaker (2015, pp. 110–111). Emotional responses to the anger of actual victims or representatives of victims might play a role in developing guilt as a response to one's own perception that one has done wrong.
[22] For some important aspects of this, see Bennett (2002).

Instead, I will suggest, what explains the implication of desert is that morally blameworthy action brings a moral imbalance in the *standing* of moral values, and in particular the standing of moral agents. While I lack space to give the idea a full defense or articulation here, my hope is that the following sketch will make it plausible enough to merit further consideration.

As understood here, the standing of something is a matter of the weight given to it in deliberation and action. The standing of some value might be most visible when we feel that it is compromised, as when someone's authority or interests or some project one cares about is ignored or downplayed: Perhaps someone's views are not taken seriously in seminars, or their preferences ignored when making plans for a night out, or perhaps the University cuts teaching and research funding while administration grows.

Crucially, moral blameworthiness is unavoidably tied to standing, so understood. The relevant moral demands are demands that we accord various weights to things, or demands that we *care* about them to certain degrees, as a Strawsonian tradition has it.[23] On the understanding I prefer, to care about a value in the relevant sense is to be disposed to notice factors promoting or thwarting it and to spend psychological, social, or material resources to promote it (Björnsson, 2017a, 2017b). Correspondingly, caring *more* about one thing than another involves being disposed to spend more resources promoting it. Given this understanding of moral demands, the morally blameworthy has always accorded less weight than morality demands to some value – to a person's perspective, well-being, or property, or to beauty, truthfulness, or human excellence, say – and this has resulted in something that is bad in relation to that value.[24] Moreover, they have given it less weight relative to their own purposes or interests than morality allows.

Importantly, when someone's relative standing is unduly lowered, this is typically not just something that was bad at the time. The imbalance in standing is an ongoing harm to that person. Perhaps when we last interacted, I gave less weight to your perspective relative to mine than morality allows. Then it remains true that I am unacceptably giving your perspective less weight than mine until this imbalance has been corrected. Compare: if I took something that was rightfully yours, it was

---

[23] See Strawson (1962), McKenna (2012), and Arpaly and Schroeder (2014). Shoemaker (2015) takes the quality of will relevant to the sort of blame that concerns us here to be quality of regard for persons; I take persons to be (very important) special cases of moral value.

[24] One might be to blame for harms of moral importance even if one cared as much as morality demands, being sufficiently disposed to notice and act on moral reasons, because one makes some other kind of mistake. But then one isn't *morally* to blame for the harm in the sense concerning us here (Björnsson, 2017b, pp. 142–144).

not just something bad that happened back then. Your right to that thing is given less weight than it should until this has been corrected.

What is it to correct an imbalance in standing? Generally speaking, it is to do more to promote the value that has been unjustly set aside or thwarted, giving less weight to that which has been unjustly favored. More concretely, if you have unduly favored your interest in some divisible good over mine, the most obvious way of correcting the imbalance is for you to favor my interest over yours by handing me some of that good. If my perspective has been unduly favored over yours in discussion, correcting the imbalance might mean giving your perspective more attention and authority while giving mine less. (A morally blameworthy agent has always unjustly favored their own perspective; typically, both perspectives and concrete material or social interests of victims have been unfairly disregarded relative to other values.)

Because standing is a matter of weight given, correcting many forms of imbalance requires the involvement of a particular weight-giver. If I haven't given enough weight to your interests, then others might compensate for that by giving you a helping hand and me the cold shoulder: The community at large might then have given our interests the right relative weight. But it remains true that *I* have, overall, inappropriately put my interests before yours. Only I can correct for that imbalance. How? Not just by coming to care about your interests to the required degree: It will still remain true that I have, overall, unduly put my interests before yours. Correcting the imbalance means putting your interest before mine in action. Similar things can be said about other forms of imbalance. If I have unduly failed to give your perspective on things the appropriate attention and weight compared to mine, correcting the imbalance does not just mean becoming more disposed to take you seriously. It means actually taking you more seriously compared to myself, in thought and action.

Based on this, here is why the morally blameworthy deserve setbacks – why such setbacks are good as a matter of justice – and why they characteristically deserve the suffering involved in feeling guilty:

First, as I understand it, the demand to give a certain weight to the perspectives or interests of others relative to your own is not just a demand to give such weight on each occasion, but a demand to properly balance *over time* the psychological and material resources invested into promoting their perspectives or interests and yours. Moreover, doing so is, in some intuitive sense, good as a matter of justice. From this it follows that if I have given your perspective or interests less weight relative to mine than required, then morality demands, as a matter of justice, that I correct this imbalance.

Second, if the guilty have an interest in avoiding the suffering characteristic of guilt, giving no weight to that interest is one way in which they can lower their own standing relative to the victim. By ignoring this interest in promoting the interests and perspective of the victim, the guilty can thus to some extent discharge the demand to rebalance after having put their own perspective over that of the victim.

This provides the outline of an explanation of why the morally blameworthy deserve to have their interests set back, in the sense that it is to some extent good, as a matter of justice. Moreover, the set-back of interest is deserved, not because of what further consequences this might have, or for contractual reasons. It is deserved exactly because the agent is morally blameworthy.

We also have an explanation of why, in central cases of moral blameworthiness, it is natural to think that the blameworthy deserves the feeling of guilt specifically, or the suffering involved in recognizing what they have done.

Still, what the guilty deserve on this explanation is not necessarily suffering. It is that their standing is lowered relative to the interests and perspectives that they have previously unduly subordinated to their own. This is why, when Jiro takes in his wrongdoing, reacts with horror, and proceeds with somber empathy-driven determination to right his wrong while setting his other interests aside, he doesn't *also* deserve to suffer. Correspondingly, while resentment, indignation, and guilt sometimes prompt action that rebalances standing by inflicting suffering on the blameworthy, rebalancing might also often be achieved by prompting the sort of response displayed by Jiro.

5 Loose Ends: Reactive Attitudes, Demands on Caring

Running out of space, I have to leave loose ends.

In particular, I have said little about the reactive attitudes that figure centrally in many accounts of moral blame, blameworthiness, and responsibility. Here I can only indicate in slogans what I find plausible given what I have said about blame and blameworthiness: *Guilt* is the sorrowful sense of having unduly disfavored someone or something,[25] *resentment* the angry sense of having been unduly disfavored, and *indignation* the angry sense that someone or something has been unduly disfavored. In each case, the object of concern is an imbalance in standing, and in each the action tendency is toward rebalancing. Because moral blame in particular presupposes that the target has unduly disfavored someone or something, it is

---

[25] Or, in an extended sense, of having been unduly favored in relation to someone or something.

naturally accompanied by one of these attitudes. And since the morally blameworthy are uniquely placed to correct the resulting imbalance, targets of moral blame are also naturally targeted by guilt, resentment, or indignation.

I have also provided only the barest outline of how demands to give weight to values over time ground reasons to rebalance in response to blameworthy action, and said nothing about how morality constrains such rebalancing, or about the nature and substance of the demands in question. Still, I hope to have made plausible in this paper not only (i) that blame doesn't in general presuppose that the blameworthy deserves to suffer, but also (ii) that the morally blameworthy might deserve setbacks exactly because they have given themselves undue weight and so harmed the relative standing of others or of other values. If the latter explanation seems promising, the exact nature of demands on caring and rebalancing are worth exploring more closely.[26]

[26] This paper has benefited greatly from discussion at the University of Gothenburg Practical Philosophy and Political Theory Research Seminar as well as from written comments from Andreas Brekke Carlsson, Doug Portmore, Dave Shoemaker, Michael McKenna, Per Milam, and Romy Eskens. Work on the paper was funded by the Swedish Research Council, grant 2015-01488.

CHAPTER 11

Reason to Feel Guilty

Randolph Clarke and Piers Rawling

Let F be a fact in virtue of which an agent, s, is blameworthy for performing an act of A-ing. For example, as some theorists have it, the fact in question might be that s freely A-ed, knowing that it was wrong for her to A, and moved by ill will when she so acted (see, e.g., McKenna, 2012, p. 61). Consider:

(**Reason**) F is (at some time) a reason for s to feel guilty (to some extent) for A-ing.

Leaving implicit the qualification concerning extent, consider, further:

(**Desert**) s's having this reason suffices for s's deserving to feel guilty for A-ing.

Here we explicate and advance these two theses (with slight qualification of the first), as well as a third thesis connecting desert of feeling guilty with the fittingness of this response.[1] We then raise a difficulty for the idea that one's desert of a feeling of guilt – or, indeed, even its fittingness – hinges simply on the truth of that feeling's constitutive thought.

In light of our three theses, we address several claims that have been made regarding responsibility and desert. We take issue with the divorce of desert from responsibility. We find acceptable a claim regarding blameworthiness and reason to induce guilt, and we defend the idea that it is noninstrumentally good that one who is blameworthy be subject to a fitting feeling of guilt. We argue against a view on which desert of blame has a teleological dimension. At the end of the chapter, we provide clarification and suggest a qualification of the thesis we call **Reason**.

1 Feeling Guilty

The feeling of guilt, like resentment and indignation, is among the negative reactive attitudes (Strawson, 1962), emotions to which we are

---

[1] More precisely, the theses advanced are generalizations of these claims.

commonly subject when we blame someone for something. In the case of feeling guilty, of course, the person blamed is oneself.

Though not uncontested, it is widely accepted that emotions are object-directed or intentional states: an emotion has an intentional object, it is about something. We endorse this view of the feeling of guilt. We suggest that in feeling guilty, one at least implicitly takes oneself to be blameworthy for something.[2] On this view, **Reason** implies that a fact in virtue of which one is blameworthy for A-ing is (at some time) a reason for one to be subject to an emotion in being subject to which one takes oneself to be blameworthy for A-ing. The implication seems eminently reasonable.

Whether the intentionality of emotion should be understood cognitively – as the emotion's having propositional content – is a question on which we shall avoid taking sides, though we return to it in Section 5. But evidently simply believing that one is blameworthy for something is not sufficient for feeling guilty. There is a felt quality – an affective aspect – of a feeling of guilt that the mere belief lacks.[3] It feels bad to feel guilty. How bad it feels varies. We shall say that as it feels worse, one's feeling of guilt is more severe; as it feels less bad, the feeling is milder. The extent to which it feels bad is what we call the extent to which one feels guilty.

A feeling of guilt commonly has a motivational aspect as well. The feeling can motivate one to apologize, make amends, or resolve to turn over a new leaf (Baumeister et al., 1994, p. 260). It can motivate self-reproach or self-punishment, though it is important to see that the emotion is not itself behavior of this kind. Indeed, it is not any kind of behavior. Nor, then, is it behavior that one might engage in with the aim of making oneself feel guilty. If on some occasion one succeeds in making oneself feel guilty, the feeling of guilt is what one brings about, not one's bringing about this feeling. The attitude is a state, not the performance of an action.

---

[2] The proposal satisfies what Rosen (2015) calls phenomenological and naivety constraints: it is consistent with the phenomenology of feeling guilty, and it is framed in terms that everyone capable of feeling guilty is capable of understanding. Several writers take the intentional content of a feeling of guilt to be considerably more complex than what we have suggested. In some cases, the aim appears to be to capture in the emotion's content all the conditions that must be satisfied if one is to be blameworthy for a certain thing. We do not think that this is an advisable strategy, and some of the resulting accounts we find psychologically unrealistic. We briefly discuss one such view in Section 5.

[3] Further, one can feel guilty for a certain thing without believing that one is blameworthy for that thing – indeed, while believing that one is *not* blameworthy. In recognition of this possibility, a reactive emotion such as feeling guilty is sometimes said to be partly constituted by a *thought*, which one might or might not accept; see, for example, Rosen (2015).

Although we have distinguished several aspects of a feeling of guilt, we do not mean to imply that these are discrete, separable components. On the contrary, the emotion seems to be a unitary thing, albeit one that we can consider in these several ways.

We take it that a reason to feel guilty is, then, a reason to be subject to an emotion that characteristically has the indicated intentional, affective, and motivational aspects. If one deserves to feel guilty, then one deserves to be in such a state.

2 Reason, Emotion, and Fit

We adopt a familiar notion of a reason for x – where x is an attitude or action – as a consideration that counts in favor of x. (Similarly, a reason against x is a consideration that disfavors x.) Thus, our concern is with a reason "in the standard normative sense" (Scanlon, 1998, p. 19). One can act or have attitudes for such a reason, in which case that consideration is (in Scanlon's terms) one's operative reason for so acting or having that attitude.

Normative evaluation of emotions is common in everyday contexts – one shouldn't stay angry forever over minor things – as well as in law – asylum is to be granted when applicants show a well-founded fear of persecution. People are asked why they are, for example, amused or disappointed, and their answers are commonly treated as purported reasons; what is cited, even if allowed to be a cause, can be dismissed as a bad reason. A recalcitrant emotion – one that persists despite one's knowledge that its object lacks the feature that, in being subject to that emotion, one takes the object to have – is, unlike a perceptual illusion such as the Müller-Lyer, said to be irrational.[4] We accept that such talk is often correct. Our emotions can be rational or irrational, based on good reasons or not.

Among considerations that favor or disfavor having a given emotion, two kinds can be distinguished. Some of the first kind concern the instrumental value or disvalue of having the emotion. For example, if fearing a dangerous animal will only make it more likely to attack, that fact disfavors fearing it.[5] The fact that the animal is dangerous is a consideration, of a second kind, that favors fearing it. Our concern with reasons to feel guilty is with a consideration of this second kind.

---

[4] This is one respect in which emotion differs from perception.

[5] Some writers deny that such a consideration is a reason against having the emotion, rather than merely a reason to want or try not to have it. We think that it is both, though we won't argue the point here.

A favoring reason of this kind renders the emotion it favors a *correct* or *fitting* response to its object. We shall call such reasons *f*-reasons. We take it that a fact in virtue of which one is blameworthy for *A*-ing can encompass all the reason required to render fitting one's feeling guilty for that deed. Thus, **Reason** can be glossed: a fact in virtue of which one is blameworthy for *A*-ing is (at some time) a sufficient *f*-reason to feel guilty for *A*-ing – sufficient, that is, to render that feeling fitting.

We allow that considerations encompassed in (but not fully encompassing) such reasons may also aptly be called reasons to feel guilty, and they can bear on the fittingness of the response. For example, the fact that it was wrong for *s* to *A* may be such a reason. Similarly, some fact partly in virtue of which it was wrong for *s* to *A*, such as that in *A*-ing *s* betrayed a friend, can be a reason for *s* to feel guilty. But these would not be considerations favoring feeling guilty *in addition* to the fact in virtue of which *s* is blameworthy for *A*-ing; they would be encompassed in, or part of the basis of, the latter.

Similarly, the fact that one is blameworthy for *A*-ing may be said to be a reason to feel guilty for *A*-ing, and one bearing on the fittingness of that response. But it would be double-counting to count this as an *f*-reason *in addition to* the fact in virtue of which one is blameworthy.

A complication: it might be that some considerations encompassed in a fact like *F* are not themselves reasons to feel guilty, but rather background conditions in which other considerations encompassed in that fact count as such reasons. Perhaps the fact that *s* acted freely in *A*-ing is not itself a reason for *s* to feel guilty, but rather a background condition required if the fact that *s* acted wrongly in *A*-ing is to count as such a reason.[6] To accommodate this possibility, **Reason** might be reformulated: *F* encompasses what is (at some time) a sufficient *f*-reason for *s* to feel guilty (to some extent) for *A*-ing. However, for the sake of simplicity, in what follows we'll often state things in terms of the original formulation.

A sufficient *f*-reason to feel guilty, like *f*-reasons generally, is a pro tanto reason favoring the fitting response. Even when feeling guilty is fitting, one might have reasons disfavoring that response, and it might be that all things considered one should not feel guilty. In that case, all things considered one should not have an emotion that would be fitting. Fittingness is but one of several normative dimensions of emotions.

---

[6] The fact that *s* freely *A*-ed would then be what Dancy (2004, p. 39) calls an enabler.

3 Fit and Desert

The desert of a response is often linked to the fittingness of that response (Feinberg, 1970, p. 82; Clarke, 2016, p. 128; Nelkin, 2016, p. 178; McKenna, 2019, p. 257). With respect to desert of feeling guilty, a linking claim might be put as follows (with the qualification concerning extent left implicit):

> (**Ground**) What grounds s's deserving to feel guilty for A-ing is simply what grounds that feeling's being a fitting response by s to her A-ing.

To clarify: evidently the relation, _ *being deserved by* _ *in response to* _, is not (identical with) the relation, _ *being a fitting response by* _ *to* _. When your belief is that p is fitting, it is certainly not deserved by *you*, and we think it is simply not deserved. Further, although your fitting resentment of your wrongdoer is, we think, deserved, it is deserved by *the wrongdoer*, not by you; one of the distinctive features of guilt is that the one who fittingly feels it is the one who deserves it. Moreover, we allow that the fact that one deserves to feel guilty can be distinguished from the fact that this feeling is fitting.

Nevertheless, we suggest that, necessarily, a feeling of guilt is fitting just in case it is deserved; and what explains the fittingness (or lack thereof) of a feeling of guilt is just what explains the desert (or lack thereof) of that feeling. As it might be put, desert of feeling guilty is fully and exclusively grounded in what grounds the fittingness of that feeling.

What we have said about reasons to feel guilty and what we say here about ground can be brought together as follows: if s has a sufficient f-reason to feel guilty for A-ing, this reason, together with any background conditions required for this consideration to count as such a reason, grounds both the fittingness and the desert of s's feeling guilty for A-ing.

Derk Pereboom accepts that "a sense of pained remorse is a morally fitting … response" to one's acknowledgment that one is blameworthy for something (2015, p. 288). But he denies that "the guilty deserve to suffer such pain" (288). The "moral fittingness" of such a feeling, he implies, does not suffice for its being deserved.[7]

For many object-directed emotions – amusement or surprise, for example – their fittingness does not, of necessity, coincide with their having any moral

---

[7] Note that, as we see it, fittingness is not itself a moral property. Rather, we hold, in the case of negative reactive emotions, fittingness necessarily coincides with a moral property, viz., being deserved. We shall construe talk of the "moral fittingness" of an attitude to concern that attitude's being fitting and (in some way) morally appropriate.

property. Pereboom and we agree that the fittingness of certain attitudes in response to one's blameworthy conduct *does* implicate some moral property. We, unlike he, think that the implicated property is that of being deserved.

One of our disagreements with Pereboom can be set aside here. He favors a view on which negative reactive attitudes such as resentment and indignation include anger toward the purported offender as well as "a belief that the agent deserves to be the target of that very anger just because of what he has done or failed to do" (2014, p. 128). Since this belief is, he holds, always false – no one ever deserves any such thing – resentment and indignation are never fitting. If a feeling of guilt likewise includes some such belief (we doubt that it need include anger), then, as Pereboom sees it, that feeling, too, is never fitting.

We do not see good reason to think that feeling guilty need include believing anything about desert. But setting this issue aside, a substantive dispute with Pereboom remains. Consider a feeling in having which one takes oneself to be blameworthy for something, which is a negative affective state, and which has the motivational profile that we characterized in Section 1. Pereboom accepts that a feeling of this kind can be a morally fitting response to conduct for which one is blameworthy – its fittingness, as he sees it, is a moral matter – but he denies that one can ever deserve to have such feeling. Why might one – why do we – think otherwise?

If you resent someone who is innocent, then, we think, your attitude is unjust. It is unjust for the same reason that it is unfitting: the person lacks the evaluative feature, blameworthiness, that in resenting that person you take her to have. Likewise, if you feel guilty for something for which you are not to blame, your attitude is unjust, and unjust for the same reason that it is unfitting. The unfittingness of these negative reactive emotions implicates not just some moral matter but, more specifically, justice.

Further, the consideration of justice that is implicated is desert. The innocent deserve not to be blamed. That is what is unjust about blaming them. Blaming the innocent is not merely gratuitous, undeserved, it is contrary to what they deserve.[8]

Blameworthiness yields a different desert status: the blameworthy do *not* deserve not to be blamed. They do not deserve this for the same reason that blame of them is not unfitting. And as blame of the blameworthy is not only

[8] In this respect, there is an asymmetry between attitudes of moral credit and those of moral blame. The former, if unfitting, are (at least generally) merely gratuitous, not responses that their objects deserve not to be objects of. Exactly why this asymmetry exists is an interesting question, one that we leave unaddressed here.

not unfitting, it is fitting, so, we hold, the blameworthy not only do not deserve not to be blamed, they deserve blame. Blame of them is not only not unjust, it is just. It is deserved, and so just, for the same reason that it is fitting. Its being deserved is grounded in what grounds its being fitting. Desert is the kind of moral matter that is at issue with the fittingness of blame.

A thoroughgoing desert denier must deny – to her disadvantage, we think – that the innocent deserve not to be blamed. A less thoroughgoing denier might accept this claim about the innocent but deny that anyone deserves to be blamed. But unless it is said that even the blameworthy deserve not to be blamed – a curious position – a difference in desert status between the innocent and the blameworthy will have been recognized: the former deserve, while the latter do not deserve, not to be blamed.

Might this be the only difference in desert status between these two, or is there the further difference that the blameworthy deserve to be blamed whereas the innocent do not? Here is a consideration that supports affirming the further difference. Consider gratitude toward someone who has not, in fact, done you any favor. The person does not deserve your gratitude, but she also does not deserve *not* to be the object of that attitude; your gratitude toward her is not contrary to justice, it is merely gratuitous. But now, if the difference in desert status between the innocent and the blameworthy is only that the latter, unlike the former, do not deserve not to be blamed, then the desert status that obtains with blame of the blameworthy is the same as that which obtains with gratitude toward the nonbenefactor: the blameworthy agent does not deserve not to be blamed, but she also does not deserve to be blamed. There is no difference in desert status that might provide an explanation of why blame of her is not, like gratitude toward a nonbenefactor, merely gratuitous. Recognizing a further difference between the desert status of the innocent and that of the blameworthy provides the understanding: the blameworthy not only do not deserve not to be blamed, they deserve blame.

Feeling guilty for something of which you are innocent is not merely gratuitous; the feeling is one that you deserve not to have. As well, feeling guilty (at the right time, and to the right extent) for something for which you are blameworthy is not merely gratuitous; the feeling is one that you deserve to have.

A theorist who accepts that feeling guilty can be morally fitting might reject **Ground** if she holds an inflated desert theory.[9] For example, the

---

[9] We take the expression from Feinberg (1970, p. 83), who makes similar points about the bearing of desert.

thesis would seem objectionable if one thought that deserving to be subject to an emotion entailed that all things considered, one should be subject to it; for fittingness clearly does not carry this entailment. But deserving to feel guilty does not, either. (Desert in general does not entail such all-things-considered judgments.) One can have a reason to feel guilty, one's having which suffices for one's deserving to feel guilty, and yet that reason can be outweighed by considerations that favor one's not feeling guilty. We reckon that it is not so rare that one who deserves to feel guilty has such overriding reasons. One has things to do, and feeling guilty can interfere with getting them done. When this is so, it makes feeling guilty no less fitting, and no less deserved, but it might have the result that all things considered, one should not, at present, feel guilty. With these matters taken into account, we wonder what desert of feeling guilty is thought to be if the moral fittingness of that response is said not to suffice for it.

An association of the notion of desert with viciousness and savagery might lead one to reject the notion. We, too, reject viciousness and savagery. But, as we think Pereboom would agree, there need be nothing vicious or savage about a morally fitting pained feeling in response to one's culpable conduct. What should be rejected, we think, is not the notion of desert but the mistaken association.

4   Just Emotions

The consideration of justice that we have invoked is a matter of certain object-directed emotions, such as guilt and resentment, being directed toward those who deserve to be objects of these attitudes, and of these attitudes not being directed toward those who deserve not to be objects of them. Such justice is not a matter of the administration of sanctions, the infliction of punishment, or payback for prior wrongs; it is not retributive in a familiar sense. It is a variety of distributive justice, though plainly not a matter of the distribution of economic benefits, and it does not concern economic, political, or social institutions or practices.

W. D. Ross recognizes a form of justice that is in an important respect similar to what we have in mind, one that consists of "the apportionment of pleasure and pain to the virtuous and the vicious respectively" (1988, p. 138). The just apportionment, he says, is distribution "in accordance with the merit of the persons concerned" (21).

Ross's notion nevertheless differs from the one that we have invoked. Although a feeling of guilt is painful, resentment need not pain the one resented; it might remain uncommunicated, or be felt only after the blamed person is deceased. The relevant distribution, then, is not one of pleasure and pain. Nor is it a distribution of benefit and harm. It is not obvious that blame of the dead harms them at all. Perhaps the best case for thinking that it might is that, when it is undeserved, it is an injustice to them. But then the injustice of the blame will be prior to its being a harm – what its being a harm consists in – rather than something consisting in the malapportionment of harm.

Further, unlike Ross's notion, ours concerns only the responses of moral agents to the conduct of one another. The distribution that matters is not one of just anything that might be wanted or unwanted but, specifically, that of reasons-responsive attitudes. Justice, we contend, has a place in this sphere.

Joel Feinberg suggests that "responsive attitudes are the basic things persons deserve and ... 'modes of treatment' are deserved only in a derivative way, insofar as they are the natural or conventional means of expressing the morally fitting attitudes" (1970, p. 82). We note that whether this or that mode of treatment is deserved can depend not just on what would be natural or conventional expressions of a deserved attitude but on moral matters as well. Still, Feinberg's suggestion agrees with our view that the desert of reactive attitudes is a basic consideration of justice.

Such desert is a moral matter in two senses. First, one deserves a certain negative reactive attitude, when one does, due to some fact in virtue of which one has a certain moral property, that of being blameworthy for something. And second, one's desert of such an attitude is itself a matter of there being a certain moral reason favoring it.

This notion of desert, with its associated notion of justice, can be elucidated by articulating their interconnections with each other and with other normative phenomena. We have identified some of these connections, tying desert of negative reactive attitudes to the fittingness of these attitudes and to what we've called *f*-reasons, and thus to blameworthiness and facts in virtue of which one is blameworthy, and situating the feeling of guilt among these phenomena. We will later – in Section 6 – discuss a connection with reasons for action and – in Section 7 – with value. The view that emerges is, we hope, one that many readers will find both familiar and plausible.

5 Fit as Accuracy

An influential construal of the fittingness of an emotion stems from Justin D'Arms and Daniel Jacobson (2000). Emotions, D'Arms and Jacobson hold, present their objects as possessing certain evaluative features. For an emotion to be fitting is for it to accurately present its object. The approach has been applied by several writers (e.g., Portmore, 2019a; Strabbing, 2019) to the fittingness of reactive attitudes, including feeling guilty.[10] If, as **Ground** implies, the fittingness of a feeling of guilt suffices for its being deserved, the approach yields the result that accuracy of presentation of this feeling suffices for its desert.

Care would be needed in spelling out such a view. Both feelings of guilt and blameworthiness are gradable: both come in degrees. One's feeling of guilt can be more or less severe – one can feel guilty to a greater or lesser extent – where this is at least in part an affective matter, a matter of how bad one feels in feeling guilty. And, of course, one can be more or less blameworthy, where this is not a matter of being more or less worthy of something, but of being worthy of more or less (perhaps more or less severe) blame.

Whether one's feeling of guilt is deserved is, we contend, partly a matter of whether its severity is in some sense proportional to how blameworthy one is (though, as we will soon note, the matter is complicated). Fit, understood in an ordinary way, encompasses such proportionality. And proportionality (or disproportionality) of this sort implicates a moral matter: an overly severe feeling of guilt, just as overly severe blame of another, is unjust.

How might this proportionality be captured in terms of accuracy of presentation of the emotion? Consider a cognitivist construal of the intentionality of a feeling of guilt: it represents *that something or other is the case* – its content is a proposition. The accuracy of its presentation can then be seen as a matter of *truth*.[11] If the fittingness of a feeling of guilt is said to suffice for that feeling's being deserved, the view will then be that the feeling's truly representing things suffices for one's deserving to have that feeling.

Suppose that one's feeling of guilt represents that one is blameworthy for *A*-ing. One might indeed be blameworthy for *A*-ing – one's feeling of guilt might truly represent that one has this feature – and yet it might be that one does not deserve to have this feeling, for the feeling might be far more severe than anything that one deserves. One might not deserve to feel so bad.

The problem is not solved simply by incorporating a degree of blameworthiness into the content of the representation. One can, in feeling

---

[10] Portmore (2019a) writes mostly of an emotion's being "appropriate," though he sometimes says "fitting."

[11] Writers who hold that the "appropriateness" of reactive attitudes is just a matter of the truth of a constitutive thought include, in addition to Portmore and Strabbing, Graham (2014) and Rosen (2015).

guilty, have the thought that one is very blameworthy without feeling very bad, or think that one is worthy of only mild blame while feeling very bad.

Such possibilities might be denied. It might be suggested (we have encountered the suggestion) that in object-directed emotions there is a necessary connection between the cognitive and affective aspects, such that, necessarily, a feeling of guilt represents that one is very blameworthy if and only if one feels very bad. But reflection on how feeling guilty for a past offense often evolves over time casts doubt on this claim. Shortly after a youthful offense, in recognizing my blameworthiness for it, I might both take myself to be very blameworthy and feel very bad. Decades later, I don't feel so bad about it, but in so responding I still take myself to be very blameworthy for the misdeed, just as blameworthy as I earlier thought. Resentment likewise can fade in intensity of feeling without alteration of one's view of how blameworthy the offender is.

The observation raises a question about fittingness: might the milder later feeling be fitting, just as fitting as was the more severe earlier feeling? Or is this a case of justifiably having a feeling of guilt less severe than what would be fitting? We incline toward the first view of the matter.[12] If over some period of time one has blamed oneself quite a lot for a certain offense, the emotional response from oneself that is now fitting might be less severe than what was fitting earlier, though we do not think that one has become less blameworthy.[13] If this is correct, then the proportionality between intensity of affect and degree of blameworthiness that figures in fit will depend in part on what has occurred since the offense.

Returning to the problem we raised at the start of this section, here is a way to ensure that a feeling of guilt – whatever its severity – is deserved just in case its intentional content – construed as a proposition – is true: take the feeling to represent oneself as deserving *that very token feeling*. If no overly severe feeling of guilt is ever deserved, then none will truly represent things.

Consider, in this light, Douglas Portmore's view that the thought that is constitutive of a feeling of guilt for *A*-ing is that one deserves to experience the unpleasantness of this feeling in virtue of having violated a legitimate demand in *A*-ing (2019a, p. 12). Although we are not sure that this is Portmore's intent, the idea might be that the feeling refers to itself, rather than simply to the kind of feeling that it is. Assuming that desert requires

---

[12] Na'aman (2021) advances a view of the fittingness of certain emotions that agrees with our judgment here.
[13] Similarly, one's sense of amusement at a certain joke, or one's grief over a loss, tends to fade with time, and it does not seem to us unfitting that it does.

proportionality (however complicated a matter that is) between intensity of affect and degree of blameworthiness, a feeling of guilt will truly represent things only if it is proportional to one's degree of blameworthiness.

Portmore does not aim to explicate desert in terms of fittingness. On the contrary, since in his view the fittingness of a feeling of guilt is explained in terms of the truth of a constitutive thought, and since the truth of that thought would be explained, in part, by desert of the feeling, his view explains fittingness in terms of desert. Whereas we take the desert and the fittingness of the feeling to have a common ground, on Portmore's view desert of the feeling is part of what grounds its being fitting.

In any case, we are skeptical that a feeling of guilt has the sophisticated intentional content that Portmore attributes to this emotion. He rejects a construal of the feeling's intentionality in terms of blameworthiness, arguing, for one thing, that young children can feel guilty even if they lack this concept. We find the content that Portmore attributes to the feeling considerably more demanding, requiring possession of concepts of desert, of the ground of desert, and of legitimate demand, as well as (perhaps) involving reference to the very feeling with that content.

Even setting aside the relation of fittingness to desert – and prescinding from a commitment to cognitivism – it is challenging to spell out the fittingness of feeling guilty in terms of accuracy of presentation. D'Arms and Jacobson observe that "considerations of fittingness can be divided into two kinds, corresponding to two dimensions of fit: one can criticize an emotion with regard to its *size* and its *shape*" (2000, p. 73). An emotion that presents its object as having an evaluative feature that, in fact, the object lacks is unfitting on grounds of shape. An overreaction might be fitting with respect to shape but is unfitting on grounds of size. Accuracy of presentation is meant to capture both of these dimensions of fit.

The intensity of a token feeling of guilt would, we imagine, be at least part of what constitutes its size. The strength or breadth of its motivational profile might also be thought to matter. The motivational tendencies of guilt, too, can change over time without one's take on how blameworthy one is having changed. How, then, to think of fit as accuracy of presentation is a question we leave unsettled.

6   Reason to Act

Reason identifies a reason to be subject to an emotion: a fact in virtue of which one is blameworthy for something is (at some time) a reason (what we have called an *f*-reason) for one to feel guilty for that thing. As we observed, being subject to an emotion is not performing an action. But is there a reason for action in play when someone has an *f*-reason to feel guilty?

Dana Nelkin (2019) argues *against* the following thesis: there is a *pro tanto* reason to induce feelings of guilt in the blameworthy. Imagine, she suggests, that one person has culpably wronged another. (The offense is not trivial, but it is not grave, either.) You have the power of The Look: simply by looking at a person in a certain way, you can bring about in her a feeling of guilt.[14] But the offender has resolved never to do this kind of thing again. Either her relationship with her victim is irreparably damaged, or all has been forgiven. And no one besides you and the offender is around to notice what she feels now. Nelkin maintains that you would not be making a mistake, leaving a reason on the table, by taking a pass on inducing a feeling of guilt.

Suppose that the fact in virtue of which the offender is blameworthy is (at present) a sufficient *f*-reason for her to feel guilty. (We say more about the parenthetical addition in Section 9.) Then we are committed to affirming something that Nelkin denies. But we find the affirmation acceptable.

Granted, the mere fact that a certain attitude would be fitting does not entail that anyone has a reason to act so as to induce that attitude. If you've been told a funny joke, your feeling amused would be fitting; there is a consideration that favors your so responding. But there need be no one who has a reason to induce in you that response. Things differ, we think, when a fitting attitude is deserved and one's having it would be just.

Having a sufficient *f*-reason to feel guilty, we have said, suffices for deserving to be subject to that emotion. Were the offender to have a fitting feeling of guilt, then, her feeling would be just, what she deserves to feel. Someone's having a feeling that is just is in one respect (with respect to just emotions) good. Given that you have the power of The Look, then, there is a state of affairs accessible to you that is, with respect to just emotions, better than one in which you stand pat and the offender does not feel guilt. There is then, we accept, a consideration that favors your giving The Look.

But unless more is said about the case, this reason appears insufficient to justify your intervention. Although the offender deserves to feel guilty, she does not thereby deserve to be caused by you to feel guilty. Indeed, she

---

[14] To clarify, what you can bring about is the real deal – an emotion in having which the offender would recognize her blameworthiness for the misdeed – not simply an unpleasant feeling. Thanks to Derk Pereboom for suggesting this clarification.

does not thereby deserve to be caused by anyone to feel that way. Although her having the reason she has to feel guilty suffices for her deserving to feel that way, your having the reason you have to give The Look doesn't suffice for her deserving that you induce in her that feeling.

Anyone inducing in her the feeling of guilt would be harming her, bringing about a state of affairs that is worse (than the status quo ante) for her, presumably without her consent. Imagine that she possesses The Shield: with a mere thought she can neutralize The Look. Would she be within her rights to protect herself from your intervention? It seems to us that she would. It would be just were she to feel guilty, but she is not obligated to submit to your intervention to produce that state of affairs.

Even when what is deserved is an action administering justice, it can be wrong for agents lacking authority to carry it out. Your neighbor's child might deserve to be disciplined, but it might be wrong of you to administer the discipline. A thief might deserve to have what she stole taken from her and returned to its rightful owner, but it might be wrong of you to carry out this rectification.

Things might be otherwise if you stand in some special relation to the offender. If she is your nonadult child, for example, you might have the authority, as well as a responsibility to help cultivate virtuous dispositions in her, that would justify your giving her The Look.

Indeed, such a case is not entirely fanciful. We do have something approaching the power of The Look with respect to those with whom we are intimate. And we do sometimes make them feel guilty by looking at them in certain ways. When they deserve that feeling, the fact that they do is one reason favoring our so acting, but when we are justified, our conduct is generally supported by further considerations, such as the fact that their felt recognition of their wrongdoing is important to our ongoing relationship with them.

Although Nelkin denies that one's blameworthiness provides a reason for others to induce a feeling of guilt, she nevertheless finds it "plausible that desert offers a certain kind of *conditional* reason for bringing it about that someone gets what she deserves" (2019, p. 189). By a conditional reason, she means a fact that is, under certain conditions, a reason for someone, but otherwise is not. For example, if you are in a position in which you must harm someone, and you can either harm someone deserving of it or someone else, the fact that the former deserves to be harmed might be a reason for you to harm her.

If we take reasons to be considerations that can be fairly succinctly expressed – the fact that it is raining, for example – then they are standardly conditional, in the sense that they can count as reasons (for some agent or agents) in some circumstances but not (for that same agent or agents) in others. On the condition that I'm headed out the door, the fact that it is raining might be a reason for me to get my umbrella, but not if what I aim to do is get wet! It might be possible to avoid conditionality of this sort by, as it were, writing the circumstances into the considerations. But much of what we would be left with as reasons would then be so complicated as to be practically inexpressible, given the multitude of possible conditions that can affect whether some (succinctly expressed) consideration is a reason for someone on some occasion.

Given that a consideration might count as a reason only given certain background conditions, what does our disagreement with Nelkin come to? We say that, with the power of The Look, you have a reason to induce guilt that is likely outweighed, given the circumstances; she says that you have a conditional reason, one that might, in other circumstances, contribute to sufficient reason to give The Look. The difference, we suspect, stems from a disagreement about value, to which we now turn.

7 Value

We are committed to a qualified variant of another thesis that Nelkin (2019) denies, namely: it is noninstrumentally good that one who is blameworthy feel guilty. Again supposing that the fact in virtue of which the person is blameworthy is (at present) a sufficient f-reason for her to feel guilty, if she feels guilty to the right extent for the conduct for which she is blameworthy, then, we say, that feeling is a fitting response to her conduct. What grounds its being fitting also grounds its being deserved. In being deserved by her, her feeling of guilt is just. That she has this just feeling is in some respect good. And the goodness is noninstrumental, not a matter of this state of affairs being a means to something good.

Against such a view, Nelkin urges us to consider the No Guilt Creatures. Although they care about others as we do, they never feel guilt. Otherwise, they respond to recognition of their own wrongdoing largely as we often do, resolving to do better, making amends, and so forth. (Presumably they never sincerely say they're sorry!) Other things being equal, Nelkin suggests, their world is better than ours.

There are two importantly different ways in which we might understand the thought experiment. On the one hand, we might take it that the No Guilt Creatures are alien beings, members of another species, and utterly lacking a capacity that we humans have. On this understanding, we think that they lack any reason to feel guilty, and the question of their deserving this response simply doesn't arise. We do not find them superior to us, but none of them is a deficient one of their kind for never feeling as we often do when we do wrong. They are simply a different form of life.

Alternatively, we might think of the No Guilt Creatures as some of us. Each is as capable as the rest of us of feeling guilty, but they deal with recognition of their own wrongdoing in other ways.[15] They are spared the pain of guilt. But, again, we do not think that their way of responding to their wrongdoing is better.

We would gladly forego the pain of stomachache when we have eaten too much. But unlike that state, the pained feeling of guilt is reasons-responsive. Responding to our culpable misdeeds without ever feeling guilty, while remaining capable of that response, would be failing ever to respond in a way that we sometimes have reason to respond, with a fitting emotion, one that we deserve to feel. We do not find it better to be unresponsive to reasons in this way.

Many emotional responses – being troubled, disturbed, or horrified in response to troubling, disturbing, or horrific events – are unpleasant experiences. Yet these are fitting responses to such events, and commonly when such events occur, we have reason to be subject to these emotions. Were we to remain capable of these responses but never experience anything more than affectless replacements of them, we would be at least partly unresponsive to these reasons. We do not find this state of affairs better than that of our fitting occasional emotional response.

8 Teleology

Suppose that someone s is blameworthy for A-ing in virtue of having freely A-ed, knowing that it was wrong for her to A, and moved by ill will when she so acted. We have suggested that the fact that s so acted is (at some time) a reason for her to feel guilty (to some extent) for A-ing, and s's having this reason suffices for her deserving to feel guilty. Her action is then what is commonly called a *desert basis* for that feeling: she deserves this response because she has so acted (Feinberg, 1970, p. 58).

Why is an action of *this* kind a desert basis for feeling guilty? We might say: because it renders one blameworthy for one's conduct. But why does an action of *this* kind render one blameworthy?

---

[15] Nelkin comes to the thought experiment by way of discussing Harman's (2009) claim that he never feels "non-trivial guilt" (by which he means anything more than simply believing that he has done wrong).

Manuel Vargas offers a theory that answers these questions by appeal to teleology. The "responsibility system" is his term for the array of responses that people exhibit to those regarded as morally responsible agents – responses including judgments of blameworthiness, reactive emotions, blaming behavior such as reprimand and criticism, and the imposition of sanctions (2013, p. 6). Participants in this system internalize norms governing the responses in question. A specific set of such norms is justified, Vargas maintains, insofar as participation in a system of responses governed by these norms cultivates moral-considerations-responsive agency – insofar as it contributes to our greater responsiveness to moral reasons.

The theory provides a two-tiered account of the normative status of reactive emotions such as feeling guilty (Vargas, 2015, 2019). A feeling of guilt is deserved just in case it responds to a desert basis for such a feeling. The norm governing feeling guilty is thus backward-looking. But this norm is in turn justified by forward-looking considerations. Something counts as a desert basis for feeling guilty just in case a norm prescribing response to things of that kind with such an emotion figures in a responsibility system that optimally cultivates moral agency. We think that Vargas goes wrong on this second point.

In feeling guilty, we have suggested, one takes oneself to be blameworthy for something. One's deserving to have such a feeling is grounded in what grounds the fittingness of that feeling; and the feeling is a fitting response only if one is indeed blameworthy for the thing in question. The desert basis for the feeling will be something for which one is blameworthy.

Whether one is blameworthy for something is distinct from whether it is worthwhile – in any particular case or generally – blaming one for that thing or blaming anyone for things of that kind. Blame's serving some purpose can bear on the latter question, but it does not bear on the former. Whether participation in a system of responses cultivates moral-considerations-responsive agency depends on contingencies – for example, on whether we commonly take note of moral criticism or just find it boring – on which blameworthiness does not depend.

Vargas says: "If there were a community that never accepted blame, then it is hard to see how blame could play much role in cultivating the relevant forms of agency. In such a community, blame would not be deserved" (2013, p. 264). But no failure to accept blame would imply that no one is ever blameworthy for anything, even if universal rejection made it pointless to blame.

Feeling guilty on some occasion can be normatively flawed in some respect for failing to serve some purpose. But it is not for that reason unfitting or undeserved. To think that it is is to conflate fittingness or desert with other normative matters.

Analogous things may be said of the fittingness of other emotions. Whether fear of lions is fitting is one thing; whether (in general) fearing lions serves some purpose is another. In fearing something one takes it to be dangerous. And whether something is dangerous does not depend on whether generally fearing such things serves some purpose. Fear might be in some way normatively flawed for failing to serve a purpose; but the flaw is not one of being unfitting.

9   Qualification

We come, finally, to clarification and a suggested qualification of the thesis we call **Reason**. First, this thesis says that a certain fact is *at some time* a reason to feel guilty. Perhaps if you have felt guilty enough, for long enough, then a fact in virtue of which you are blameworthy for something is no longer a reason for you to feel guilty for that thing. You might have felt all the guilt that you should for lying to your mom when you were five about eating an extra cookie. Though the misdeed (still) counts among things for which you are to blame, perhaps you no longer have any reason to feel the least bit guilty for it.

Whether the same qualification applies to fittingness and desert we are not sure, though we think that it does. It might no longer be fitting for you to feel guilty for that childhood peccadillo, and you might no longer deserve to feel bad about it. We incline, then, toward the following possibility: if you have felt sufficient guilt for a past misdeed, then although you remain blameworthy for it, the fact in virtue of which you are blameworthy no longer provides a reason for you to feel guilty, and it no longer grounds the fittingness or desert of feelings of guilt on your part.

We part company with those who hold that sufficient atonement can eliminate one's blameworthiness, and thus the fittingness of blame altogether. Atonement cannot exonerate; it cannot render one not guilty of a moral offense. And as one remains guilty, so, we think, blame remains fitting. In brief: if one is guilty of an offense, then one is culpable for it. And one who is culpable for an offense is to blame for it. If one is to blame for something, then one is blameworthy, or worthy of blame for it. And one who is worthy of blame for something is a fitting target of blame for it.[16]

Andreas Carlsson (2017) has advanced a view on which one is blameworthy for something if and only if one deserves to feel guilty for it, and one's desert explains one's blameworthiness. Having felt sufficiently guilty for some offense, having sincerely apologized, having made appropriate reparation, and having been forgiven, he argues, one may no longer deserve to feel guilty for it (see his chapter in this volume). One is then no longer blameworthy for the misdeed.[17]

We do not tie blameworthiness to desert of feeling guilty in this way. Even subsequent to one's atonement, another person first learning of one's misdeed might fittingly blame one for it. One remains to blame; blame by others can still be deserved, even if one no longer deserves to feel guilty. But neither do we tie blameworthiness to desert of blame by any particular other. Just as one's guilt can become unfitting over time, so, we think, another's resentment can become unfitting. Neither change renders one no longer blameworthy. A third person's proportionate blame might still be fitting and deserved. Thus, we do not find here an asymmetry between self-blame and blame by others.

Second, a qualification of **Reason**: there might be infractions for which one is blameworthy that are so minor that *any* feeling of guilt would be an overreaction. An affectless recognition of one's fault might be all, in the way of intentional attitudes, that is fitting in such a case. Although there are facts in virtue of which one is blameworthy for such things, one might never have any reason to feel guilty for them.

Third, if one is blameworthy for something but utterly incapable of feeling guilt, then, we suggest, one does not have a reason to feel guilty for that thing. Reasons to be subject to emotions, we think, resemble reasons for action in this respect. No consideration is a reason for us to give you the moon, because we are incapable of doing that. Similarly, it seems, an individual incapable of a given emotion has no reason to be subject to it.

In fact, everyone who is ever blameworthy for anything will at some time cease to be capable of feeling guilty, for all such agents eventually die

---

[16] Clarke (forthcoming) provides a more thorough response to the view that atonement can diminish or eliminate blameworthiness.

[17] Portmore (this volume) similarly holds that one can come to deserve to suffer less (or even no more) guilt for an offense as a result of already having suffered guilt for it, and that one thereby becomes less blameworthy (or no longer blameworthy at all) for that offense.

(and, we assume, no one is capable of any emotion after her death). This fact provides another reason to hold that a consideration that counts as a reason to feel guilty can cease to be such a reason. The fact that Nixon prolonged the Vietnam War is not now a reason for him to feel guilty, since he is not now capable of having that or any other emotion. Still, he is to blame for the offense.[18]

---

[18] For comments and discussion, many thanks to Ben Bramble, Tori McGeer, participants at the Workshop on Self-Blame and Moral Responsibility, University of Oslo, September 2019, and participants at the Laurance S. Rockefeller Seminar, Princeton University, October 21, 2019.

References

Adams, R. M. (1985). Involuntary sins. *The Philosophical Review*, *94*(1), 3–31.

Adolphs, R. (2017a). How should neuroscience study emotions? By distinguishing emotion states, concepts, and experiences. *Social Cognitive and Affective Neuroscience*, *12*(1), 24–31.

Adolphs, R. (2017b). Reply to Barrett: Affective neuroscience needs objective criteria for emotions. *Social Cognitive and Affective Neuroscience*, *12*(1), 32–33.

Alicke, M. D. (2000). Culpable control and the psychology of blame. *Psychological Bulletin*, *126*(4), 556–574.

Alicke, M. D., Davis, T. L., & Pezzo, M. V. (1994). A posteriori adjustment of a priori decision criteria. *Social Cognition*, *12*(4), 281–308.

Alicke, M. D., Rose, D., & Bloom, D. (2012). Causation, norm violation, and culpable control. *The Journal of Philosophy*, *108*(12), 670–696.

Aristotle. (1954). *Aristotle: Rhetoric*. (W. Rhys Roberts, Trans.). Modern Library.

Arpaly, N. (2000). On acting rationally against one's best judgment. *Ethics*, *110*(3), 488–513.

Arpaly, N. (2006). *Meaning, merit, and human bondage*. Princeton University Press.

Arpaly, N., & Schroeder, T. (2014). *In praise of desire*. Oxford University Press.

Baier, A. (1990). What emotions are about. *Philosophical Perspectives*, *4*(2), 1–29.

Baker, K. (2011). The myth of the home run that drove an angels pitcher to suicide. *The Atlantic* (October 27, 2011).

Barrett, L. F. (2017a). *How emotions are made: The secret life of the brain*. Houghton Mifflin Harcourt.

Barrett, L. F. (2017b). The theory of constructed emotion: An active inference account of interoception and categorization. *Social Cognitive and Affective Neuroscience*, *12*(1), 1–23.

Barrett, L. F. (2017c). Functionalism cannot save the classical view of emotion. *Social Cognitive and Affective Neuroscience*, *12*(1), 34–36.

Bastian, B., Jetten, J., & Fasoli, F. (2011). Cleansing the soul by hurting the flesh: The guilt-reducing effect of pain. *Psychological Science*, *22*(3), 334–335.

Baumeister, R. F. (1990). Suicide as escape from self. *Psychological Review*, *97*(1), 90–113.

Baumeister, R. F., Stillwell, A. M., & Heatherton, T. F. (1994). Guilt: An interpersonal approach. *Psychological Bulletin*, *115*(2), 243–267.

Beardsley, E. L. (1970). Moral disapproval and moral indignation. *Philosophy and Phenomenological Research, 31*(2), 161–176.

Bell, M. (2013). The standing to blame. In D. J. Coates & N. Tognazzini (Eds.), *Blame: Its nature and norms* (pp. 263–281). Oxford University Press.

Benbaji, H. (2013). How is recalcitrant emotion possible? *Australasian Journal of Philosophy, 91*(3), 577–599.

Bennett, C. (2002). The varieties of retributive experience. *The Philosophical Quarterly, 52*(207), 145–163.

Björnsson, G. (2017a). Explaining (away) the epistemic condition on moral responsibility. In P. Robichaud & J. W. Wieland (Eds.), *Responsibility: The epistemic condition* (pp. 146–162). Oxford University Press.

Björnsson, G. (2017b). Explaining away epistemic skepticism about culpability. In D. Shoemaker (Ed.), *Oxford studies in agency and responsibility* (pp. 141–164). Oxford University Press.

Björnsson, G. (2017c). Review of Rik Peels, responsible belief: A theory in ethics and epistemology. *Notre Dame Philosophical Reviews.* https://ndpr.nd.edu/reviews/responsible-belief-a-theory-in-ethics-and-epistemology/

Björnsson, G. (2020a). Being implicated: On the fittingness of guilt and indignation over outcomes. *Philosophical Studies, 178,* 3543–3560. https://doi.org/10.1007/s11098-021-01613-4

Björnsson, G. (2020b). Collective responsibility and collective obligations without collective agents. In S. Bazargan-Forward & D. Tollefsen (Eds.), *The Routledge handbook of collective responsibility* (pp. 127–141). Routledge.

Björnsson, G. (n.d.). Skills, values, and demands: A map of blame and its surroundings. Manuscript.

Björnsson, G., & Persson, K. (2012). The explanatory component of moral responsibility. *Noûs, 46*(2), 326–354.

Blanchfield, A. W., Hardy, J., De Morree, H. M., Staiano, W., & Marcora, S. M. (2014). Talking yourself out of exhaustion: The effects of self-talk on endurance performance. *Medicine and Science in Sports and Exercise, 46*(5), 998–1007.

Boehm, C. (1999). *Hierarchy in the forest: The evolution of egalitarian behavior.* Harvard University Press.

Bok, H. (1998). *Freedom and responsibility.* Princeton University Press.

Brady, M. S. (2007). Recalcitrant emotions and visual illusions. *American Philosophical Quarterly, 44*(3), 273–284.

Brady, M. S. (2009). The irrationality of recalcitrant emotions. *Philosophical Studies, 145*(3), 413–430.

Brink, D. O., & Nelkin, D. (2013). Fairness and the architecture of responsibility. In D. Shoemaker (Ed.), *Oxford studies in agency and responsibility Volume 1* (pp. 284–313). Oxford University Press.

Brink, D. O., & Nelkin, D. (in press). The nature and significance of blame. In J. Doris & M. Vargas (Eds.), *The Oxford handbook of moral psychology.* Oxford University Press.

Brown, J. (2020). What is epistemic blame? *Noûs, 54,* 389–407.

Brownstein, M. (2018). Self-control and overcontrol: Conceptual, ethical, and ideological issues in positive psychology. *Review of Philosophy and Psychology, 9*(3), 585–606.

Bryant, R. A., & Guthrie, R. M. (2007). Maladaptive self-appraisals before trauma exposure predict posttraumatic stress disorder. *Journal of Consulting and Clinical Psychology, 75*(5), 812–815.

Calhoun, C. (2004). Subjectivity and emotion. In R. C. Solomon (Ed.), *Thinking about feeling: Contemporary philosophers on emotions* (pp. 107–124). Oxford University Press.

Callard, A. (2017). The reason to be angry forever. In M. Cherry & O. Flanagan (Eds.), *The moral psychology of anger* (pp. 123–137). Rowman & Littlefield.

Carlsson, A. B. (2017). Blameworthiness as deserved guilt. *The Journal of Ethics, 21*(1), 89–115.

Carlsson, A. B. (2019). Shame and attributability. In D. Shoemaker (Ed.), *Oxford studies in agency and responsibility*, Vol. 6 (pp. 112–139). Oxford University Press.

Caruso, G. D. (2021). *Rejecting retributivism: Free will, punishment, and criminal justice.* Cambridge University Press.

Cherry, M. (2018). The errors and limitations of our 'anger-evaluating' ways. In M. Cherry & O. Flanagan (Eds.), *The moral psychology of anger* (pp. 49–66). Rowman & Littlefield.

Chislenko, E. (2019). Blame and protest. *The Journal of Ethics, 23*(2), 163–181.

Clarke, R. (2013). Some theses on desert. *Philosophical Explorations, 16*(2), 153–164.

Clarke, R. (2016). Moral responsibility, guilt, and retributivism. *The Journal of Ethics, 20*(1–3), 121–137.

Clarke, R. (Forthcoming). Still guilty. *Philosophical Studies.*

Coates, D. J. (2017). A wholehearted defense of ambivalence. *The Journal of Ethics, 21*(4), 419–444.

Coates, D. J., & Tognazzini, N. (2013). The contours of blame. In D. J. Coates & N. Tognazzini (Eds.), *Blame: Its nature and norms* (pp. 3–26). Oxford University Press.

Coleman, J., & Sarch, A. (2012). Blameworthiness and time. *Legal Theory, 18*, 101–137.

Connelly, K. (n.d.). Blame and respect. Manuscript.

Coplan, R. J., & Armer, M. (2005). Talking yourself out of being shy: Shyness, expressive vocabulary, and socioemotional adjustment in preschool. *Merrill-Palmer Quarterly, 51*, 20–41.

Craig, T. K. J., & Brown, G. W. (1984). Goal frustration and life events in the aetiology of painful gastrointestinal disorder. *Journal of Psychosomatic Research, 28*(5), 411–421.

Dancy, J. (2004). *Ethics without principles.* Oxford University Press.

D'Arms, J. (2005). Two arguments for sentimentalism. *Philosophical Issues, 15*, 1–21.

D'Arms, J. (2013). Value and the regulation of the sentiments. *Philosophical Studies, 163*(1), 3–13.

D'Arms, J., & Jacobson, D. (1994). Expressivism, morality, and the emotions. *Ethics, 104*(4), 739–763.

D'Arms, J., & Jacobson, D. (2000). The moralistic fallacy: On the 'appropriateness' of emotions. *Philosophical and Phenomenological Research, 61*, 65–90.

D'Arms, J., & Jacobson, D. (2003). The significance of recalcitrant emotions (or, antiquasijudgmentalism). *Royal Institute of Philosophy Supplements, 52*, 127–145.

D'Arms, J., & Jacobson, D. (2017). Whither sentimentalism? On fear, the fearsome, and the dangerous. In R. Debes & K. Stueber (Eds.), *Ethical sentimentalism: New perspectives* (pp. 230–249). Cambridge University Press.

D'Arms J., & Jacobson, D. (Forthcoming). *Rational sentimentalism*. Oxford University Press.

Darwall, S. (2006). *The second-person standpoint: Morality, respect, and accountability*. Harvard University Press.

Darwall, S. (2010). But it would be wrong. *Social Philosophy and Policy, 27*(2), 135–157.

Davidson, D. (1985). Incoherence and irrationality. *Dialectica, 39*(4), 345–354.

Davidson, D. (2006a). How is weakness of will possible? In *The essential Donald Davidson* (pp. 72–89). Oxford University Press.

Davidson, D. (2006b). Paradoxes of irrationality. In *The essential Donald Davidson* (pp. 138–152). Oxford University Press.

De Hooge, I. E. (2012). The exemplary social emotion guilt: Not so relationship-oriented when another person repairs for you. *Cognition and Emotion, 26*(7), 1189–1207.

Deigh, J. (1994). Cognitivism in the theory of emotions. *Ethics, 104*(4), 824–854.

Dennett, D. (1984). *Elbow room: The varieties of free will worth wanting*. MIT Press.

Dennett, D. (2003). *Freedom evolves*. Viking.

Dennett, D., & Caruso, G. D. (2020). *Just deserts*. Polity Press.

Deonna, J. A., & Teroni, F. (2012a). From justified emotions to justified evaluative judgements. *Dialogue, 51*(1), 55–77.

Deonna, J. A., & Teroni, F. (2012b). *The emotions: A philosophical introduction*. Routledge.

Dill, B., & Darwall, S. (2014). Moral psychology as accountability. In J. D'Arms & D. Jacobson (Eds.), *Moral psychology & human agency: Philosophical essays on the science of ethics* (pp. 40–83). Oxford University Press.

Donohue, M. R., & Tully, E. C. (2019). Reparative prosocial behaviors alleviate children's guilt. *Developmental Psychology, 55*, 2102–2113.

Döring, S. A. (2015). What's wrong with recalcitrant emotions? From irrationality to challenge of agential identity. *Dialectica, 69*(3), 381–402.

Driver, J. (1992). The suberogatory. *Australasian Journal of Philosophy, 70*(3), 286–295.

Duggan, A. P. (2018). Moral responsibility as guiltworthiness. *Ethical Theory and Moral Practice, 21*(2), 291–309.

Duggan, A. P. (n.d.). A genealogy of retributive intuitions. Manuscript.

Duhigg, C. (2019). The real roots of American rage. *The Atlantic*. January/February. www.theatlantic.com/magazine/archive/2019/01/charles-duhigg-american-anger

Ebels-Duggan, K. (2019). Beyond words: Inarticulate reasons and reasonable commitments. *Philosophy and Phenomenological Research, 98*(3), 623–641.

Ellsworth, P. C., & Tong, E. M. (2006). What does it mean to be angry at yourself? Categories, appraisals, and the problem of language. *Emotion, 6*(4), 572–586.

Enoch, D., & Marmor, A. (2007). The case against moral luck. *Law and Philosophy, 26*(4), 405–436.

Fehr, E., & Gächter, S. (2002). Altruistic punishment in humans. *Nature, 415*(6868), 137–140.

Feinberg, J. (1970). Justice and personal desert. In *Doing & deserving: Essays in the theory of responsibility* (pp. 55–94). Princeton University Press.

Fischer. J. M. (1994). *The metaphysics of free will.* Blackwell.

Fischer, J. M. (2007). Compatibilism. In J. M. Fischer, R. Kane, D. Pereboom, & M. Vargas (Eds.), *Four views on free will.* Blackwell.

Fischer, J. M., & Ravizza, M. (2000). *Responsibility and control: A theory of moral responsibility.* Cambridge University Press.

Foot, P. (1978). *Virtues and vices.* Oxford University Press.

Frank, R. (1988). *Passions within reasons.* Norton.

Frankfurt, H. (1969). Alternate possibilities and moral responsibility. *Journal of Philosophy, 68*, 5–20.

Franklin, C. E. (2013). Valuing blame. In D. J. Coates & N. A. Tognazzini (Eds.), *Blame: Its nature and norms* (pp. 207–223). Oxford University Press.

Fricker, M. (2016). What's the point of blame? A paradigm based explanation. *Noûs, 50*, 165–183.

Frijda, N. H. (1986). *The emotions.* Cambridge University Press.

Frijda, N. H. (1994). The lex talionis: On vengeance. In S. van Goozen, N. E. Van de Poll, & J. A. Sergeant (Eds.), *Emotions: Essays on emotion theory* (pp. 263–289). Psychology Press.

Gibbard, A. (1990). *Wise choices, apt feelings: A theory of normative judgment.* Harvard University Press.

Gintis, H., Smith, E. A., & Bowles, S. (2001). Costly signaling and cooperation. *Journal of Theoretical Biology, 213*(1), 103–119.

Girodo, M., & Wood, D. (1979). Talking yourself out of pain: The importance of believing that you can. *Cognitive Therapy and Research, 3*(1), 23–33.

Goldberg, J. H., Lerner, J. S., & Tetlock, P. E. (1999). Rage and reason: The psychology of the intuitive prosecutor. *European Journal of Social Psychology, 29*(5–6), 781–795.

Gollwitzer, M., & Denzler, M. (2009). What makes revenge sweet: Seeing the offender suffer or delivering a message? *Journal of Experimental Social Psychology, 45*(4), 840–844.

Graham, P. A. (2014). A sketch of a theory of moral blameworthiness. *Philosophy and Phenomenological Research, 88*(2), 388–409.

Greenspan, P. S. (1988). *Emotions and reasons: An inquiry into emotional justification.* Routledge & Kegan Paul.

Greenspan, P. S. (1992). Subjective guilt and responsibility. *Mind, 101*(402), 287–303.

Greenspan, P. S. (1995). *Practical guilt: Moral dilemmas, emotions, and social norms.* Oxford University Press.

Griffiths, P. (1997). *What emotions really are.* University of Chicago Press.

Gross, T. (2019). Conan O'Brien needs a friend' is a joke name for a Podcast— Sort of. Fresh Air. NPR, 2 Oct. 2019. Radio.

Haidt, J. (2003). The moral emotions. In R. J. Davidson, K. R. Sherer, & H. H. Goldsmith (Eds.), *Handbook of affective sciences* (pp. 852–870). Oxford University Press.

Haidt, J., Sabini, J., Gromet, D., & Darley, J. (2010). *What exactly makes revenge sweet? How anger is satisfied in real life and at the movies* [Unpublished manuscript]. Retrieved October 7, 2019, from https://bit.ly/35858c6

Haji, I. (1998). *Moral accountability*. Oxford University Press.

Hanser, M. (2005). Permissibility and practical inference. *Ethics, 115*(3), 443–470.

Hardy, J. (2006). Speaking clearly: A critical review of the self-talk literature. *Psychology of Sport and Exercise, 7*(1), 81–97.

Hardy, J., Hall, C. R., & Alexander, M. R. (2001). Exploring self-talk and affective states in sport. *Journal of Sports Sciences, 19*(7), 469–475.

Harman, G. (2009). Guilt-free morality. In R. Shafer-Landau (Ed.), *Oxford studies in metaethics*, Vol. 4 (pp. 203–214). Oxford University Press.

Hatzigeorgiadis, A., Zourbanos, N., Goltsios, C., & Theodorakis, Y. (2008). Investigating the functions of self-talk: The effects of motivational self-talk on self-efficacy and performance in young tennis players. *The Sport Psychologist, 22*(4), 458–471.

Helm, B. W. (2001). *Emotional reason: Deliberation, motivation, and the nature of value*. Cambridge University Press.

Helm, B. W. (2015). Emotions and recalcitrance: Reevaluating the perceptual model. *Dialectica, 69*(3), 417–433.

Hieronymi, P. (2001). Articulating an uncompromising forgiveness. *Philosophy and Phenomenological Research, 62*(3), 529–555.

Hieronymi, P. (2004). The force and fairness of blame. *Philosophical Perspectives, 18*(1), 115–148.

Howard, C. (2018). Fittingness. *Philosophy Compass, 13*(11), e12542.

Inbar, Y., Pizarro, D. A., Gilovich, T., & Ariely, D. (2013). Moral masochism: On the connection between guilt and self-punishment. *Emotion, 13*(1), 14–18.

Izard, C. E. (1997). Emotions and facial expressions: A perspective from differential emotions theory. In J. A. Russell & J. M. F. Dols (Eds.), *The psychology of facial expression*, Vol. 10 (pp. 57–77). Cambridge University Press.

Jäger, C., & Bartsch, A. (2006). Meta-emotions. *Grazer Philosophische Studien, 73*(1), 179–204.

Jaggar, A. M. (1989). Love and knowledge: Emotion in feminist epistemology. *Inquiry, 32*(2), 151–176.

James, W. (1894). Discussion: The physical basis of emotion. *Psychological Review, 1*(5), 516–529.

Janoff-Bulman, R. (1979). Characterological versus behavioral self-blame: Inquiries into depression and rape. *Journal of Personality and Social Psychology, 37*(10), 1798–1809.

Jaworska, A. (2007). Caring and internality. *Philosophy and Phenomenological Research, 74*(3), 529–568.

Jeppsson, S. (2016). Accountability, answerability, and freedom. *Social Theory and Practice, 42*(4), 681–705.

Jones, K. (2003). Emotions, weakness of will, and the normative conception of agency. *Royal Institute of Philosophy Supplements, 52*, 181–200.

Jones, W. H., & Kugler, K. (1993). Interpersonal correlates of the Guilt Inventory. *Journal of Personality Assessment, 61*(2), 246–258.

Kalis, A. (2018). Self-control as a normative capacity. *Ratio, 31*, 65–80.

Kant, I. (1797/1963). *The Metaphysical elements of justice*, JohnLadd, tr. Bobbs-Merrill.

Kassinove, H., Sukhodolsky, D. G., Tsytsarcv, S. V., & Solovyova, S. (1997). Self-reported anger episodes in Russia and America. *Journal of Social Behavior and Personality, 12*(2), 301–324.

Ketelaar, T., & Tung Au, W. (2003). The effects of feelings of guilt on the behaviour of uncooperative individuals in repeated social bargaining games: An affect-as-information interpretation of the role of emotion in social interaction. *Cognition and Emotion, 17*(3), 429–453.

Khoury, A. C. (2018). The objects of moral responsibility. *Philosophical Studies, 175*(6), 1357–1381.

Khoury, A. C., & Matheson, B. (2018). Is blameworthiness forever? *Journal of the American Philosophical Association, 4*(2), 204–224.

King, M. (2019). Skepticism about the standing to blame. In D. Shoemaker (Ed.), *Oxford studies in agency and responsibility*, Vol. 6 (pp. 265–288). Oxford University Press.

Kneer, M., & Machery, E. (2019). No luck for moral luck. *Cognition, 182*, 331–348.

Kolodny, N. (2005). Why be rational?. *Mind, 114*(455), 509–563.

Korsgaard, C. (1996). *The sources of normativity*. Cambridge University Press.

Korsgaard, C. M. (2009). *Self-constitution: Agency, identity, and integrity*. Oxford University Press.

Lamb, R. (1987). Objectless emotions. *Philosophy and Phenomenological Research, 48*(1), 107–117.

Lane, A. M., Thelwell, R. C., Lowther, J., & Devonport, T. J. (2009). Emotional intelligence and psychological skills use among athletes. *Social Behavior and Personality: An International Journal, 37*(2), 195–201.

Latus, A. (2001). Moral luck. In J. Feiser (Ed.), *The Internet encyclopedia of philosophy*. ISSN 2161-0002, https://iep.utm.edu/

Lazarus, R. (1991). *Emotion and adaptation*. Oxford University Press.

Lazarus, R. S. (1982). Thoughts on the relations between emotion and cognition. *American Psychologist, 37*(9), 1019–1024.

Lenman, J. (2006). Compatibilism and contractualism: The possibility of moral responsibility. *Ethics, 117*(1), 7–31.

Lerner, J. S., Goldberg, J. H., & Tetlock, P. E. (1998). Sober second thought: The effects of accountability, anger, and authoritarianism on attributions of responsibility. *Personality and Social Psychology Bulletin, 24*(6), 563–574.

Lerner, J. S., & Keltner, D. (2001). Fear, anger, and risk. *Journal of Personality and Social Psychology, 81*(1), 146–159.

Lewis, H. B. (1971). *Shame and guilt in neurosis*. International Universities Press.

Lewis, M. (1993). The development of anger and rage. In R. A. Glick & S. P. Roose (Eds.), *The role of affect in motivation, development, and adaptation*, Vol. 2. Rage, power, and aggression (pp. 148–168). Yale University Press.

Lewis, M. (2000). Self-conscious emotions: Embarrassment, pride, shame, and suilt. In M. Lewis & J. M. Haviland-Jones (Eds.), *Handbook of emotions*, 2nd ed. (pp. 623–636). Guilford.

Lewis, M., Alessandri, S. M., & Sullivan, M. W. (1990). Violation of expectancy, loss of control, and anger expressions in young infants. *Developmental Psychology*, *26*(5), 745.

Litvak, P. M., Lerner, J. S., Tiedens, L. Z., & Shonk, K. (2010). Fuel in the fire: How anger impacts judgment and decision-making. In M. Potegal, G. Stemmler, & C. Spielberger (Eds.), *International handbook of anger* (pp. 287–310). Springer.

Luby, J. L., Barch, D. M., Whalen, D., Tillman, R., & Freedland, K. E. (2018). A randomized controlled trial of parent-child psychotherapy targeting emotion development for early childhood depression. *American Journal of Psychiatry*, *175*(11), 1102–1110.

Macnamara, C. (2013). Taking demands out of blame. In D. J. Coates & N. Tognazzini (Eds.), *Blame: Its nature and norms* (pp. 141–161). Oxford University Press.

Macnamara, C. (2015a). Blame, communication and moral responsible agency. In R. Clarke, M. McKenna, & A. Smith (Eds.), *The nature of moral responsibility: New essays* (pp. 211–235). Oxford University Press.

Macnamara, C. (2015b). Reactive attitudes as communicative entities. *Philosophy and Phenomenological Research*, *90*(3), 546–569.

Macnamara, C. (2020). Guilt, desert, fittingness, and the good. *The Journal of Ethics*, *24*, 449–468.

Markovits, J. (2010). Acting for the right reasons. *Philosophical Review*, *119*(2), 201–242.

Marušić, B. (2020). Accommodation to injustice. In R. Shafer-Landau (Ed.), *Oxford studies in metaethics*, Vol. 15 (pp. 263–283). Oxford University Press.

Mason, E. (2019). *Ways to be blameworthy*. Oxford University Press.

Matheson, B., & Milam, P.-E. (2021). The case against non-moral blame. In M. Timmons (Ed.), *Oxford studies of normative ethics*, Vol. xi.

McGeer, V. (2013). Civilizing blame. In D. J. Coates & N. Tognazzini (Eds.), *Blame: Its nature and norms* (pp. 162–188). Oxford University Press.

McHugh, C. (2017). Attitudinal control. *Synthese*, *194*(8), 2745–2762.

McKenna, M. (2008). Putting the lie on the control condition for moral responsibility. *Philosophical Studies*, *139*(1), 29–37.

McKenna, M. (2012). *Conversation and responsibility*. Oxford University Press.

McKenna, M. (2013). Directed blame and conversation. In D. J. Coates & N. Tognazzini (Eds.), *Blame: Its nature and norms* (pp. 119–140). Oxford University Press.

McKenna, M. (2019). Basically deserved blame and its value. *Journal of Ethics and Social Philosophy*, *15*, 255–282.

McRae, E. (2012). A passionate buddhist life. *Journal of Religious Ethics*, *40*, 99–121.

Mele, A. R. (1987). *Irrationality: An essay on Akrasia, self-deception, and self-control*. Oxford University Press.

Mele, A. R. (1989). Akratic feelings. *Philosophy and Phenomenological Research*, *50*(2), 277–288.

Menges, L. (2017a). Grounding responsibility in appropriate blame. *American Philosophical Quarterly*, *54*(1), 15–24.

Menges, L. (2017b). The emotion account of blame. *Philosophical Studies*, *174*(1), 257–273.

Mikula, G. (1986). The experience of injustice: Toward a better understanding of its phenomenology. In H. W. Bierhoff, R. L. Cohen, & J. Greenberg (Eds.), *Justice in social relations* (pp. 103–124). Plenum.

Milam, P. E., & Brunning, L. (2018). Oppression, forgiveness, and ceasing to blame. *Journal of Ethics and Social Philosophy*, *14*(2), 143–178.

Mill, J. S. (1991). [1861]. *Utilitarianism*. Reprinted in J. M. Robson (Ed.), *Collected Works of John Stuart Mill*, Vol. 10 (pp. 203–259). Routledge.

Millikan, R. G. (1984). *Language, thought, and other biological categories: New foundations for realism*. MIT Press.

Moore, M. (2009). *Causation and responsibility: An essay in law, morals, and metaphysics*. Oxford University Press.

Morris, H. (1976a). *On guilt and innocence: Essays in legal philosophy and moral psychology*. University of California Press.

Morris, H. (1976b). Guilt and suffering. In H. Morris (Ed.), *On guilt and innocence: Essays in legal and moral psychology* (pp. 95–125). University of California Press.

Murphy, J. (2005). *Getting even: Forgiveness and its limits*. Oxford University Press.

Na'aman, O. (2021). The rationality of emotional change: Toward a process view. *Noûs*, *55*(2), 245–269.

Nadelhoffer, T. (2006). Bad acts, blameworthy agents, and intentional actions: Some problems for juror impartiality. *Philosophical Explorations*, *9*(2), 203–219.

Nelissen, R., & Zeelenberg, M. (2009). When guilt evokes self-punishment: Evidence for the existence of a Dobby Effect. *Emotion*, *9*(1), 118–122.

Nelissen, R. M. (2012). Guilt-induced self-punishment as a sign of remorse. *Social Psychological and Personality Science*, *3*(2), 139–144.

Nelkin, D. K. (2011). *Making sense of freedom and responsibility*. Oxford University Press.

Nelkin, D. K. (2013a). Desert, fairness, and resentment. *Philosophical Explorations*, *16*(2), 117–132.

Nelkin, D. K. (2013b). Freedom and forgiveness. In I. Haji & J. Caouette (Eds.), *Free will and moral responsibility* (pp. 165–188). Cambridge Scholars Press.

Nelkin, D. K. (2016). Accountability and desert. *The Journal of Ethics*, *20*(1–3), 173–189.

Nelkin, D. K. (2017). Blame. In K. Timpe, M. Griffith, & N. Levy (Eds.), *The Routledge companion to free will* (pp. 374–388). Routledge.

Nelkin, D. K. (2019). Guilt, grief, and the good. *Social Philosophy and Policy*, *36*(1), 173–191.

Nichols, S. (2007). After incompatibilism: A naturalistic defense of the reactive attitudes. *Philosophical Perspectives*, *21*, 405–428.

Nichols, S. (2013). Brute retributivism. In T. Nadelhoffer (Ed.), *The future of punishment* (pp. 25–46). Oxford University Press.

Niedenthal, P. M., Tangney, J. P., & Gavanski, I. (1994). "If only I weren't" versus "If only I hadn't": Distinguishing shame and guilt in counterfactual thinking. *Journal of Personality and Social Psychology*, *67*(4), 585–595.

Nussbaum, M. (2001). *Upheavals of thought: The intelligence of emotions*. Cambridge University Press.

Nussbaum, M. (2004). Emotions as judgments of value and importance. In R. Solomon (Ed.), *Thinking about feelings: Contemporary philosophers on emotions* (pp. 183–199). Oxford University Press.

Nussbaum, M. (2016). *Anger and forgiveness*. Oxford University Press.

O'Connor, C. (2016). The evolution of guilt: A model-based approach. *Philosophy of Science*, *83*(5), 897–908.

Ohtsubo, Y., Matsunaga, M., Komiya, A., Tanaka, H., Mifune, N., & Yagi, A. (2014). Oxytocin receptor gene (OXTR) polymorphism and self-punishment after an unintentional transgression. *Personality and Individual Differences*, *69*, 182–186.

Ortony, A., Clore, G. L., & Collins, A. (1988). *The cognitive structure of emotions*. Cambridge University Press.

Pagel, M. D., Becker, J., & Coppel, D. B. (1985). Loss of control, self-blame, and depression: An investigation of spouse caregivers of Alzheimer's disease patients. *Journal of Abnormal Psychology*, *94*(2), 169–182.

Parkinson, B. (1996). Emotions are social. *British Journal of Psychology*, *87*(4), 663–683.

Parkinson, B. (2019). *Heart to heart: How emotions affect other people*. Cambridge University Press.

Peels, R. (2016). *Responsible belief: A theory in ethics and epistemology*. Oxford University Press.

Pereboom, D. (1995). Determinism al dente. *Noûs*, *29*(1), 21–45.

Pereboom, D. (2001). *Living without free will*. Cambridge University Press.

Pereboom, D. (2014). *Free will, agency, and meaning in life*. Oxford University Press.

Pereboom, D. (2015). A notion of moral responsibility immune to the threat from causal determination. In R. Clarke, M. McKenna, & A. M. Smith (Eds.), *The nature of moral responsibility: New essays* (pp. 281–296). Oxford University Press.

Pereboom, D. (2017). Responsibility, regret, and protest. In D. Shoemaker (Ed.), *Oxford studies in agency and responsibility*, Vol. 4 (pp. 121–140). Oxford University Press.

Pereboom, D. (2019). What makes the free will debate substantive? *The Journal of Ethics*, *23*(3), 257–264.

Pereboom, D. (2020). Forgiveness as renunciation of moral protest. In M. McKenna, D. K. Nelkin, & B. Warmke (Eds.), *Forgiveness*. Oxford University Press.

Pereboom, D., & McKenna, M. (2022). Manipulation arguments. In D. Nelkin & D. Pereboom (Eds.), *The Oxford handbook of moral responsibility*. Oxford University Press.

Pickard, H. (2013). Irrational blame. *Analysis*, *73*(4), 613–626.

Plato. (1992). Republic. (G. M. A. Grube, Trans.). Revised by C. D. C. Reeve. Hackett.

Polger, T. W. (2019). Functionalism. *The Internet Encyclopedia of Philosophy*, ISSN 2161-0002. Retrieved May 21, 2019, from www.iep.utm.cdu/

Portmore, D. W. (2019a). Control, attitudes, and accountability. In D. Shoemaker (Ed.), *Oxford studies in agency and responsibility*, Vol. 6 (pp. 7–32). Oxford University Press.

Portmore, D. W. (2019b). Desert, control, and moral responsibility. *Acta Analytica*, *34*(4), 407–426.

Portmore, D. W. (2019c). *Opting for the best: Oughts and options*. Oxford University Press.

Price, C. (2006). Affect without object: Moods and objectless emotions. *European Journal of Analytic Philosophy*, *2*(1), 49–68.

Prinz, J. (2004). *Gut reactions: A perceptual theory of emotion*. Oxford University Press.

Prinz, J. (2005). Are emotions feelings? *Journal of Consciousness Studies*, *12*(8–9), 9–25.

Prinz, J. J., & Nichols, S. (2010). Moral emotions. In J. M. Doris (Ed.), *The moral psychology handbook* (pp. 111–146). Oxford University Press.

Quiles, Z. N., & Bybee, J. (1997). Chronic and predispositional guilt: Relations to mental health, prosocial behavior, and religiosity. *Journal of Personality Assessment*, *69*(1), 104–126.

Radzik, L. (2009). *Making amends: Atonement in morality, law, and politics*. Oxford University Press.

Räikkä, J. (2005). On irrational guilt. *Ethical Theory and Moral Practice*, *7*(5), 473–485.

Reis-Dennis, S. (2019). Anger: Scary good. *Australasian Journal of Philosophy*, *97*(3), 451–464.

Richards, N. (1986). Luck and desert. *Mind*, *95*(378), 198–209.

Riek, B. M., Luna, L. M. R., & Schnabelrauch, C. A. (2014). Transgressors' guilt and shame: A longitudinal examination of forgiveness seeking. *Journal of Social and Personal Relationships*, *31*(6), 751–772.

Roberts, R. C. (1988). What an emotion is: A sketch. *The Philosophical Review*, *97*(2), 183–209.

Roberts, R. C. (1991). What is wrong with wicked feelings? *American Philosophical Quarterly*, *28*(1), 13–24.

Roberts, R. C. (2003). *Emotions: An essay in aid of moral psychology*. Cambridge University Press.

Rosch, E. (1972). Universals in color naming and memory. *Journal of Experimental Psychology*, *93*, 10–20.

Rosch, E. H. (1973). Natural categories. *Cognitive Psychology*, *4*(3), 328–350.

Rosen, G. (2015). The alethic theory of moral responsibility. In R. Clarke, M. McKenna, & A. Smith (Eds.), *The nature of moral responsibility. New essays* (pp. 65–88). Oxford University Press.

Rosenstock, S., & O'Connor, C. (2018). When it's good to feel bad: An evolutionary model of guilt and apology. *Frontiers in Robotics and AI*, *5*(9), 1–14.

Ross, W. D. (1988). *The Good and the right*. Hackett.

Russell, P. (2004). Responsibility and the condition of moral sense. *Philosophical Topics*, *32*(1/2), 287–305.

Russell, P. (2017). *The limits of free will*. Oxford University Press.

Sartorio, C. (2016). *Causation and free will*. Oxford University Press.

Scanlon, T. M. (1998). *What we owe to each other*. Belknap Press of Harvard University Press.

Scanlon, T. M. (2008). *Moral dimensions: Permissibility, meaning, blame*. Belknap Press of Harvard University Press.

Scanlon, T. M. (2013a). Giving desert its due. *Philosophical Explorations*, *16*(2), 101–116.

Scanlon, T. M. (2013). Interpreting blame. In D. J. Coates & N. Tognazzini (Eds.), *Blame: Its nature and norms* (pp. 84–99). Oxford University Press.

Scarantino, A. (2010). Insights and blindspots of the cognitivist theory of emotions. *The British Journal for the Philosophy of Science*, *61*(4), 729–768.

Scarantino, A. (2014). The Motivational theory of emotions. In J. D'Arms & D. Jacobson, (Eds.), *Moral psychology and human agency* (pp. 156–185). Oxford University Press.

Scarantino, A., & Griffiths, P. (2011). Don't give up on basic emotions. *Emotion Review*, *3*(4), 444–454.

Schwitzgebel, E. (2013). A dispositional approach to attitudes: Thinking outside the belief box. In N. Nottleman (Ed.), *New essays on belief: Constitution, content and structure* (pp. 75–99). Palgrave Macmillan.

Seidman, J. (2016). The unity of caring and the rationality of emotion. *Philosophical Studies*, *173*(10), 2785–2801.

Shabo, S. (2012). Where love and resentment meet: Strawson's intrapersonal defense of compatibilism. *Philosophical Review*, *121*(1), 95–124.

Sharadin, N. (2016). Reasons wrong and right. *Pacific Philosophical Quarterly*, *97*(3), 371–399.

Shaver, P., Schwartz, J., Kirson, D., & O'Connor, C. (1987). Emotion knowledge: Further exploration of a prototype approach. *Journal of Personality and Social Psychology*, *52*(6), 1061–1086.

Sher, G. (2006). *In praise of blame*. Oxford University Press.

Shoemaker, D. (2011). Attributability, answerability, and accountability: Toward a wider theory of moral responsibility. *Ethics*, *121*(3), 602–632.

Shoemaker, D. (2013). Blame and punishment. In D. J. Coates & N. Tognazzini (Eds.), *Blame: Its nature and norms* (pp. 100–118). Oxford University Press.

Shoemaker, D. (2015). *Responsibility from the margins*. Oxford University Press.

Shoemaker, D. (2017). Response-dependent responsibility; or, a funny thing happened on the way to blame. *Philosophical Review*, *126*(4), 481–527.

Shoemaker, D. (2018). You oughta know: Defending angry blame. In M. Cherry & O. Flanagan (Eds.), *Moral psychology of the emotions. The moral psychology of anger* (pp. 67–88). Rowman & Littlefield.

Shoemaker, D. (2019). Blameworthy but unblamable: A Puzzle of corporate responsibility. *The Georgetown Journal of Law and Public Policy, 17*, 897–918.

Shoemaker, D. (2021). The forgiven. In M. McKenna, D. Nelkin, & B. Warmke (Eds.), *Forgiveness and it's moral dimensions* (pp. 29–56). Oxford University Press.

Shoemaker, D., & Vargas, M. (2019). Moral torch fishing: A signaling theory of blame. *Noûs.* https://doi.org/10.1111/nous.12316

Silfver, M. (2007). Coping with guilt and shame: A narrative approach. *Journal of Moral Education, 36*(2), 169–183.

Smart, J. J. (1961). Free-will, praise and blame. *Mind, 70*(279), 291–306.

Smith, A. M. (2004). Conflicting attitudes, moral agency, and conceptions of the self. *Philosophical Topics, 32*, 331–352.

Smith, A. M. (2005). Responsibility for attitudes: Activity and passivity in mental life. *Ethics, 115*(2), 236–271.

Smith, A. M. (2008). Control, responsibility, and moral assessment. *Philosophical Studies, 138*(3), 367–392.

Smith, A. M. (2012). Attributability, answerability, and accountability: In defense of a unified account. *Ethics, 122*(3), 575–589.

Smith, A. M. (2013). Moral blame and moral protest. In D. J. Coates & N. Tognazzini (Eds.), *Blame: Its nature and norms* (pp. 27–48). Oxford University Press.

Smith, A. M. (2015a). Attitudes, tracing, and control. *Journal of Applied Philosophy, 32*(2), 115–132.

Smith, A. M. (2015b). Responsibility as answerability. *Inquiry, 58*(2), 99–126.

Solomon, R. C. (1988). On emotions as judgments. *American Philosophical Quarterly, 25*(2), 183–191.

Solomon, R. C. (2007). *True to our feelings: What our emotions are really telling us.* Oxford University Press.

Spelman, E. (1989). Anger and insubordination. In A. Garry & M. Pearsall (Eds.), *Women, knowledge, and reality: Explorations in feminist philosophy* (pp. 263–274). Routledge.

Stocker, M. (1987). Emotional thoughts. *American Philosophical Quarterly, 24*(1), 59–69.

Strabbing, J. T. (2019). Accountability and the thoughts in reactive attitudes. *Philosophical Studies, 176*(12), 3121–3140.

Strawson, G. (1986). *Freedom and belief.* Oxford University Press.

Strawson, P. F. (1962). Freedom and resentment. *Proceedings of the British Academy, 48*, 187–211.

Stroud, S. (2006). Epistemic partiality in friendship. *Ethics, 116*(3), 498–524.

Swannell, S., Martin, G., Page, A., Hasking, P., Hazell, P., Taylor, A., & Protani, M. (2012). Child maltreatment, subsequent non-suicidal self-injury and the mediating roles of dissociation, alexithymia and self-blame. *Child Abuse & Neglect, 36*(7–8), 572–584.

Szigeti, A. (2015). Sentimentalism and moral dilemmas. *Dialectica*, *69*(1), 1–22.

Talbert, M. (2012). Moral competence, moral blame, and protest. *The Journal of Ethics*, *16*(1), 89–109.

Tanaka, H., Yagi, A., Komiya, A., Mifune, N., & Ohtsubo, Y. (2015). Shame-prone people are more likely to punish themselves: A test of the reputation-maintenance explanation for self-punishment. *Evolutionary Behavioral Sciences*, *9*(1), 1–7.

Tangney, J. P., & Dearing, R. L. (2002). *Shame and guilt*. Guilford.

Tangney, J. P., Stuewig, J., & Mashek, D. J. (2007). Moral emotions and moral behavior. *Annual Review of Psychology*, *58*, 345–372.

Tappolet, C. (2012). Emotions, perceptions, and emotional illusions. In C. Calabi (Ed.), *Perceptual illusions* (pp. 205–222). Palgrave Macmillan.

Taylor, C. (1985). Self-interpreting animals. In *Human agency and language: Philosophical papers*, Vol. 1. Cambridge University Press.

Teroni, F. (2007). Emotions and formal objects. *Dialectica*, *61*(3), 395–415.

Thomason, K. K. (2018). *Naked: The dark side of shame and moral life*. Oxford University Press.

Thomson, J. J. (1993). Morality and bad luck. In D. Statman (Ed.), *Moral luck*. State University of New York Press.

Tierney, H. (2021a). Guilty confessions. In D. Shoemaker (Ed.), *Oxford studies in agency and responsibility*, Vol. 7. Oxford University Press.

Tierney, H. (2021b). Hypercrisy and standing to self-blame. *Analysis*, *81*, 262–269.

Tilghman-Osborne, C., Cole, D. A., & Felton, J. W. (2012). Inappropriate and excessive guilt: Instrument validation and developmental differences in relation to depression. *Journal of Abnormal Child Psychology*, *40*(4), 607–620.

Todd, C. (2014). Relatively fitting emotions and apparently objective values. In S. Roeser & C. Todd (Eds.), *Emotions and value* (pp. 90–104). Oxford University Press.

Tognazzini, N. A. (2010). Persistence and responsibility. In J. Campbell, M. O'Rourke, & H. Silverstein (Eds.), *Time and identity*. MIT Press.

Tognazzini, N., & Coates, D. J. (2018). "Blame." Edward N. Zalta, ed. *The Stanford encyclopedia of philosophy*. https://plato.stanford.edu/archives/fall2018/entries/blame/

Tracy, J. L., & Robins, R. W. (2006). Appraisal antecedents of shame and guilt: Support for a theoretical model. *Personality and Social Psychology Bulletin*, *32*(10), 1339–1351.

Trost, Z., Vangronsveld, K., Linton, S. J., Quartana, P. J., & Sullivan, M. J. (2012). Cognitive dimensions of anger in chronic pain. *Pain*, *153*(3), 515–517.

Ullman, S. E. (1996). Social reactions, coping strategies, and self-blame attributions in adjustment to sexual assault. *Psychology of Women Quarterly*, *20*(4), 505–526.

Van Kleef, G. A., De Dreu, C. K., & Manstead, A. S. (2004). The interpersonal effects of anger and happiness in negotiations. *Journal of Personality and Social Psychology*, *86*(1), 57–76.

Van Raalte, J. L., Brewer, B. W., Lewis, B. P., & Linder, D. E. (1995). Cork! The effects of positive and negative self-talk on dart throwing performance. *Journal of Sport Behavior*, *18*(1), 50.

Van Raalte, J. L., Brewer, B. W., Rivera, P. M., & Petitpas, A. J. (1994). The relationship between observable self-talk and competitive junior tennis players' match performances. *Journal of Sport and Exercise Psychology, 16*(4), 400–415.

Vargas, M. (2004). Responsibility and the aims of theory: Strawson and revisionism. *Pacific Philosophical Quarterly, 85*(2), 218–241.

Vargas, M. (2005). The trouble with tracing. *Midwest Studies in Philosophy, 29,* 269–291.

Vargas, M. (2013). *Building better beings: A theory of moral responsibility.* Oxford University Press.

Vargas, M. (2015). Desert, responsibility, and justification: A reply to Doris, McGeer, and Robinson. *Philosophical Studies, 172*(10), 2659–2678.

Vargas, M. (2019). Responsibility, methodology and desert. *Journal of Information Ethics, 28*(1), 131–147.

Veling, H., Ruys, K. I., & Aarts, H. (2012). Anger as a hidden motivator: Associating attainable products with anger turns them into rewards. *Social Psychological and Personality Science, 3*(4), 438–445.

Velleman, J. D. (2003). Don't worry, feel guilty. *Royal Institute of Philosophy Supplements, 52,* 235–248.

Vilhauer, B. (2004). Hard determinism, remorse, and virtue ethics. *The Southern Journal of Philosophy, 42*(4), 547–564.

Walker, M. U. (1991). Moral luck and the virtues of impure agency. *Metaphilosophy, 22*(1/2), 14–27.

Wallace, R. J. (1994). *Responsibility and the moral sentiments.* Harvard University Press.

Wallace, R. J. (2010). Hypocrisy, moral address, and the equal standing of persons. *Philosophy & Public Affairs, 38*(4), 307–341.

Wallace, R. J. (2011). Dispassionate opprobrium: On blame and the reactive sentiments. In R. J. Wallace, R. Kumar, & S. Freeman (Eds.), *Reasons and recognition: Essays on the philosophy of T.M. Scanlon* (pp. 348–372). Oxford University Press.

Wallace, R. J. (2019). *The moral nexus.* Princeton University Press.

Waller, B. (1990). *Freedom without responsibility.* Temple University Press.

Waller, B. (2011). *Against moral responsibility.* MIT Press.

Watanabe, E., & Ohtsubo, Y. (2012). Costly apology and self-punishment after an unintentional transgression. *Journal of Evolutionary Psychology, 10*(3), 87–105.

Watson, G. (1987). Responsibility and the limits of evil: Variations on a strawsonian theme. In F. Schoeman (Ed.), *Responsibility, character, and the emotions* (pp. 256–286). Cambridge University Press.

Watson, G. (1996). Two faces of responsibility. *Philosophical Topics, 24*(2), 227–248.

Watson, G. (2004). *Agency and answerability.* Oxford University Press.

Watson, G. (2011). The trouble with psychopaths. In R. J. Wallace, R. Kumar, & S. Freeman (Eds.), *Reasons and recognition: Essays on the philosophy of T.M. Scanlon* (pp. 307–331). Oxford University Press.

Watson, G. (2013). Standing in judgment. In D. J. Coates, & N. Tognazzini (Eds.), *Blame: Its nature and norms* (pp. 282–301). Oxford University Press.

Wiggins, D. (1987). A sensible subjectivism. In *Needs, values truth*. Blackwell.

Williams, B. (1981). *Moral luck*. Cambridge University Press.

Windsor, M. (2019). What is the uncanny? *British Journal of Aesthetics*, *59*, 51–65.

Wittgenstein, L. (1953). *Philosophical investigations*. G. E. M. Anscombe & R. Rhees (Eds.; G. E. M. Anscombe, Trans.). Blackwell.

Wolf, S. (2001). The moral of moral luck. *Philosophic Exchange*, *31*(1), 1.

Wolf, S. (2011). Blame italian style. In R. J. Wallace, R. Kumar, & S. R. Freeman (Eds.), *Reasons and recognition: Essays on the philosophy of T. M. Scanlon* (pp. 332–347). Oxford University Press.

Yang, S. (2016). Do emotions have directions of fit? *Organon F*, *23*(1), 32–49.

Young, L., Nichols, S., & Saxe, R. (2010). Investigating the neural and cognitive basis of moral luck: It's not what you do but what you know. *Review of Philosophy and Psychology*, *1*(3), 333–349.

Zeelenberg, M., & Breugelmans, S. M. (2008). The role of interpersonal harm in distinguishing regret from guilt. *Emotion*, *8*(5), 589–596.

Zhu, R., Shen, X., Tang, H., Ye, P., Wang, H., Mai, X., & Liu, C. (2017). Self-punishment promotes forgiveness in the direct and indirect reciprocity contexts. *Psychological Reports*, *120*(3), 408–422.

Zimmerman, M. J. (1987). Luck and moral responsibility. *Ethics*, *97*(2), 374–386.

Zimmerman, M. J. (1988). *An essay on moral responsibility*. Rowman & Littlefield.

Index